Macmillan Computer Science Series

Consulting Editor: Professor F. H. Sumner, University of I

A. Abdellatif, J. Le Bihan and M. Limame, *Oracle – A user's guide*
S. T. Allworth and R. N. Zobel, *Introduction to Real-time Software Design. second edition*
Ian O. Angell, *High-resolution Computer Graphics Using C*
Ian O. Angell and Gareth Griffith, *High-resolution Computer Graphics using FORTRAN 77*
Ian O. Angell and Gareth Griffith, *High-resolution Computer Graphics Using Pascal*
M. Azmoodeh, *Abstract Data Types and Algorithms, second edition*
C. Bamford and P. Curran, *Data Structures, Files and Databases, second edition*
Philip Barker, *Author Languages for CAL*
A. N. Barrett and Mackay, *Spatial Structure and the Microcomputer*
R. E. Berry, this book is kings and M. D. Soren, *A Book on C, second edition*
P. Davies, *Information Systems Development*
G. M. Birtwistle, *Discrete Event Modelling on Simula*
B. G. Blundell, C. N. Daskalakis, N. A. E. Heyes and T. P. Hopkins, *An Introductory Guide to Silvar Lisco and HILO Simulators*
B. G. Blundell and C. N. Daskalakis, *Using and Administering an Apollo Network*
Richard Bornat, *Understanding and Writing Compilers*
Linda E. M. Brackenbury, *Design of VLSI Systems – A Practical Introduction*
Alan Bradley, *Peripherals for Computer Systems*
G. R. Brookes and A. J. Stewart, *Introduction to occam 2 on the Transputer*
J. K. Buckle, *Software Configuration Management*
W. D. Burnham and A. R. Hall, *Prolog Programming and Applications*
P. C. Capon and P. J. Jinks, *Compiler Engineering Using Pascal*
J. C. Cluley, *Interfacing to Microprocessors*
J. C. Cluley, *Introduction to Low Level Programming for Microprocessors*
Robert Cole, *Computer Communications, second edition*
Derek Coleman, *A Structured Programming Approach to Data*
E. Davalo and P. Naïm, *Neural Networks*
S. M. Deen, *Principles and Practice of Database Systems*
C. Delannoy, *Turbo Pascal Programming*
Tim Denvir, *Introduction to Discrete Mathematics for Software Engineering*
D. England et al., *A Sun User's Guide*
A. B. Fontaine and F. Barrand, *80286 and 80386 Microprocessors*
J. S. Florentin, *Microprogrammed Systems Design*
J. B. Gosling *Design of Arithmetic Units for Digital Computers*
M. G. Hartley, M. Healey and P. G. Depledge, *Mini and Microcomputer Systems*
J. A. Hewitt and R. J. Frank, *Software Engineering in Modula-2 – An Object-oriented Approach*
Roger Hutty, *Z80 Assembly Language Programming for Students*
Roger Hutty, *COBOL 85 Programming*
Roland N. Ibbett and Nigel P. Topham, *Architecture of High Performance Computers, Volume I*
Roland N. Ibbett and Nigel P. Topham, *Architecture of High Performance Computers, Volume II*
Patrick Jaulent, *The 68000 – Hardware and Software*
P. Jaulent, L. Baticle and P. Pillot, *68020-30 Microprocessors and their Coprocessors*
M. J. King and J. P. Pardoe, *Program Design Using JSP – A Practical Introduction*
E. V. Krishnamurthy, *Introductory Theory of Computer Science*
V. P. Lane, *Security of Computer Based Information Systems*
Graham Lee, *From Hardware to Software – An Introduction to Computers*
M. Léonard, *Database Design Theory*
David Lightfoot, *Formal Specification Using Z*
A. M. Lister and R. D. Eager, *Fundamentals of Operating Systems, fourth edition*
Elizabeth Lynch, *Understanding SQL*

continued overleaf

Tom Manns and Michael Coleman, *Software Quality Assurance*
A. Mével and T. Guéguen, *Smalltalk-80*
R. J. Mitchell, *Microcomputer Systems Using the STE Bus*
R. J. Mitchell, *Modula-2 Applied*
Y. Nishinuma and R. Espesser, *UNIX – First contact*
Pim Oets, *MS-DOS and PC-DOS – A Practical Guide, second edition*
Pham Thu Quang and C. Chartier-Kastler, *MERISE in Practice*
A. J. Pilavakis, *UNIX Workshop*
Christian Queinnec, *LISP*
E. J. Redfern, *Introduction to Pascal for Computational Mathematics*
Gordon Reece, *Microcomputer Modelling by Finite Differences*
W. P. Salman, O. Tisserand and B. Toulout, *FORTH*
L. E. Scales, *Introduction to Non-Linear Optimization*
Peter S. Sell, *Expert Systems – A Practical Introduction*
A. G. Sutcliffe, *Human–Computer Interface Design*
M. Thorin, *Real-time Transaction Processing*
M. R. Tolhurst *et al.*, *Open Systems Interconnection*
A. J. Tyrrell, *COBOL from Pascal*
M. J. Usher, *Information Theory for Information Technologists*
Colin Walls, *Programming Dedicated Microprocessors*
I. R. Wilson and A. M. Addyman, *A Practical Introduction to Pascal – with BS6192, second edition*

Non-series
Roy Anderson, *Management, Information Systems and Computers*
I. O. Angell, *Advanced Graphics with the IBM Personal Computer*
B. V. Cordingley and D. Chamund, *Advanced BASIC Scientific Subroutines*
N. Frude, *A Guide to SPSS/PC+*
Percy Mett, *Introduction to Computing*
Tony Royce, *COBOL – An introduction*
Barry Thomas, *A PostScript Cookbook*

Database Design Theory

Michel Léonard

Centre for Informatics
University of Geneva

MACMILLAN

Authorised English-language translation of *Structures des
bases de données,* by Michel Léonard, © Bordas, Paris,
1988

Translated by M. J. Stewart

First published 1992 by
MACMILLAN EDUCATION LTD
Houndmills, Basingstoke, Hampshire RG21 2XS
and London
Companies and representatives
throughout the world

ISBN 0–333–53813–7

A catalogue record for this book is available from the
British Library.

Printed in Hong Kong

Contents

PART 3   DECOMPOSITION OF A RELATION

PART 4   PERSPECTIVES

Preface

A new subject for study

Our aim is to work on a subject which we will call *structured information*. As databases become more and more numerous in the world of organisations and businesses, it seems to us that this subject is going to become more and more recognised, especially since its importance is independent of the type of DBMS chosen (for example, relational or object oriented).

This subject is not a traditional part of dataprocessing material. Its principal subject concerns the appropriateness of information processing tools developed with the help of database management systems, for one or several management processes in an organisation. Nor is this subject a traditional part of the management of organisations because its other principal subject is the realisation of databases in an organisational environment. This matter appears to us as a link between dataprocessing material and control of organisational material. It is for us like a transfer between on one hand the analysis of a management process and its computerisation with the help of databases and on the other hand the analysis of the appropriateness of a database for a process of control. In this book we are presenting a study of the properties of *structured information* to facilitate exchanges between information processing skills and control skills. Thus the very essence of this subject is for us to provide an intellectual space common to the two subject matters that are connected to it. In particular it must allow the expression of results of analysis of a control process in terms which are easily translatable to terms of information processing specifications and the carrying out of information processing, and on the other hand, it must allow an easy understanding of the functioning of information processing applications working on a database by those who are carrying out the control process which has thus been computerised. We are going to limit the study of this subject to the bases necessary for the design of structures of databases, although we are extremely interested in the work relative to the design of treatment (ROLLAND78; BODART-PIGNEUR83; WASSERMAN83; GUYOT86).

Plan of the work

The first part concerns the modelling of a field of application. Having introduced the classic concepts of the relational data model (CODD70), we present the rules of integrity and the different varieties of dependencies. Chiefly we introduce the reference dependencies and the relative dependencies which are as far as we know original and which are essential for the study of structures of data which allow cycles. We are trying to show that the usefulness of rules of integrity is not limited to assuring the consistency of the database but that they are efficient aids to the difficult process of modelling a field of application which includes its observation, its analysis and the expression of results of analysis in precise terms.

This part finishes with the importance of the data dictionary which is going to contain the model.

The second part assumes that the model obtained previously forms the core of the final structure of the database. In the case of complex models, the third part will show that it is necessary to work on the first model and to change it into an equivalent model so that the controls of integrity can be efficiently verified.

As this third part is much more complex, we will first of all, in the course of the second part, present the transformation of a relational data model into a computing data structure.

At the beginning of this second part, we shall show why in our opinion, the relational data model cannot be accepted as a computer model of data storage. We present such a model which we call an access paths graph (APG). In the second part we supply an algorithmic approach for the transformation of a relational data model into an access paths graph then into a computer data structure. We are led to supply a representation in a graph equivalent to a set of relations which we call a relation graph (RG). This representation is much more simple than the one frequently used, that of the hypergraphs (BERGE70), and it can be considered as a distinctive hypergraph.

In the third part, "Decomposition of a relation", we study the quality of the initial relational model in relation to the future database.

The essential concept here is that of decomposition of a relation. It is a question of replacing a relation R by a set of relations $(R_1...R_i...R_n)$ so that all information stored in R is potentially able to be stored in $(R_1...R_i...R_n)$ and vice versa.

As we have already shown in the first part, it is the dependencies which are going to allow the decomposition of relations. The study of decompositions has made it necessary for us to study the extension and inversely the projection of rules of integrity.

Next we present straightforward decompositions (the validity of rules of integrity at the level of each of the relations $R_1...R_i...R_n$ is sufficient to guarantee the validity at the level of R) and the impervious decompositions (a user who wants to extract an item of data from the database can consider that the n relations are independent and thus forget the existence of R).

We will show in a special case how it is possible to construct open decompositions and how it is sometimes impossible to obtain an open and safe decomposition.

This situation leads us to return to a solution commonly put forward (BERSTEIN76) as a satisfactory solution for obtaining an efficient database structure. We are led to introduce new mechanisms which ought to form part of database management systems and which would allow certain decompositions to be guaranteed safe.

The presence of these mechanisms allows us to put forward another solution for obtaining an efficient database structure, which seems to us to possess amongst others the following advantage over the previous solution: that of placing before the database designer of choices which can only be expressed in terms of information and not in technical terms.

The fourth part is intended to give different perspectives:

- it emphasises the necessity of having at one's disposal models of data which are more sophisticated, not only for the modelling phase, but also for the establishment of dataprocessing. We quote our own attempt which was made concrete by the ECRINS DBMS (LEONARD-GALLARD-JUNET- TSCHOPP85) as well as attempts by other teams (for example TIGRE (VELEZ-LOPEZ87));

- it stresses the necessity of increasing the functions of a DBMS so that the setting up of dataprocessing applications using DBMS's may be efficient. The mechanisms pointed out in the third part are encompassed in other mechanisms which are all equally necessary and we show by the proof of a theorem how these mechanisms can be very useful.

The fundamental objective

We suggest the study of points which we consider as fundamental in the design of a database structure. We think that they will be very useful for all designers of databases especially when they become more and more complex.

On the other hand we do not suggest any particular method (which would put forward different design stages and would place them in a chronological order by giving details of how to move from one to the other in a context which would of necessity be repetitive). Nor do we suggest any tool or methodology (which would have to encompass not only aspects of the conduct of dataprocessing projects but also cognitive aspects linked with modelling processes, the process for integrating dataprocessing tools into the organisation, a process for following up on this integration, and another for reorganisation and restructuring, and aspects of the dynamics of groups of persons affected by the database).

We shall try to contribute to the setting up of a *basis* of knowledge for the design and realisation of databases where users will be happy to deposit and collect their data, whether relational or object oriented.

Finally, I should like to acknowledge the assistance of former students, researchers and staff in the preparation of this book.

Abbreviations used in the book

If R designates a relation then:

R^+	designates the set of the attributes of R.
‖R‖	designates the predicate of R.
r	designates an entity of R.
iR	designates an instance of R, that is, a set of entities of R.
KR	designates a key to R.
KR^+	designates the set of the attributes of R which belong to at least one key to R.

If in the context of a paragraph there is no likelihood of confusion with other relations then: r'r"r_i also designate entities of R.

If A designates an attribute, then a designates a value of its domain; if there is no likelihood of confusion with other attributes, then a'a"a_i also designate other values of A.

If D is a decomposition then D^+ designates the set of the attributes of the relations of D.

If f is a functional dependency then:

f^+ designates the set of the attributes of f,
g(f) designates the left part of f,
d(f) designates the right part of f.

jd	:	join dependency.
dd	:	dimensioning dependency.
dec	:	decomposition.
fd	:	functional dependency.
APG	:	access paths graph.
APG_r	:	raw access paths graph.
RG	:	relation graph.
ir	:	integrity rule.
DBMS	:	database management system.

PART 1

DATA MODELLING

1 A relational data model

1.1 Concepts of the relational data model

1.1.1 Domain

A *domain* is a non-empty set D. To express that element a belongs to D, we write: a ED. We call the elements of a domain its *values* or its *objects*. A domain D is *composed* if it is defined using several domains $D_1...D_n$. Its set is the cartesian product of sets $D_1...D_n$, perhaps reduced by elements that verify a precise condition.

The *type* of a domain indicates the operations that are defined on its elements; the following is a non-exhaustive list of these.
A domain is of type *text* if no operation is permitted.
It is of type *word* if the comparison operators "equality" and "difference" are defined in it; a special case of type word is type *ordered word*, in which in addition to the previous operations those of "inferior" and "superior" are also defined; if the order relation is not obvious, it must be defined.
It is of type *numeric* if in addition to the above the operations of addition and subtraction are defined in it. Rather than numeric, which may not be sufficiently precise, the type can be described as integer, positive integer, decimal, real, etc. It is of type *boolean* if it only contains two values and if the boolean algebra operations (NOT, AND, OR) are defined in it. It is of type *monomer* if it is made up of several domains of type boolean.
For domains of type numeric and possibly of types word and ordered word it may be necessary to specify the *unit* relating to the value of the field (km, kg, s, etc).
To *define* a domain, one can specify the values it contains by enumeration in the case of domains of type word or boolean or ordered word, or by definition intervals in the case of domains of type numeric or ordered word, or by a mathematical or algorithmic formalism. The type of a domain must always be provided.

Special case
There are domains used very frequently in management applications for which
it is unnecessary to provide a definition on each occasion. Here are some
examples:

dom DAYNUMBER	: increasing ordered word (1,31).
dom MONTH	: word (january, february, march, april, may, june, july, august, september, october, november, december).
dom YEAR	: increasing ordered word (1900, -).
dom DATE	: ordered word made up of DAYNUMBER MONTH YEAR less leap year days.

Leap year days are calculated by an algorithm that give the set of leap days,
such as Tuesday, 30 February 1985.

dom HOUR	: increasing ordered word (0,23).
dom MINUTE	: increasing ordered word (0,59).
dom TIME	: ordered word made up of HOUR MINUTE.

1.1.2   Attribute

An attribute is a class of data that behaves homogenously in the database; its
meaning is based solely on the fact that it belongs to that class.
E..ch attribute is assigned to one and only one domain.
An item of data belonging to the class of an attribute is represented in the
database by one of the values of the domain of this attribute.

An attribute is *joined* if its domain is joined or if it is defined from several
attributes; then its domain is a subset of the cartesian product of the domains of
these attributes; this subset is determined by an algorithmic process (this subset
may possibly be equal to the cartesian product itself).

Notation

Take c to be a value of attribute C. If attribute C is made up of attributes
$C_1...C_n$, then notations $c.C_1$ and $c(C_1)$ designate the value taken by c for
attribute C_1. Now if attribute C allows a domain made up of domains $D_1...D_n$
then $c.D_1$ designates the value taken by value c for domain D_1.

1.1.3 Relation

A *relation* n-ary R is a set R^+ of attributes of R and a predicate described as ‖R‖ whose free variables (that is, those that are not quantified by either of the two quantifiers $\exists$ $\forall$) correspond to the attributes of R^+ and take their values in the domains of these attributes.

An *n-tuple* of R is an element of the cartesian product of the domains of the n attributes of R.

An *entity* r of relation R is an n-tuple of R that verifies the predicate:
‖R‖(r) = true.

Note

The fact that an n-tuple of the cartesian product is or is not an entity of relation R arises from no algorithmic process: the database user decides this by either asking or not asking for this tuple to be stored in the database. This highlights the fundamental difference between the concepts of relation and joined attribute.

Notation

If r is an entity of R (or an n-tuple of the cartesian product of domains of R) $r.A_i$ or $r(A_i)$ or $r[A_i]$ designates the value taken by r for attribute A_i. If X^+ designates a set of attributes of R^+, $r.X^+$ designates the values taken by r for the different attributes of X^+.

1.1.4 Unknown values

When defining a relation R, one has to specify for every attribute of R whether the entities of R may take its unknown value.

A entity r of R is *clear* if for every attribute A of R, r does not take the unknown value. It is *obscure* if there is at least one attribute for which it takes an unknown value.

1.1.5 Instance

An *instance* of a relation R is a set of entities of this relation that we describe by iR (and perhaps more simply by R if there is no possible ambiguity with relation R). It is *clear* if all its entities are clear.

There is a special instance of R, which groups together all the clear entities of R that have been stored in the database throughout its life. This is called the *closure* of R. From the formal point of view, it is equivalent to the predicate of

R since it contains the set of all the tuples of R that verify this predicate. This is simply described by R. We are only interested in the instances of a relation formed from clear entities.

The notation $r \in R$ is used to indicate that the tuple r of the cartesian product of the domains of the attributes of R is an entity of R.

An *instance* of a database formed from relations $R_1...R_n$ is a set of relation instances, one for each of the relations $R_1...R_n$.

1.1.6   Key

A *key* to a relation R is a minimal set of attributes of R such that if two entities of R take the same values for these attributes in the same instance, they are identical.

A key K to R is *mandatory* if for every entity r of R and for every attribute A of K, r.A must always be clear.

We assume that every relation allows at least one key possibly formed from all the attributes of the relation. It may allow several keys. We will give a more formal definition of the concept of a key in section 2.4.3.

Thus, a mandatory key allows us to distinguish between the entities of the same relation R depending on the values that they take for the attributes forming that key.

We propose the following rule: every relation must have at least one mandatory key. If relation R allows a single key K then it is mandatory and no entity of R may take the unknown value for a attribute of key K.

A key allows the entities of a relation to be identified and it is for this reason that we prefer the word *identifier* instead of the word key, as (HAINAUT86) proposes.

1.1.7   Order relation defined on relations

$R < S$ if and only if the closure of R is included in that of S. This is a partial order relation. The equality of two relations derives from the equality of their predicates and thus of their closures.

1.2   Operations defined on a set of relations

The proofs of the properties in this chapter may be found in the appendix to the chapter.

1.2.1 Normal operations defined on a set of relations

1.2.1.1 Product and join of two relations

The product of two relations R and S is a new relation T such that $\|T\| = \|R\| \wedge \|S\|$ and $T^+ = R^+ \| S^+$:

all the attributes of R and of S are marked in T^+ by the name of their origin relation: thus if A is an attribute of R and of S, it gives rise to two attributes of T: A of R and A of S.

We describe this by T = R**S.

The join of two relations R and S is a new relation T such that $T^+ = R^+ \cup S^+$ (union of sets of attributes of R^+ and of S^+) and $\|T\| = \|R\| \wedge \|S\|$.

We describe this by T = R*S.

Note that whether T is obtained by product or by join of the two relations R and S, every entity t of T verifies that $t.R^+$ is an entity of R and $t.S^+$ is an entity of S.

The *hinge* of R and of S is the set of attributes common to R and to S; we describe it as $RS^+ = R^+ \wedge S^+$.

If RS^+ is empty, there is no difference between the product and join. Otherwise, every entity of T obtained by join verifies $t.RS^+ = r.RS^+ = s.RS^+$.

1.2.1.2 Sum of two relations

The sum of two relations R and S gives a new relation T such that $T^+ = R^+ \cup S^+$ and $\|T\| = \|R\| \cup \|S\|$.

We write T = R + S.

Thus every entity t of T verifies that:

$t.R^+$ is an entity of R or $t.S^+$ is an entity of S.

Since the operation for the union of sets and that of the logical or of predicates are associative and commutative operations, the operation for summing relations is also an associative and commutative operation.

1.2.1.3   Complement of a relation

The complement of relation R is a new relation S such that $S^+ = R^+$ and $\forall s \in S$ $s.R^+$ is not an entity of R.
We write S = not R.

1.2.1.4   Projection of a relation

The projection of a relation R on a set of attributes X is only defined if X is included in R^+. In this case, a new relation S is defined on the set of attributes $S^+ = X$ and for which the predicate $\|S\|$ verifies: $\forall s \in S \exists r \in R$ such that $r.X = s$.
We say that s is the projection of r on X^+.
We write S = R[X].

1.2.1.5   Selection of a relation

The selection of a relation R by a predicate P is only defined if the variables of P are attributes of $R (P^+ \subset R^+)$ and if they are free. This operation constructs a new relation T such that its set of attributes is that of R: $T^+ = R^+$ and its predicate verifies $\|T\| = \|R\| \wedge P$.
We write $T = (*P)R$.

Property
It is possible to assign to the predicate P a relation PR such that $PR^+ = P^+$ and $\|PR\| = P$. Then $T = (*P)R = PR*R$.

This property allows us to set aside consideration of the selection operation in our subsequent study of the properties of relational operations.

1.2.1.6   P-product of two relations

The P-product of two relations R and S is defined using a predicate P whose variables P^+ are attributes of R or of S and are free. It is a new relation such that: $T^+ = R^+ \| S^+$ and $\|T\| = \|R\| \wedge \|S\| \wedge P$.
We write $T = R (**P)S$.

Property (**P)

R(**P)S = (*P)(R**S).

In fact, these two relations are defined on the same attributes and have the same predicate. This property allows us to set aside consideration of the P-product in our subsequent study of the properties of relational operations. It is similarly possible to define the *P-join* of two relations.

1.2.2 Relations that are formally noteworthy

U^+ is a set of attributes that contains all other sets.

Relation 1 is defined on U^+ and its predicate is always verified: the relation 1_x designates the projection of 1 on the set of attributes X.

Relation 0 is defined on U^+ and its predicate is never verified; the relation 0_x designates the projection of 0 on X.

The *enlargement* of a relation R is a new relation described by R^e defined on U^+ such that $R^e = 1*R$. R^e is said to be the *enlarged relation* of R.

1.2.2.1 Properties of enlargement

(e1) $R^e[R^+] = R$.

(e11) $1[X] = 1_x$ and $(1_x)^e = 1$.

(e12) $0[X] = 0_x$ and $(0_x)^e = 0$.

(e2) If $X \subset R^+$ then $R^e[X] = R[X]$.

(e21) If $X \wedge R^+ = \emptyset$ then $R^e[X] = 1_x$.

(e3) $(R*S)^e = R^e *S^e$.

(e31) $(R^e *S^e) = R^e *S = R*S^e$.

(e4) $(R+ S)^e = R^e + S^e$.

(e41) $(R^e + S^e) = R^e + S = R + S^e$.

(e5) $(\text{not } R)^e = \text{not } (R^e)$.

(e6) $((*P)R)^e = (*P)(R^e)$.

(e7) $(R = S) \Rightarrow (R^e = S^e)$ and $(R^e = S^e) \wedge (R^+ = S^+) \Rightarrow R = S$.

1.2.2.2 Boolean algebra of relations

Take (U) to be the set of relations defined on U^+ or on a subset of U^+ and take (U^e) to be the set of enlarged relations of the relations (U). The closure $(U^e)^*$

of (U^e) designates the set of relations that can be constructed from the relations of (U^e) using the operations of sum, join and complement.

Theorem (e8)

The sum and join operations form a boolean algebra defined on (U^e)* because:
- *and,* or *or* operations defined on the predicates are associative, commutative and doubly distributive one to the other: thus the same applies for the summing and join of two relations of (U^e)*;
- the idempotence of the summing and the join of two relations of (U^e)* derives from the idempotence of the *and* and *or* operations defined on the predicates;
- the neutral element of the sum is relation 0 and that of the join is relation 1;
- not R is the complement of relation R of (U^e)* because it can easily be verified that:

$$\text{not } R + R = 1,$$
$$\text{not } R * R = 0.$$

Corollary (e9)

Listed below are the noteworthy classical properties of a boolean algebra that are applied to the boolean algebra of the relations of (U^e)* as a particular case:
$1 + R = 1.$
$0 * R = 0.$
$R + (R * S) = R.$
$R + (\text{not } R * S) = R + S.$
$R = R * S$ is equivalent to $R + S = S.$
The complement of a relation is unique.
The neutral elements are unique.
$\text{not } (\text{not } R) = R.$
$\text{not } (R + S) = (\text{not } R) * (\text{not } S).$
$\text{not } (R * S) = (\text{not } R) + (\text{not } S).$

1.2.2.3   Focus operation

The focus operation allows both the projection of a relation R on a set of attributes X included in R^+, as well as the enlargement of relation R to a set of attributes Y containing R^+.
Generally, it defines a new relation: focus (R/X) from a relation R and from a set of attributes X included in U^+ in the following manner:

$$\text{focus}(R/X) = R^e[X].$$

Properties of the focus operation

(f1) focus $(R/U^+) = R^e$ (enlargemnt);

if $X \subset R^+$ then focus $(R/X) = R[X]$ (projection).

(f2) focus $(1_x/Y) = 1_y$ (with $Y \subset U^+$).

focus $(0_x/Y) = 0_y$.

(f3) focus $(R*S/X) \subset$ focus' $(R/X) *$ focus (S/X);

if X contains the hinge $R^+ \wedge S^+$ then

focus $(R*S/X) =$ focus $(R/X) *$ focus (S/X).

(f4) focus $(R+S/X) =$ focus $(R/X) +$ focus (S/X).

(f5) not focus $(R/X) \subset$ focus (not R/X);

if X contains R^+ then not focus $(R/X) =$ focus (not R/X).

(f6) If $Y \subset X \subset R^+$ then

focus (focus $(R/X)/Y) =$ focus $(R/Y) = R[Y]$.

If X contains R^+ then focus (focus$(R/X)/Y) =$ focus (R/Y).

1.2.3   Properties of normal relational operations

Take (U) to be the set of relations defined on U^+ or on a subset of U^+ and take
(U)* to be the closure of (U), that is, the set of relations that can be constructed
from relations (U) using the sum, join, complement and projection operations.

1.2.3.1   Properties of sum, join and complement operations

(01) The sum and the join of relations are operations that are idempotent,
commutative, associative and doubly distributive one to the other. These
properties derive directly from the corresponding properties of the *or* and *and*
operations defined on the predicates.

(02) If $X = R^+$ then not $R + R = 1_x$,

not $R * R = 0_x$,

$R * 0_x = 0_x$,

$R + 0_x = R * 1_x = R$,

$R + 1_x = 1_x$.

(03) $R + (R*S) =$ focus $(R/R^+ \cup S^+)$.

$R + ($not $R*S) = R + S$.

(04) not (not $R) = R$.

not $(R+S) =$ not $R *$ not S.

not $(R*S) =$ not $R +$ not S.

The proofs of the properties are to be found in the appendix to this chapter. They are founded on the boolean algebra of the relations defined on U^+ and on property (e7).

1.2.3.2   Properties of sum, composition and complement operations in relation to the projection operation

(p1) If $Y \subset X \subset R^+$ then $(R[X])[Y] = R[Y]$.

(p2) If $X \subset R^+ \wedge S^+$ then $(R*S)[X] \subset R[X] * S[X]$;
        if X is equal to the hinge of R and of S, then there is equality.

(p3) If $X \subset R^+ \wedge S^+$ then $(R+S)[X] = R[X] + S[X]$.

(p4) If $X \subset R^+$ then not $R[X] \subset (\text{not } R)\,[X]$.

These properties are corollaries of the focus operation properties (f3, f4, f5, f6).

1.2.3.3   Properties of the selection operation

(s1) $(*P)((*Q)R) = (*(P \wedge Q))R$.

(s2) If P^+ is included in X, $(*P)(R[X]) = ((*P)R)[X]$.

(s3) $((*P)R) + ((*Q)R) = (*(P+Q))R$.

(s4) If P^+ is included in R^+, then $(*P)(R*S) = ((*P)R) * S$.

(s5) If P^+ is included in R^+ and in S^+,
        then $(*P)(R+S) = ((*P)R) + ((*P)S)$.

These properties derive from the definition of the selection operation (s1 and s3) and from the properties (s, p2, associativity of join, distributivity of summing and join).

1.2.4   Relational expression

A relational expression is constructed using relations, the preceding relational operators, predicates for selection operations, sets of attributes and square brackets for the projection operation, and parentheses.

A *well formulated* relational expression is defined recursively in the following manner: a relation is a well formed relational expression; take X to be a set of attributes, E_1 and E_2 to be two well formed relational expressions and P_1 to be a predicate, then expressions (E_1), not E_1, $E_1[X]$, $(*P_1)E_1$, $E_1 * E_2$, $E_1 + E_2$, E_1 ** E_2 are well formed.

They are *well constructed* only if $X \subset E_1{}^+$ and $P_1{}^+ \subset E_1{}^+$.

We adopt the following convention in order to simply the writing of relational expressions:

a) Unary operators take priority over binary operators:
   not $R * T[X^+]$ means $(\text{not}R) * (T[X^+])$.
b) Projection takes priority over complement and selection:
   not $R[X^+]$ means not $(R[X^+])$.
c) Complement and selection have the same level of priority:
   the operator written closest to the relation has priority:
   not $(*P)R$ means not $((*P)R)$.
d) Join takes priority over product;
   $R*S**T$ means $(R*S)**T$.
e) Product takes priority over sum.
f) With the above rules being respected, binary operations are carried out from left to right.

1.3 Normal operations defined on a set of instances

The *product* of two instances iR and iS of two relations R and S constructs a set of n-tuples N defined on $T^+ = R^+ \| S^+$, such that:

$\forall\ n \in N\quad n.R^+ \in iR$ and $n.S^+ \in iS$,

and $\forall r \in iR\ \forall s \in iS\ \exists n \in\ N$ such that $n.R^+ = r$ and $n.S^+ = s$.

We write: $N = iR **iS$.

It is easy to prove that N is an instance of the relation $T = R**S$.

The *join* of two instances iR and iS, containing clear entities, of relations R and S constructs a set of n-tuples N defined on

$T^+ = R^+ \cup S^+$, such that:

$\forall n \in N\ n.R^+ \in iR$ and $n.S^+ \in iS$

and $\forall r \in iR,\ \forall s \in iS$ such that $r.R^+ \wedge S^+ = s.R^+ \wedge S^+$, then $\exists n \in\ N$ such that $n.R^+ = r$ and $n.S^+ = s$.

We write: $N = iR * iS$.

It is easy to prove that N is an instance of relation $T = R * S$.

The *projection* of an instance of iR of relation R on a set of attributes S^+, is only defined if S^+ is included in R^+; it constructs a set of n-tuples N defined on S^+ such that:

$\forall n \in N$, $\exists r \in iR$ such that $r.S^+ = n$

and $\forall r \in iR$, $\exists n \in N$ such that $r.S^+ = n$.

We write: $N = iR[S^+]$.

It is easy to prove that N is an instance of $S = R[S^+]$.

The *selection* of an instance iR of relation R by a predicate P is only defined if the variables of P are attributes of $R(P^+ \subset R^+)$ and if they are free. It constructs a new set of   n-tuples N defined on R^+ that is the subset of entities of iR verifying P.

We write: $N = (*P) \, iR$.

It is easy to prove that N is an instance of the relation $(*P)R$.

1.4   Synthesis: data dictionary

1.4.1   Relevance of the relational data model

The aim of this chapter is to present the main concepts of the simplest relational data model. We have provided the formal definitions and have shown some of their mathematical properties. Finally, we will illustrate them using a concrete example. At this stage, we hope as a synthesis to show the relevance of such an approach which is already detectable in this first chapter.

a)   This relevance concerns the necessary common language between on the one hand managers who are very interested in the use of databases, but who are relatively unfamiliar with the languages of technical computing, and on the other hand IT practitioners, who are database specialists, but who do not fully understand all the subleties, that are sometimes quite significant, of real management processes and which may sometimes even appear to them to be incoherent, because they are not sufficiently informed about the procedures for installing a database within an organisation.

The relational database model provides for data the possibility of a common language. We have seen that it is easily understandable by managers when we have not formally tried to teach them the concepts, but have simply discussed with them the relational model that we obtained in their domain. This common language does not appear to us to be the relational data model itself, but the relational application model itself.

The relational data model then appears as a *superstructure* (some refer to it as a metastructure) known to database specialists, which allows these specialists to maintain a dialogue with the managers.

b)   Another fundamental point concerns on the one hand the design of a database and on the other its follow-up. One very important phase in the design of a database relates to the observation of all the data that must be taken account of in the database. This phase which we call data modelling of the application field, generally confronts designers with a mass of data of varying interest. They need to be able to quickly classify and arrange such data. The relational data model suggests that they classify this data in terms of relations, attributes, domains, entities, domain values, integrity rules (chapter 2) or non-important data. There appear to be two basic characteristics of this phase:
the one recognises that a model only attains its stability after much reflection and numerous observations; very often, during the course of this phase the designer may notice that such and such a relation should be removed, that another should be created, that such an attribute of such a relation should be deleted (or added). The designer needs to have an aid to keep his model up to date. The other characteristic confirms that the modelling of a rather complicated database is not the work of one person, but a team.
Both in order to increase efficiency and to reduce nervous tension within the group, it seems indispensable for the members of the team to share not only a common language but also a logistical aid to ensure that the file of the team's model is clearly kept up to date in a complete way, that is, taking into account the work of every member of the team.

The first response to these two characteristics of the modelling phase is the establishment of a data dictionary whose superstructure is provided by the concepts of the relational data model. This data dictionary will be stored like a small database and will provide all the update facilities for the current model.

The data dictionary which contains the model is not just required when the database is to be designed. It is in fact required to record all the semantics of the data contained in the database. So, if during the course of the database follow-up, it is necessary to alter the information in the database (by adding or removing) in order to respond to alterations in the database environment, it is by consulting and carefully altering this dictionary that those responsible will be able to restructure the database satisfactorily.

c)   A third fundamental point concerning the relevance of the relational model is the relative facility for transcribing the results of a data model into computing terms. It is therefore no coincidence that all developments of new database management systems (DBMS) since 1974 have been based on the concepts of the relational model.

We believe that the relational data model has emphasised the clear and relevant design architecture of the new DBMSs that are called relational. In particular, they have a data dictionary which brings together the database structure. It is itself managed like a small database and can often be interrogated using the same query language as that of the main database.

During the course of this book, the relevance of this relational model will allow us to introduce the main aspects of the necessary cohesion between on the one hand a data model and on the other a data information structure that may or may not be taken into account by a relational DBMS.

We will now explain the architecture of a data dictionary in broad outline and at the same time fill in the role that we see for the relational data model, namely to be the structure for such a dictionary.

In part 3 we will show how it is possible to enrich this relational data model to take into account more easily more complex database structures.

1.4.2   Rules of the relational model

The relational data model considers the existence of three basic concepts: relation, attribute and domain. We say that a *category* is a relation or an attribute or a domain.

A data model of an application field constructed from the relational model will define a data structure in terms of these three categories: it therefore comprises a list of relations, attributes and domains that provide all the types of data in the application field. Then every object in the application field is referenced as a data item of one of these types.

There are thus in fact three levels:
    1)   that of categories,
    2)   that of types,
    3)   that of data.

These three levels are common both to the analysis of an application field and to the modelling process, as well as to the architecture of a relational database management system and to relational databases.

For example, for a relational database, level 2) corresponds to the logical data structure and level 3) to data storage.

Level 1) then appears as the *superstructure* of a data model, a DBMS or a database.

The *data dictionary,* both as a data model and a DBMS or a database corresponds to level 1 and level 2; its purpose is to store in an orderly fashion all the information about an application field relating to this data and to provide an easy means of access to this information. A data dictionary is therefore a small database whose structure is exactly the superstructure mentioned above and whose data is all of the type of the data in the application field.

This superstructure can be described using the graph shown in figure 1.1 (ABRIAL74), in which:
- every node is assigned to a category;
- an edge directed from node N_1 to node N_2 means that a type of category N_1 can be assigned to one or more types of category N_2. Thus for example a type of category "relation", that is a relation, can be assigned to one or more types of category attribute, that is, one or more attributes.
There are two parameters assigned to each edge, the minimal and maximal cardinalities, that is, respectively the minimal and maximal numbers of types of the category of N_2 that can be assigned to a type of the category of N_1. (We have adopted the convention of using a single arrow to show a maximal cardinality equal to 1, and two arrows to show the opposite.)

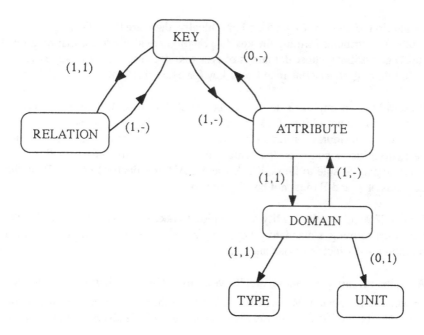

Figure 1.1 Relational data model

The following are the implicit rules contained in the graphical representation:

(m1)   a relation must be defined on at least one attribute;
(m2)   an attribute must be an attribute of at least one relation;
(m3)   a key is a key to a single relation;
(m4)   a relation has always at least one key (possibly formed on the set of attributes of the relation);
(m5)   a key is a set formed from at least one attribute;
(m6)   an attribute can belong to no key or it can belong to several;
(m7)   an attribute has one and only one domain;
(m8)   a domain is the domain of at least one attribute but several attributes can have the same domain;
(m9)   a domain has one and only one type;
(m10)   a domain can be assigned to one unit at most.

Rules m1, m4, m5, m7, m9 m10 are implicit rules of the relational data model. Rules m2, m8 must be verified for the model to be described as *well formulated*: they show that an attribute (respectively a domain) is only preserved in a model if it is assigned to at least one relation (respectively an attribute). Rule m3 indicates that the dictionary does not allow relations having the same key.

In addition to these rules described graphically, there are the following:
(m20) the attributes forming the key to a relation are attributes of that relation;
(m21) an attribute whose domain is of type text does not belong to any key;
(m22) there is at least one mandatory key for every relation.

Rule m20 is an implicit rule of the relational data model. Rule m21 derives partly from the definition of a key and partly from the text type of a domain: if AB are two attributes forming a key to relation R, this means that there cannot be two entities r and r' of R having the same values for AB. It is therefore necessary to be able to know if r.AB and r.'AB are identical or not. Thus the domains of A and B must not be of type text.

Rule m22 requires every entity of a relation to take not unknown values for the attributes forming a mandatory key; one is thus sure that all the entities of a relation are distinct from one another.

All rules $m_1...m_{21}$ are automatically verifiable when the dictionary is created or when it is updated. We will introduce two others which on the other hand can only be verified by those responsible for the database at the time of making the model.

(m30) The fact that a key K_i to a relation R_i contains a key K_j to a relation R_j, means that every entity r_i of R_i such that $r_i.K_j$ is clear, can only exist in the database if there is entity r_j of R_j such that $r_j.K_j = r_i.K_j$.

The inclusion of keys between relations for us expresses implicitly a referential dependency between the entities of these relations; so the deletion of entity r_j must cause the deletion of entities r_i of R_i such as $r_i.K_j = r_j.K_j$ if K_i is a mandatory key, otherwise an alteration of r_i such as $r_i.K_j$ becomes obscure.

(m31) If two relations R_i and R_j allow common attributes, it is possible to join these two relations and thus obtain a third relation which has a meaning for those responsible for the database.

Those in charge of the database must verify these last mentioned rules and perhaps alter the contents of the dictionary to ensure that these rules are respected. The example in the next section will allow us to illustrate this verification.

1.4.3   Conclusion

To conclude, we should like to insist on the very name of the relational data model. This name for us reinforces the fact that an item of data has no meaning except *in relation* to another item of data. So the definition of a relation, an attribute or a domain only has a sense with reference to other relations, attributes or domains and rarely in itself. It is relatively easy to establish that for a given field of application there is not a single correct model; there are generally several. What is important is that every element in a model is defined in a coherent way in relation to the definitions of the other elements.

A data model may be considered to be a space of names that are all in semantic relation with other names; these semantic relations are expressed explicitly in the model. In this sense a model provides a *"universe of conversation"* (TARDIEU-ROCHFELD-COLLETTI83); in fact, the data modelling of an application field in relational terms serves as a language in which all conversation concerning the database must be expressed. This language is formed from a vocabulary comprising the names of the relations, attributes, and the domain values principally; these phrases are ready-made phrases, the predicates of the relations, or new phrases that may be constructed from the first using relational operators.

It should be noted that for a database user this data model becomes the *reality* of the database: he cannot express phrases other than those contained in the conversation universe. This conversation universe becomes, with familiarity, the *reality* of the field of application itself for the uninformed user: therein lies a great danger, we believe, because this behaviour turns the modification into its opposite. In fact, the model is only a partial and distorted reality of the field of application.

During the course of the next exercise we will try to illustrate this important point, by posing some questions on the meaning of the model.

1.5   Example: production workshop

1.5.1   Scenario

This *model* is concerned with a production workshop (any resemblance to an existing workshop being completely fortuitous) organised as follows:

- it can manufacture a wide variety of products;
- the unit of time is the hour;
- once the manufacture of production units is set in motion, it lasts for at least one hour and leads to the manufacture of a minimum number of units of the product (MMQ) which represents the number of units manufactured in an hour. Manufacture is thus by product *batches* of at least MMQ units. The manufacture of a batch is carried out within one day.
- The manufacture of batches of the same product always requires the same raw materials in the same quantities; the latter are proportional to the number of product units manufactured,.
- Batches of the same product may be manufactured by any of the machines having a particular function; all these machines have the same performance. The manufacturing time for a batch is proportional to the number of units in the batch. A batch is manufactured by the same machine, and several batches of different products or of the same product can be manufactured in parallel on different machines. One machine can manufacture a single batch in a given hour.
- A technician can operate several machines: this depends on his technical competency. If he is competent to operate a machine for a particular function, then he can operate all the machines having that same function. There are generally several technicians who are competent to operate the same machine.
- One and only one technician is assigned to operate a machine during a given hour and a technician can only operate one machine at a time during a given hour.

The model proposed is intended to produce a computing tool that will allow a daily timetable to be set up from the set of daily batches to be manufactured; it of course only relates to those technicians who are fit for work and to the machines that are available; it is also conceived on the basis of the quantities of raw materials currently in stock.

1.5.2   Relations and attributes

TECHNICIAN (NTEC NAMTEC).

Predicate:	the technician number (NTEC) identifies the technician; the technician's name is assigned to it.	
NTEC	technician number	integer word (1,100).
NAMTEC	technician name	text.

ACTIVITY (NTEC NH ACTIVE).

Predicate:	technician number (NTEC) is active at the required time (NH) if he is not on leave at that time; otherwise he is inactive.	
ACTIVE	state of activity	word (active, inactive).
NH	hourly work shift	integer word (1,8).

MACHINE (NMH FUNCTION).

Predicate:	the machine number (NMH) identifies machines; each machine has a single function (FUNCTION).	
FUNCTION	a machine's function	word.
NMH	machine number	word.

MACHINE-AVAILABILITY (NMH NH MHAVAIL).

Predicate:	machine number (NMH) is at a given time either broken down, being serviced (in both cases it cannot be used for batch manufacture), or available (in this case it is, or is not, used for the manufacture of batches).	
MHAVAIL	state of machine availability	word (available, broken, being serviced).

PRODUCT (NP MMQ).

Predicate:	the product number (NP) identifies a product. There is a corresponding quantity of product units for each product number: this is the minimum manufacturing quantity for this product batch (MMQ).	
NP	product number	positive integer word.
MMQ	minimum manufacturing quantity of a batch	positive numeric integer.

BATCH (NP NBATCH NBH NMH).

Predicate:	the batch number (NBATCH) identifies a batch from all others of the same product. Manufacture of this batch is planned to be spread over so many hours (NBH) by a particular machine (NMH).	
NBATCH	batch number	positive integer word.
NBH	number of hours	numeric integer (1,8).

R-M (NRM QRM).

Predicate	the raw material number (NRM) identifies the particular raw material. There is a corresponding stock quantity of raw material (QRM) for each raw material number.	
NRM	raw material number	positive integer word.
QRM	quantity of raw material	positive numeric integer.

PROVISION (NP NRM MMQ).

Predicate:	there corresponds to a product number (NP) and to a raw material number (NRM) the quantity (MMQ) of this raw material necessary for the manufacture of the minimum batch of this product (PROVISION).	
MMQ	minimum quantity of raw material	positive numeric integer.

COMPETENCE (NTEC NMH).

Predicate	the technician with such a number (NTEC) is competent to operate the machine with such a number (NMH).

UTILISATION (NP) FUNCTION).

Predicate:	the product with such number (NP) can be manufactured only by machines with the specified function (FUNCTION).

TIME-TABLE (NH NP NBATCH NTEC NMH).

Predicate:	on this day, at this hour (NH) it is planned that batch (NBATCH) of product (NP) is to be manufactured by machine number (NMH) operated by technician number (NTEC).

1.5.3   Exercises based on this model

Determine the keys to each relation.

Indicate whether the following statements are compatible with the model. Justify your responses.

a) There is a product whose manufacture only requires one raw material.

b) It is possible to schedule in the timetable the manufacture of a batch that only takes 1 hour 35 minutes.

c) A technician can be replaced by another for the manufacture of the same batch within a given hour.

d) There are more than 5 machines for the same function.

e) Units of the same batch can be manufactured together.

Our answers are given in section **1.5.5.**

1.5.4   An illustration of the different concepts of the relational model

1.5.4.1   Relation, entity, key

An entity of relation MACHINE-AVAIL is an element of the cartesian product of the domains of attributes NMH, NH, MHAVAIL.

(1, 1, available) is such an element; it corresponds to an entity only if it verifies the predicate of the relation, that is, only if a user confirms that machine number 1 is available during the first hour.

An instance of a relation is a set of entities of the relation.

A key to the relation MACHINE-AVAIL is a minimum set of its attributes such that if two entities of MACHINE-AVAIL take the same values for these attributes in the same instance, these two entities are identical. If NMH is a key then it will not be possible to consider the availability of a machine during the course of several hours in the same instance! This is of course unacceptable.

If NH is a key to MACHINE-AVAIL then the availability of a single machine for a given hour could be stored in an instance! Again, unacceptable.

On the other hand, there must correspond to a value of NMH NH a single entity in every instance of MACHINE-AVAIL, because there is only a corresponding single state of availability. Since this set of attributes is minimal - since neither NH nor NMH verifies this property - NMH NH is a key to MACHINE-AVAIL.

It is the only key. We leave it to the reader to deduce why. The exercise in the following chapter will provide a full approach to determining keys to relations.

1.5.4.2   Relation projection, hinge to two relations, composition of two relations

The projection of relation TIME-TABLE on attributes NH NP NBATCH leads to a new relation whose predicate may be expressed as follows:

at time (NH) the manufacture of batch (NBATCH) of product (NP) is planned.

The hinge between the relations of MACHINE-AVAIL and TIME-TABLE is formed from the set of attributes common to the two relations NMH NH.

The join of these two relations will provide a new relation constructed on attributes NMH NH NP NBATCH NTEC MHAVAIL, whose predicate can be formulated as follows:
at time (NH) the manufacture of batch (NBATCH) of product (NP) by machine (NMH) is planned which is operated by technician (NTEC) and whose availability at this time (NH) is (MHAVAIL).

1.5.4.3   Mandatory key

NTEC NH forms a key to TIME-TABLE; it is not the only one, because NP NBATCH NH and NH NMH are also keys to TIME-TABLE. But it can in addition be declared as mandatory, in which case every entity of every instance of TIME-TABLE must take clear values for attributes NTEC NH.

1.5.5   Solutions to problems

1.5.5.1   Keys to relations

In the following chapter, we examine this aspect in more detail.

keys to		
	TECHNICIAN:	NTEC,
	ACTIVITY:	NTEC NH,
	MACHINE:	NMH,
	MACHINE-AVAIL:	NMH NH,
	PRODUCT:	NP,
	BATCH:	NP NBATCH,
	R-M:	NRM,
	PROVISION:	NP NRM,
	COMPETENCE:	NTEC NMH,
	UTILISATION:	NP,
	TIME-TABLE:	NH NTEC,
		NH NMH,
		NH NP NBATCH.

NAMETEC cannot be a key to the relation TECHNICIAN: its domain is in fact declared as having type text. Two values of NAMTEC cannot be compared and therefore NAMTEC cannot belong to any key.

1.5.5.2 Answers to questions on modelling

The questions suggested in section 1.5.3 are intended to make the reader aware of the distance between the "real world" and that of the database obtained from the proposed model. The following are our answers:

a) The fact that a product only requires a single raw material for its manufacture can be taken into account in the future database: in fact, the model provides for a product to be assigned in a general way, with several raw materials being used in its manufacture (key to relation PROVISION is NP NRM).

b) It is possible that "in reality" the manufacture of a batch will only last 1 hour 35 minutes. However, the current model only counts in hours. So this fact could not be taken into account on the future database with such precision; the manufacture of this batch would take two hours so far as the database was concerned.

c) In "reality", if it is permissible to replace one technician by another during a given hour for the manufacture of a given batch, it must be understood that at the database level with the current model one could also replace one technician by another; but the database would then regard the second as having done all the work during that hour. In fact, NH NP NBATCH is a key to TIME-TABLE and thus one can only assign one technician (NTEC) to one hour and to one batch.

d) The model provides for one function to be completed by several machines (MACHINE relation). If every function can be fulfilled by at most five machines, this fact is not recorded in the current model. It is expressed by means of an integrity rule as we shall show in the following chapter.

e) It is possible that units of the same batch may be manufactured at the same time. But the "conversation universe" of the model does not contain the concept of batch unit. So this fact is not carried forward into the future database.

1.6   Appendix

1.6.1   Proofs of the properties of enlargement

(e1) $R^e[R^+] = R$.

$\forall r \in R$, it is sufficient to consider any value of every attribute of U^+-R^+ to form with r an entity re of R^e such that re.R^+ = r; so R is included in $R^e[R^+]$.

$\forall s \in R^e[R^+]$, there exists an entity re of R^e such that s = re.R^+ (definition of projection). If re is an entity of R^e then re.R^+ is an entity of R (definition of enlargement) and so s is an entity of R.

(e11) $1[X] = 1_x$ and $(1_x)^e = 1$.

(e12) $0[X] = 0_x$ and $(0_x)^e = 0$.

The proofs of these two properties are obvious.

(e2)   If $X \subset R^+$ then $R^e[X] = R[X]$.

$\forall x \in R^e[X]$, there exists an entity re of R^e such that re.$X = x$ according to the definition of projection; there exists an entity r of R such that re.$R^+ = r$ according to the definition of enlargement. Since X is included in R^+, re.$X = ($re.$R^+).X = r.X$; thus there exists an entity r of R such that $x = r.X$. $R^e[X]$ is included in $R[X]$.

$\forall x \in R[X]$, there exists an entity r of R such that $x = r.X$. By the enlargement of R, there exists an entity re of R^e such that re.$R^+ = r$. Since X is included in R^+, $x = r.X = ($re.$R^+).X = $re.$X$. Thus x belongs to $R^e[X]$ and $R[X]$ is included in $R^e[X]$.

(e21)   If $X \wedge R^+ = \varnothing$ then $R^e[X] = 1_x$.

$\forall x \in X \ \exists r \in R$ and $\exists re \in R^e$ such that re.$R^+ = r$ and re.$X = x$; thus x belongs to $R^e[X]$. The reciprocal is obvious.

(e3) $(R*S)^e = R^e*S^e$.

$\forall rse \in (R*S)^e \ \exists rs \in R*S$ such that rse.$R^+ \cup S^+ = rs$.

According to the definition of join, $\exists r \in R$ and $\exists s \in S$ such that rs.$R^+ = r$ and rs.$S^+ = s$.

Thus rse$\in R^e$ and rse$\in S^e$.

Thus rse$\in (R^e * S^e)$.

Reciprocally

$\forall rse \in R^e * S^e$, rse$\in R^e$ and rse$\in S^e$ because R^e and S^e are relations defined on the same set of attributes U^+. Thus $r = $ rse.R^+ and $s = $ rse.S^+ are respectively entities of R and of S such that:

r.$R^+ \wedge S^+ = s.R^+ \wedge S^+ = $ rse.$R^+ \wedge S^+$.

Thus rse.$R^+ \cup S^+$ is an entity of R*S and rse is an entity of $(R*S)^e$.

(e31) $R^e * S^e = R^e * S = R * S^e$.

The proof follows the same reasoning as the previous proof.

(e4) $(R + S)^e = R^e + S^e$.

The proof follows the same reasoning as the previous proof.

(e41) $R^e + S^e = R^e + S = R + S^e$.

$\forall rse \in R^e + S^e$, $rse \in R^e$ or $rse \in S^e$;

thus $rse \in R^e$ or $rse.S^+ \in S$ and so $rse \in R^e + S$.

Reciprocally: $\forall rse \in R^e + S$, $rse \in R^e$ or $rse.S^+ \in S$;

thus $rse \in R^e$ or $rse \in S^e$; finally $rse \in R^e + S^e$.

(e5) $(not\ R)^e = not\ (R^e)$.

$\forall re \in (not\ R)^e$, $r = re.R^+$ is an entity of not R and is therefore not an entity of R; re is therefore not an entity of R^e, it is an entity of not (R^e).

Reciprocally:

$\forall re \in not\ (R)^e$, re is not an entity of R^e and therefore $r = re.R^+$ is not an entity of R. r is an entity of not R and re is an entity of $(not\ R)^e$.

(e6) $((*P)R)^e = (*P)\ R^e$.

There exists a relation PR such that:

$PR^+ = P^+$ and $\|PR\| = P$ and $(*P)R = PR * R$.

$((*P)R)^e = (PR*R)^e = PR^e * R^e$ (according to e3)

          $= PR*R^e$ (according to e31)

          $= (*P)R^e$.

(e7) $(R = S) \Rightarrow (R^e = S^e)$ and $(R^+ = S^+) \wedge (R^e = S^e) \Rightarrow (R = S)$

The proofs of these two properties are obvious.

1.6.2   Proofs of the properties of the focus operation

(f1a) focus $(R/U^+) = R^e$

        because focus $(R/U^+) = R^e[U^+] = R^e$.

(f1b) If $X \subset R^+$ then focus $(R/X) = R[X]$

        because focus $(R/X) = R^e[X] = R[X]$.   (from e2).

(f2) focus $(1_x/Y) = (1_x)^e[Y] = 1[Y] = 1_y$ (from e11).

      focus $(0_x/Y) = (0_x)^e[Y] = 0[Y] = 0_y$ (from e12).

(f3) focus $(R*S/X) \subset$ focus $(R/X) *$ focus (S/X).

      If X contains the hinge RS^+ then

      focus $(R*S/X) =$ focus $(R/X) *$ focus (S/X).

focus $(R*S/X) = (R*S)^e[X] = (R^e * S^e)[X]$ (from e3).

$\forall rsx \in (R^e * S^e)[X]$ $\exists rse \in (R^e * S^e)$ such that $rse.X = rsx$.

Therefore $\exists rse \in R^e$ and $\exists rse \in S^e$ such that $rse.X = rsx$.

Therefore $\exists rse \in R^e$ such that $rse.X = rsx$, and $\exists$ $rse \in S^e$ such that $rse.X = rsx$;

finally, rsx is an entity of $R^e[X] * S^e[X]$.

Reciprocally (in the case where $RS^+ \subset X$):

$\forall rsx \in R^e[X] * S^e[X]$, $rsx \in R^e[X]$ and $rsx \in S^e[X]$,

$\exists re \in R^e$ such that $re.X = rsx$ and $\exists se \in S^e$ such that $se.X = rsx$.

Thus $\exists r \in R$ such that $re.R^+ = re$ and $\exists s \in S$ such that $se.S^+ = s$.

Since $RS^+ \subset X$, $re.RS^+ = rsx.RS^+ = se.RS^+ = s.RS^+ = r.RS^+$.

Thus $\exists rs \in R*S$ such that $rs.R^+ = r$ and $rs.S^+ = s$;

then $re.R^+ \cup S^+ = rs$ and thus re is an entity of $(R*S)^e$.

Consequently, rsx is an entity of $(R*S)^e[X]$.

(f4) focus $(R + S/X) =$ focus $(R/X) +$ focus (S/X).

   focus $(R + S/X) = (R + S)^e[X] = (R^e + S^e)[X]$.

The proof follows the same reasoning as the previous case.

(f5) not focus $(R/X) \subset$ focus $(not R/X)$.

   If X contains R^+ then there is equality.

not focus $(R/X) =$ not $(R^e[X])$.

$\forall x \in$ not $(R^e[X])$ then $\forall re \in R^e$ $re.X \neq x$;

thus $\forall$ re' tuple formed on U^+ such that $re'.X = x$, $re' \in$ not R^e:

x belongs to $(not R^e)[X]$.

Thus not focus $(R/X) \subset$ focus $(not R/X)$.   (from e5).

Reciprocally $(R^+ \subset X)$:

focus $(not R/X) = (not R^e)[X]$.

$\forall x \in (not R^e)[X]$ and $\forall re \in U$ such that $re.X = x$.

We know that there exists at least such an entity re of not R^e by definition of projection.

But if there exists re' in R^e such that $re'.X = x$, then $re'.R^+$ belongs to R; since R^+ is included in X, $re'.R^+ = re.R^+$ and so re does not belong to not R^e .

Thus $\forall re \in U$ such that $re.X = x$, $re \in$ not R^e .

Thus $x \in$ not $(R^e[X])$ and focus $(not R/X) \subset$ not focus (R/X).

(f6a) If $Y \subset X \subset R^+$ then focus (focus $(R/X)/Y$) = focus (R/Y) = $R[Y]$.
The proof is simple,

(f6b) If $R^+ \subset X$ then focus (focus $(R/X)/Y$) = focus (R/Y).
focus (focus $(R/X)/Y$) = (focus $(R/X))^e[Y]$ = $(R^e[X])^e[Y]$.
$\forall re \in (R^e[X])^e$ $x = re.X \in R^e[X]$ and $\exists re' \in R_e$ such that $re'.X = x$;
therefore $re'.R^+ \in R$.
Since $R^+ \subset X$, $re'.R^+ = re.R^+$ is therefore an entity of R.
re is an entity of R^e .

Reciprocally:
$\forall re \in R^e$ $re.R^+ \in R$.
$x = re.X$ is an entity of $R^e[X]$ by construction.
Thus re is an entity of $(R^e[X])^e$.
Thus $(R^e[X])^e = R^e$.
focus (focus $(R/X)/Y$) = $R^e [Y]$ = focus (R/Y).

1.6.3   Proofs of the properties of the operations: sum, product, complement, projection

(02) We systematically apply property (e7). $X = R^+$.

$(\text{not } R + R)^e$	$= (\text{not } R)^e + R^e$	(e4)
	$= \text{not } (R^e) + R^e$	(e5)
	$= 1$	(e8).
$(\text{not } R * R)^e$	$= (\text{not } R)^e * R^e$	(e3)
	$= \text{not } (R^e) * R^e$	(e5)
	$= 0$	(e8).
$(R * 0_x)e^e$	$= R^e * (0_x)^e$	(e3)
	$= R^e * 0$	(e12)
	$= 0$	(e9).
$(R + 0_x)^e$	$= R^e + (0_x)^e$ $= R^e + 0 = R^e$.	
$(R * 1_x)^e$	$= R^e * (1_x)^e$ $= R^e * 1 = R^e$.	
$(R + 1_x)^e$	$= R^e + (1_x)^e$ $= R^e + 1 = 1$.	

(03) $R + (R*S) = focus (R/R^+ v S^+)$.

This property derives directly from properties (e7, e3, e4, e5, e9).

$$(R + (not R*S))^e \quad = R^e + (not R*S)^e \qquad (e4)$$
$$= R^e + ((not R)^e * S^e) \qquad (e3)$$
$$= R^+ + (not R^e * S^e) \qquad (e5)$$
$$= R^e + S^e \qquad (e9)$$
$$= (R + S)^e \qquad (e4).$$

2 Integrity rules

2.1 Introduction

(For a rapid overview, the reader is advised to read sections 2.1, 2.2, 2.7, 2.8, 2.9 and 2.10.)

An integrity rule is is an non-variable of the field of application which concerns any of its states or any of its changes of state. Translated into database terms and applied only to data (excluding processes on the database), this concept of an integrity rule becomes a property that it is possible to express from relations in the model, and which must always be verified by means of an algorithmic process at each state of the database or at each modification made to it.

During this difficult phase in the modelling of a field of application, the work of analysing and formalising these non-variables is of a remarkable efficiency and relevance for at least two reasons. The first of these lies in the fact that every non-variable relating to the data is such a significant property of the field of application that it must be able to be described in the model. If this is not possible, the designers must complete the model. Every final data model is *complete* with regard to the non-variables if it contains a description of all the non-variables relating to the data.

The second reason derives from the very position of the designers who analyse a field of application. Their main task is to observe and synthesise their observations into a model that obeys, for example, the formalism of the relational data model. They are thus in a position to listen attentively to all information concerning the field of application. They are faced with the problem of having to remain rather passive; we could say that information is brought to them and they make a model from it.

Alternatively, they might adopt a more "active" position and gather information that they require to establish the data model. Designers adopting

31

the "active" role immediately encounter a major problem; how do they find pertinent information? How can they understand the field of application better? Here again, a study of the non-variables provides a precise aid to database designers. We will show how every relational model, even (and often) an incomplete one, contains special situations that are likely to include non-variables. These situations suggest relevant ideas on the possible existence of non-variables in this part of the model: if there is a non-variable, one must be able to express it and, if the model does not allow this, it must be completed. On the other hand, if there is no non-variable, the designer must assure himself that the model is quite correct, despite a certain propensity towards the existence of a non- variable.

Furthermore, faced with the dangers of the "active" stance in an analytical process which result from conscious or unconscious lapses on the part of designers, it is important to note that such situations contained in a model must be studied by the designers, whether they have adopted a more or less passive or active stance.   We will describe such a model as *verified in relation to non-variables* when all these situations have been analysed.

A data model must contain not only the relations, attributes and domains as we have described in the previous chapter, but also the integrity rules. These have a very important role to play in the use of the database, namely that of ensuring its coherence. This is their normal role. What does this involve? The entities of a relation are tuples of values that verify the predicate of the relation. But this verification is only the responsibility of a user at his terminal or a program operating on the database. It is one or other of these that decides whether or not a particular tuple is an entity. Because there is always some risk of a false step, designers and users wish to be protected against such risks. The non-variables in the field of application, described in terms of integrity rules in the database, provide such protection: every alteration to the database will have to verify these integrity rules in order to be accepted. Thus, one can be sure that certain errors will be detected and that some incoherences in the database will be avoided.

The problem that remains for designers is a classic one for any enterprise. Should every possible precaution be taken, whatever the cost? Should every integrity rule be verified, or can one be satisfied with only the most important? In the second case some integrity rules (and therefore some non-variables) are not retained generally for a combination of the following reasons:
- the assurance provided by their verification covers a minimal risk;
- the price of the assurance provided by their verification is much too high, that is, the computing costs, losses of efficiency, losses of time, resources, etc are too high in comparison with the risks run.

A *database* is said to be *coherent* (in relation to the integrity rules) if all instances of its relations verify all the integrity rules retained to ensure this coherence. Each integrity rule must have its range assigned to it, that is, the set of update primitives that require its verification in order for the database to be remain coherent.

Finally, even if the designers have taken every precaution by retaining all the integrity rules, it is nevertheless impossible to guarantee the absolute coherence of the database in an algorithmic way since precisely the predicates of relations cannot be verified by the execution of an algorithm; the users of the database will still be responsible for maintaining its coherence.

2.2 Integrity rule

2.2.1 Definition of an integrity rule

An *integrity rule* (ir) is a condition that is defined in relation to either a relation (intra-relation integrity rule) or to several relations (inter-relation ir), and whose verification test can be carried out in an algorithmic manner on the instances of the relations concerned.

The *context* of an integrity rule designates the relations on which the integrity rule is defined.

The *condition* of an integrity rule must be verified for every state of the database (static integrity rule) or for every alteration to the state of the database (behaviour rule) by instances of the context relations.
A static integrity rule is applied to each entity of a relation instance (individual static integrity rule) or to an instance relation (group static integrity rule).
A behaviour rule relates to an operation to alter one or more entities of a relation instance; that is, creating, deleting, querying an entity or a set of entities, updating the value taken by an entity for an attribute. It expresses a logical condition between the state of the database before the alteration and its state afterwards.

The *range* of an integrity rule designates the set of primitives that alter the database relations and which must contain an algorithm for the verification of the integrity rule so that the coherent state of the database will be transformed by the primitive into another coherent state.

The *response* of an integrity rule ir indicates the actions to be undertaken in the event of non-verification of ir. This involves specifying the action to be taken when, once a within range primitive has been triggered, the verification algorithm detects that complete action by the primitive would cause an incoherence relating to ir. The normal response is to refuse to execute the primitive. However, the response may be more complicated and may involve a cascade of deletions.

The *expression* of an integrity rule may take the form of a mathematical expression of an algorithmic expression terminated by a condition (for example, functional dependence, join dependence - discussed in a later section, comparison of sets of entities, automata, the predicative expression whose variables are relations or attributes forming the context of the integrity rule and take their values from the set of entities or data stored in the database relating to these relations and attributes).

2.2.2   Examples

We will give some examples of an individual static integrity rule, a group ir and a behaviour rule. Section 2.10 contains a complete example that includes a wide variety of integrity rules.
Take the relation PLAYER (NAME STATUS TEAM CAPTAIN) whose predicate is as follows:
'every player has a name (NAME), a civilian status (STATUS), belongs to a single team (TEAM) and is or is not captain of this team (CAPTAIN).'
We assume that the key to this relation is NAME. NAME has a domain of type word; STATUS has a domain of type word which contains the values: unknown, single, married, divorced, widow(er). CAPTAIN has a domain of type boolean where the value 'true' means that the player is the captain, and 'false' that he is not.

2.2.2.1   Example of individual static integrity rule

'A single player cannot be captain.' This is an individual ir. Its context is the relation PLAYER. It may be expressed as:
$\forall \ j \in$ PLAYER[STATUS = single] j.CAPTAIN = false.
Its range is the following set of primitives:
    create PLAYER,
    update PLAYER[STATUS],
    update PLAYER[CAPTAIN].

2.2.2.2   Example of group static integrity rule

'Every team has at least one captain.'
Its context is the relation PLAYER. It is expressed as:
∀ eq ∈ TEAM
     ∃ j ∈ PLAYER[TEAM = eq and CAPTAIN = true].

This is a group ir. Its range is:
    update PLAYER[CAPTAIN],
    update PLAYER[TEAM],
    delete PLAYER.

The creation of a new player in a team does not normally require the verification of this ir: because the team already exists, there is a captain. But if "create PLAYER" does not lie within the range, there is the risk of the database being incoherent: in fact, when entities of PLAYER relating to this team are created, it would be possible to create a team without its captain. It would not be very precise for this sole case to introduce "create PLAYER" into this range. It would be better to define a new primitive "create TEAM" which would allow one to create PLAYER entities of a new team, and insert this new primitive into the range.
Note how the study of integrity rules has brought about an enrichment of the model by causing the designer to create this new primitive "create TEAM".

2.2.2.3   Example of behaviour rules

Consider the status of a player. It is an obvious fact that a married person cannot belong in the single status. So any change in the status of a player obeys an automaton that can be shown graphically as in figure 2.1 (cf BODART-PIGNEUR83).

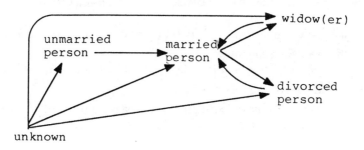

Figure 2.1 Example of behaviour rule

The nodes represent the different domain values and the only changes authorised are those described by the arcs.

More detailed examination will reveal that this automaton will not allow one of the clear values (single, widow) into an unknown value. If the application requires this possibility, then a new unknown value must be introduced for every clear value. In fact, it would not be enough to change only the unknown value already in position, because this would allow the following sequence of changes for a player: married - unknown - single.

Again, a more detailed study of this integrity rule enriches the model, since it leads to the completion of the model with 4 new values: 4 unknown values assigned to each clear value.

The context of this integrity rule is the relation PLAYER. Its range is: update PLAYER[STATUS].

2.2.3   Definitions of a relation structure and of a data collection

We now introduce two additional definitions to the concept of a relation, which specify the structural links that exist between a relation and an integrity rule.

A *structure of a relation* R or *schema of a relation* R is formed from the definition of this relation and of the set of integrity rules I(R) that allows it as context.

A *collection of data* of a relation R is an instance of R that verifies all the static integrity rules contained in I(R).

2.2.4   Equivalence relation and order relation

Take two integrity rules ir_1 and ir_2 having the same context: $R_1...R_n$ (if n = 1, the irs are intra-relational; otherwise they are inter-relational).

ir_1 and ir_2 are *equivalent* if every set of instances $(iR_1...iR_n)$ that verifies one, verifies the other, and inversely.

ir_1 is *more restrictive than* ir_2 if every set of instances $(iR_1...iR_n)$ that verifies ir_1 , verifies ir_2 - described as $ir_1 \leq ir_2$.

ir_1 is *trivial* (or equal to 1) if every set of instances $(iR_1...iR_n)$ verifies ir_1 .

ir_1 is *empty* (or is equal to 0) if no set of instances $(iR_1...iR_n)$ verifies it.

The first relation is an equivalence relation; the second is a partial order relation.

2.3 Introduction to dependencies

This generic term embraces a complete class of group static integrity rules which the scientific community has identified as significant if we are to judge from the quantity of scientific papers devoted to this subject. For us, their importance lies in the fact that they are a convergence point for a number of topics linked with data structures.

The first of these considers that the dependencies allow the expression of a class of non-variables that are essential to understand a model. We shall try to illustrate this by the example discussed in section 2.10.

Another topic deals with the role of dependencies in the obtaining of equivalent models from the semantic point of view, but leading to database structures that are more or less efficient for the verification of these dependencies.
A third topic concerns the fundamental role of dependencies in the coherent use of a database, both when querying and extracting data and when making alterations to the database.
A fourth topic is linked with the difficult phase of modelling or the difficult problem of the evolution of a database: the dependencies appear to us to be a valuable guide to the understanding of a model, its criticism and perhaps its modification. They seem to us to prompt the designer to ask perceptive questions, first concerning the model and then concerning the faithfulness of this model for the field of application.
A final topic is their extremely close link with the problem of data redundancy in a database.

We will examine these topics both in the following sections and in Part 3 on the decomposition of a relation. In fact, the concepts of the dependencies and the decomposition of relations are closely interrelated. In this chapter, we will present the different dependencies, their properties, the concept of the decomposition of a relation, and the properties of a decomposition which derive directly from those of join dependencies. These properties allow us to show the advantage of dependencies in the modelling process of a field of application (topics 1, 3 and 4 above). We study topics 2 and 5 in a later chapter.

Note
Note that since our aim is not to present the theory of dependencies, we refer the reader to the works mentioned in the references, in particular those of ULLMANN80, DELOBEL-ADIBA82 and MAIER83 for a more detailed treatment.

2.4   Functional and dimensional dependencies

2.4.1   Functional dependencies

Functional dependencies (fd) are the first dependencies that were introduced into the domain of databases (CODD70).

DEFINITIONS

A relation R is provided with the functional dependency (fd) described by $X \rightarrow C$ if and only if:

- X is a subset of R^+ and C is an attribute of R,
- for each value x of X there is a value c of C such that for every entity r of R, if r.X = x then r.C = c.

The fd $X \rightarrow A$ is said to be *trivial* if A is an attribute of X.

Example

Take the relation EXAMINATION (STUDENT COURSE MARK DEGREE PROFESSOR) which assigns the courses of a degree to students enrolled for this degree and to the professor in charge of this course; each student receives a mark for each course that he has taken.

STUDENT COURSE $\rightarrow$ MARK means that in EXAMINATION a student receives a single mark per course.

COURSE $\rightarrow$ PROFESSOR means that in EXAMINATION a single professor is in charge of a course.

Notation: the fd f: $X \rightarrow A$ allows as its lefthand part $l(f) = X$ and as its righthand part $r(f) = A$.

2.4.2   Dimensional dependencies

To generalise the fds, we will identify two important aspects of the definition of fds:

- every value x of X has *at most* a corresponding value c in R;
- the value c corresponding to x is known independently of the entities r of R that take the value x for X.

We generalise the first by introducing a new type of dependency, namely dimensional dependencies.

We generalise the second by introducing relative dependencies and reference dependencies (see 2.6.3 and 2.6.4).

DEFINITION

A relation R is provided with *dimensional dependency* (dd), described by $X \to n \to C$ where X is a subset of R^+, C an element of R^+, n a positive integer, if

- there corresponds to every value x of X at most n values c of C in R.

If n is equal to 1, the dd is a simple fd.

A dd is a group static integrity rule. We will illustrate this new dependency by means of the following example.

Example DD

Consider the contracts of a computing services company. For simplicity, we will consider a single relation CONTRACT, defined as follows:

CONTRACT (NOCONTRACT EMPLOYEE CLIENT SUBJECT DURATION STARTDATE RESPONSIBILITY) with as predicate:

a contract number (NOCONTRACT) to distinguish between all contracts. A contract is fulfilled by 10 employees at most (EMPLOYEE) and each employee has a particular responsibility (RESPONSIBILITY) for each contract that he is involved with. A contract is made with a single client (CLIENT) for work on a single subject (SUBJECT) which must be completed within so many months (DURATION) starting from a given date (STARTDATE).

The domain of SUBJECT is formed from numerous areas of computing such as databases, expert systems, information systems, etc.

The following are some functional dependencies:

NOCONTRACT $\to$ CLIENT SUBJECT DURATION STARTDATE

NOCONTRACT EMPLOYEE $\to$ RESPONSIBILITY.

Since up to 10 employees can be assigned to a contract, there is the following dimensional dependency:

NOCONTRACT $\to 10 \to$ EMPLOYEE.

2.4.3 Properties of fds

W X Y Z designate subsets of attributes of R+. It is relatively easy to demonstrate the following properties:

(fd1) Reflexivity

If X is included in Y then $Y \to X$ is an fd of R. We describe it as *trivial* since X is included in Y.

(fd2) Augmentation

If $X \to Y$ is an fd of R and if $Z \subset W$ then $X W \to YZ$ is an fd of R.

(fd3) Transitivity
If $X \rightarrow Y$ and $Y \rightarrow Z$ are fds of R then $X \rightarrow Z$ is another.

(fd4) Pseudo-transitivity
If $X \rightarrow Y$ and $Y W \rightarrow Z$ are fds of R then $X W \rightarrow Z$ is another.

(fd5) Union
If $X \rightarrow Y$ and $X \rightarrow Z$ are fds of R then $X \rightarrow Y Z$ is another.

(fd6) Decomposition
If $X \rightarrow Y$ is an fd and if Z is included in Y then $X \rightarrow Z$ is an fd.

BASIC RESULTS (fd)

Each of these properties may be considered to be a derivation rule. In fact, given a set F of functional dependencies of R, it is possible to add to it new functional dependencies by applying these mathematical properties. The latter then appear in their 'derivation rule' role to permit the derivation of new fds of R from F. Since the number of attributes of R is finite, the set of all the fds that can be derived from F by repeated application of the derivation rules leads to a unique finite set of functional dependencies of R called the *closure* F** of F. This closure F** of F is obtained using the derivation rules fd1, fd2 and fd3.
The derivation rules fd1, fd2, and fd3 constitute a valid and complete system (ARMSTRONG74)(BEERI FAGIN HOWARD77). That is, on the one hand it is valid because they allow the effective derivation of new functional dependencies of R from F; on the other hand, it is complete because if all the instances of R verifying the fds of F in addition verify a particular fd f1, then f1 belongs to the closure F**.

Property
If f and h are two functional dependencies verifying:
$d(f) = d(h)$ and $g(f) \subseteq g(h)$ then f is said to be greater than h: $f > h$ and this relation is an order relation.

Definitions and properties
The *complete base* F* of F is the set of the maximal functional dependencies of F** in comparison with the preceding order relation: these functional dependencies are called *elementary*.
G, a set of functional dependencies, is a *covering* of F if $G** = F**$; it is a *base* of F if G is included in F* (or equal to F*).

A covering C of F is *non-redundant* if no functional dependency f of C belongs to (C-f)**. A *non-redundant base* of F is a covering of F which is non-redundant and which is also a base of F.

Example

F = (AB → C; A → DE; D → B; C → A)

The closure F** contains A → B (transitivity of A → D and D → B) and also A → C (pseudo-transivity A → B and AB → C).

Therefore A → C is greater than AB → C and AB → C is not elementary.

F* = (A → C; A → DEB; D → B; C → A; C → DEB).

The following is a non-redundant base of F:

$F1^+$ = (A → C; A → DE; D → B; C → A)

Note

The closure F** of F contains all the coverings and bases of F; in particular it contains F* and F itself which is a covering of F.

Key to a relation

The fds allow us now to give a more formal definition of the concept of a key to a relation than in the previous chapter. In section 2.11 we give an example of an algorithm for obtaining all the keys to a relation.

K is a key to a relation R if and only if

K is included in R^+;

for every attribute A of R, K → A is an fd of R;

for every subset K' of K, there is an attribute B of R such that K' → B is not an fd of R.

Intrinsic functional dependency

The fd X → A of the relation R is an intrinsic fd of R if X is a key to R.

2.4.4 Properties of dds

We will leave it to the reader to show that dimensional dependencies also verify the properties of reflexivity, transitivity augmentation, pseudo-transitivity, union and decomposition, defined as in the case of fds.

We will simply note that if A → n → B and B → m → C are two dds, then by transitivity we can deduce A → n m → C.

The dds also verify another augmentation property:

Augmentation (bis) If A → n → B is a dd, then A → p → B is another for every p > n.

Multiple key to a relation

KM is a multiple key to R if and only if:

- KM is included in R^+;
- for every attribute A of R, KM → n → A is a dd of R;
- for every subset KM' of KM, there is an attribute B of R such that KM' → n → B is not a dd of R.

In the example DD relating to CONTRACT, the relation CONTRACT allows a key: NOCONTRACT EMPLOYEE and a multiple key NOCONTRACT; in fact NOCONTRACT → CLIENT SUBJECT DURATION STARTDATE is an fd, NOCONTRACT → 10 → EMPLOYEE is a dd; furthermore, by psuedo-transitivity we obtain:
NOCONTRACT → 10 → RESPONSIBILITY.

2.5   Join and decomposition dependencies

The concepts of join dependencies defined on a relation and of decomposition of a relation are very close to one another from the formal point of view. This is why we present them both in this section by pointing out their differences. The concept of decomposition is so important that it forms the subject matter of part 3.

Base property (jd)

For every relation R and for every set of attributes R_i^+ of R such that:

$$R^+ = \bigcup_{k=1}^{n} R_k^+ \quad \text{then} \quad R \subseteq \overset{n}{\underset{k=1}{*}} R[R_k^+],$$

and for every clear instance iR: $iR \subseteq \overset{n}{\underset{k=1}{*}} iR[R_k^+]$.

The proofs are obvious.

Example

Below are three instances of relations R, R_1 , R_2 :

$R(ABC)$ $R_1 = R[AB]$ $R_2 = R[AC]$

$a_1\ b_1\ c_1$ $a_1\ b_1$ $a_1\ c_1$
$a_1\ b_2\ c_1$ $a_1\ b_2$ $a_1\ c_2$
$a_1\ b_1\ c_2$

iR does not contain $(a_1\ b_2\ c_2)$ which belongs to $iR_1 * iR_2$. If they are the closures of the relations, then R does not allow $(a_1\ b_2\ c_2)$ as entity, although it is an entity of $R_1 * R_2$.

2.5.1   Definitions and first properties

DEFINITION

A *decomposition* D of a relation R is a set of relations $R_1\ R_2...R_k...R_n$ verifying:

a) $R_k = R[R_k^+]$

b) $R = \overset{n}{\underset{k=1}{*}}\ R[R_k^+].$

D^+ designates the set of attributes of relations R_k: $D^+ = R^+$.

D is a *total* decomposition of R. If there is a relation RR for which R is a projection, then D is a *partial* decomposition of RR.

Note

Property b) implies property   c): $\overset{n}{\underset{k=1}{\cup}} R_k^+ = R^+$.

Notation

From now on D_k D D' designate implicitly decompositions respectively of R_k R and R'.

DEFINITION

If the set of relations $R_1...R_k...R_n$ is a decomposition D of relation R, the entities $(r_1...r_k...r_n)$, one in relation to the decomposition, are *mutually compatible* if there is an entity r of R such that $r.R_k^+ = r_k$. The instances $iR_1...iR_k...iR_n$ are *mutually compatible* if

$$(\overset{n}{\underset{k=1}{*}} (iR_k))[R_j^+] = iR_j \qquad (\forall j \in (1,n)).$$

COMPLETENESS PROPERTY

If the relations $R_1...R_k...R_n$ form a decomposition D of relation R, then for every entity r_i, there is a set of mutually compatible entities $(r_1 \ r_2...r_k...r_n)$ that contains it, and for every clear instance iR_k, there is a mutually compatible set of instances $(iR_1 \ iR_2 ...iR_n)$ that contains it.

Proof
Since R_k is a projection of R, there is for every instance iR_k an instance iR of R such that $iR[R_k^+] = iR_k$. The compatible instances iR_j of iR_k are formed by projections of iR on R_j^+.
For every entity r_k of iR_k, we thus obtain a set of compatible entities.

DEFINITION

Take the relations $R_k = R[R_k^+]$. R allows *join dependency* (jd), shown by $* (R_j)$ (j=1...) or $(R_1...R_n)$ if and only if for every instance iR of R verifying this integrity rule we have:

$$iR = \overset{n}{\underset{j=1}{*}} iR[R_j^+].$$

The jd is total for R; it is partial for every relation for which R is a projection.

Property (jdo)
If R allows the jd $(R_1...R_n)$, then $\{R_1...R_n\}$ forms a decomposition of R.
If R decomposes according to D: $\{R_1...R_n\}$ then every instance of R is contained in an instance called *complete* of R for D which verifies the jd $(R_1...R_n)$.

Proof

All the instances of R verify jd, and in particular the closure of R: R decomposes according to D.

Take iR to be an instance of R; $iR[R_j^+]$ is an instance of R_j because $R_j = R[R_j^+]$.

$$iR' = \overset{n}{\underset{j=1}{*}} iR[R_j^+] \text{ is an instance of R because } R = \overset{n}{\underset{j=1}{*}} R[R_j^+].$$

According to the base property $iR \subseteq iR'$.

iR' is a complete instance of R for D because it verifies the jd $(R_1...R_n)$.

We describe as *associated* a decomposition D of R and a jd of R which are formed on the same relations.

Corollary

A valid system of inferences for the jds is also valid for associated decompositions.

Proof

Take a relation R which decomposes to D1 D2...Dp. Its closure verifies the associated join dependencies d_1 d_2 ...dp. By the inference rule, we can deduce that it verifies the jd d formed on $R_1...R_j...R_n$. Since it involves the closure of R, we have:

$$R = \overset{n}{\underset{j=1}{*}} R[R_j^+]$$

both at the level of the closures and at the level of the relations. R thus allows $R_1...R_j...R_n$ as decomposition.

Note

This corollary allows us to introduce at the same time valid inference rules of the jds which are also valid for the decompositions.

Differences between one jd and a decomposition of R

If the relation R(ABC) decomposes to $R_1 = R[AB]$ and $R_2 = R[AC]$, the database may contain the following two instances:

iR_1	iR_2
a b	a c
a' b'	a" c"

Instance iR associated with this state of the database contains a single entity (ab) and iR[AB] $\subseteq$ iR$_1$, and iR[AC] $\subseteq$ iR$_2$.

We consider that we do not yet know an entity (a' c') of R$_2$ and an entity (a" b") of R$_1$, but that these entities will be known in a future state of the database. So the closure of R and the closures of R$_1$ and R$_2$ will verify the jd (R$_1$ R$_2$).

Instance iR formed from entities a b c, a b' c', a b' c, is not complete: to make it complete we need to add a b c'.
On the other hand, iR does not verify the jd (R$_1$ R$_2$).

Another difference between a decomposition of R and a jd of R may be found in their role in the definition of a database. At the level of the definition of a database structure, we will try to find decompositions of a relation R and select one from them: this is done in part 3. But the entities of R are not actually stored in the database; they can be calculated from entities of the relations R$_k$ of the decomposition, which are in fact stored. Nevertheless, at the level of embedding in the database, a jd must be verified like any integrity rule.

DEFINITION

One decomposition (with regard to a jd) is *included* in another if, and only if, the set of relations forming the first is included in the set of relations forming the second.

Notation

If D$_1$ is a partial decomposition of RR,
if D$_2$ is another,
if the set of relations of (D$_1$ $\cup$ D$_2$) forms another decomposition, then the latter is described by D$_1$ D$_2$.
We will use the same convention for the jds.

2.5.2 Properties of jds and decompositions

All the properties in this section and the one that follows allow the following to be constructed from a decomposition D (with regard to a jd d): (R$_1$...R$_k$...R$_n$) of relation R:
 - a new decomposition D' (with regard to jd d') included in the first: properties of projection, generalised reflexivity, reduction, generalised reduction;

- a new decomposition D' (with regard to jd d') which contains the first: properties of extension, augmentation;
- a new decomposition (with regard to jd) using another decomposition (with regard to jd): properties of grouping, substitution, enlargement.

From the practical point of view, the first properties will serve to reveal a decomposition or a jd, of attributes or of relations: we will use them in particular to study the only relations and attributes that occur in a cyclic database structure (2.7).

The other properties will serve to determine the widest possible semantic spaces in a database (2.10.2).

(jd1) The same jd may be expressed using any permutation of the relations that go to make it.

(jd2) Extension:
If $S^+ \subseteq R^+$ and if $S = R[S^+]$ then $(R_1...R_n \ S)$ forms a jd of R.

(jd3) Augmentation:
If $(R_1^*...R_k^*...R_p)[S^+] = S$ $(p < n)$ then $(R_1...R_k...R_p...R_n \ S)$ forms a jd of R.

(jd4) Projection:
If S^+ is included in R^+ and if each attribute of $R^+ - S^+$ belongs to a single relation R_k then

$(R_1[R_1^+ \cap S^+]...R_k[R_k^+ \cap S^+]...R_n[R_k^+ \cap S^+])$ is a jd of $R[S^+]$.

All the hinges of the first jd are preserved in the second.

(jd5) Grouping:
If $(R_1...R_k...R_{n-1} \ S_1...S_j...S_p)$ forms a jd of R,
if $(S_1...S_j...S_p)$ forms a jd of R_n,
then $(R_1...R_k...R_{n-1} \ R_n)$ forms a jd of R.

(jd6) Substitution:
If $(R_1...R_k...R_{n-1} \ R_n)$ forms a jd of R,
and if $(S_1...S_j...S_p)$ forms a jd of R_n,
then $(R_1...R_k...R_{n-1} \ S_1...S_j...S_p)$ forms another jd of R.

2.5.3   Structural properties

(jd7) Generalised reflexivity:

If $(R_2^*...R_j^*...R_m)[R_1^+] = R_1$ $(m < n)$ then $(R_2...R_j...R_m...R_n)$ is another jd of R.

DEFINITION

A relation R_1 is an *extremity* of the jd d if and only if for the set of attributes Chmax of R verifying:

$$Chmax = \bigcup_{k=2}^{n} (R_k^+ \cap R_1^+): \exists k \in (2..n) \text{ such that } R_k^+ \cap R_1^+ = Chmax.$$

If R_1 is an extremity of d, it is also an extremity of the decomposition $\{R_1...R_k...R_n\}$.

Example

Take the decomposition of R: D = $\{R_1(ABC)\ R_2(BCD)\ R_3(CDE)\}$;

R_1 is an extremity of D (Chmax = BC) as well as R_3(Chmax =CD).

Take a decomposition of R':

D' = $\{R_1(ABC)\ R_2(BCD)\ R_3(CDE)\ R_4(ACG)\}$.

R_1 is not an extremity of D' because Chmax = ABC and no other relation of D' contains Chmax.

(jd8) Reduction:

If R_1 is an extremity of d, $(R_2...R_n)$ is a partial jd d' of R.

d' is obtained by *reduction* of d.

DEFINITIONS

A decomposition is said to be *linear* if the successive application of reduction leads to a decomposition reduced to one relation. Otherwise it is said to be *cyclic*.

A decomposition D_1 of R_1 is an *extremity* of a decomposition D_2 of R_2 if it is included in it, and if R_1 is an extremity of the decomposition obtained by grouping in D_2 of D_1 in R_1 (property jd5). These definitions also apply to the jds.

Example

Take the decomposition of R: $D = \{R_{11}(AB)\ R_{12}(AC)\ R_2(BCD)\ R_3(CDE)\}$.

Take the decomposition of $R_1 = R[ABC]$: $D1 = \{R_{11}(AB)\ R_{12}(AC)\}$.

D_1 is an extremity of D (Chmax = BC).

Take the decomposition of R': $D' = \{R_{11}(AB)\ R_{12}(AC)\ R_2(BCD)\ R_3(ACD)\}$.

Take the decomposition of $R_1 = R'[ABC]$: $D_1 = \{R_{11}(AB)\ R_{12}(AC)\}$.

D_1 is not an extremity of D (Chmax = ABC).

(jd9) Generalised reduction:

If the jd d' is an extremity of the jd d then the set of relations of d that does not belong to d' forms a partial jd.

(jd10) Enlargement:

Take d_1 to be a jd of R_1, d_2 a jd of R_2 and (R_1, R_2) a jd of R_{12}, then $d_1\ d_2$ is a jd of R_{12}.

2.5.4   Properties of fds and jds

(fd-jd1) Take a jd $(R_1\ R_2)$ of R and an fd $AB \rightarrow C$ of R such that A and B are attributes of R_1 and C is an attribute of R_2.

Take Ch^+ to be the set of attributes common to R_1 and R_2.

Then $Ch^+ \rightarrow C$ is an fd of R, when Ch^+ is not empty.

Proof

For every instance iR of R that verifies the jd $(R_1\ R_2)$ and $AB \rightarrow C$, and for all entities r, r' of iR such that $r.Ch^+ = r'.Ch^+ = ch$, we can then construct the following entities:

entities	A	B	Ch^+	C	
r	a	b	ch	c	$r \in R$
r'	a'	b'	ch	c'	$r' \in R$
$r.R_1^+ = r_1$	a	b	ch		$r_1 \in R_1$
$r.R_2^+ = r_2$			ch	c	$r_2 \in R_2$
$r'.R_1^+ = r_1'$	a	b	ch		$r_1' \in R_1$
$r'.R_2^+ = r_2'$			ch	c'	$r_2' \in R_2$
$r_1^* r_2' = r_{12}$	a	b	ch	c'	$r_{12} \in R$

Because of the fd AB → C, c = c' and r_{12} = r.

(fd-jd2) If the relation R(ABC) is provided with the fd A → B then (R[AB] R[AC]) is a jd of R.
Proof
For every instance iR of R that verifies A → B then ∀ re iR[AB] * iR[AC], we can construct the following entities:

entities	A	B	C	
r	a	b	c	
r_1	a	b		$r_1 \in$ iR[AB]
r_2	a		c	$r_2 \in$ iR[AC]
rab	a	b	c'	rab ∈ iR because $r_1 \in$ iR[AB]
rac	a	b'	c	rac ∈ iR because $2r_2 \in$ iR[AC]

Because of the fd A → B, b = b' and thus rac = r.r is an entity of iR.

2.5.5   Tree dependencies

DEFINITION
There is an important special case of join dependency: these are tree dependencies (td) (DELOBEL73; DELOBEL-LEONARD74). A *tree depend-ency* is a join dependency in which, two by two, the relations forming the jd have the same attributes in common which form the root of the tree dependency.
The following is an example of a jd that is a td:
(R_1(ABC) R_2(AF) R_3(ADE)); its root is A and it can also be written as a tree dependency A:BC/F/DE.

The properties of tds are derived from those of jds, as for example:
(jd1).A:F/BC/DE;
(jd4) A:F/B/D and also A:BC/DE;
(jd5) A:FBC/DE;
(jd6) If we know in addition that A:B/C then we can obtain: A:B/C/F/DE;
(jd8) The tds are linear cds;
(jd-fd1)   If F → E is an fd then A → E is also one;
            if AF → E is an fd then A → E is also one.
The tree dependencies have other properties like the one that allows one to deduce from the td considered, the following: td1) AE: BC/F/D.

2.5.6 Multivalued dependencies

Introduced by (FAGIN77), multivalued dependencies are a special case of tds. The *multivalued dependency* AB →→ C is defined in R if and only if ABC are subsets of attributes of R^+ and if AB: C/D is a td, D being a subset of attributes of R such that $D = R^+$ - ABC.

This concept of multivalued dependency should not on any account be confused with the concept of dimensional dependency.
So, in example DD, the dd NOCONTACT → 10 → EMPLOYEE is defined in the relation CONTRACT: it means that up to 10 employees may be assigned to a contract.
The multivalued dependency NOCONTRACT →→ EMPLOYEE would mean the existence of the following td:
NOCONTRACT: EMPLOYEE/CLIENT SUBJECT DURATION
STARTDATE RESPONSIBILITY.
In particular, one could deduce the following td by projection (jd4):
NOCONTRACT: EMPLOYEE/RESPONSIBILITY.
It would mean that every employee engaged in a contract assumes all the responsibilities foreseen for this contract!
One could deduce from this td and the fd:
NOCONTRACT EMPLOYEE → RESPONSIBILITY,
the following fd by application of the property (jd-fd1):
NOCONTRACT → RESPONSIBILITY.
All the employees engaged in the same contract would in fact have the same responsibility. This conclusion is not compatible with the application described.
This application allows the dd: NOCONTRACT → 10 → EMPLOYEE, but does not allow the multivalued dependency:
NOCONTRACT →→ EMPLOYEE.

Furthermore, this concept of multivalued dependency should not be confused with another concept which is expressed using inclusion dependencies (discussed in section 2.6).
We illustrate this difference with the same example as before: we assume, in addition, that an employee cannot be engaged in a contract unless he is competent in the subject of the contract.
This rule is not modelled by the following multivalued dependency:
EMPLOYEE →→ SUBJECT in the relation CONTRACT. In fact, this multivalued dependency would be written as the following td:
EMPLOYEE: SUBJECT/NOCONTRACT CLIENT DURATION
STARTDATE RESPONSIBILITY.

The latter could be projected according to the following td:
EMPLOYEE: SUBJECT/NOCONTRACT.
From the fd NOCONTRACT $\rightarrow$ SUBJECT, we could deduce (property jd-fd1)
the fd: EMPLOYEE $\rightarrow$ SUBJECT. An employee would then only be
competent for a single subject! The multivalued dependency
EMPLOYEE $\rightarrow\rightarrow$ SUBJECT is therefore not defined in CONTRACT.
The situation presented in this example requires the creation of the relation
COMPETENCE (EMPLOYEE SUBJECT), whose predicate is obvious, and
the introduction of the following integrity rule:
CONTRACT [EMPLOYEE SUBJECT] $\subseteq$ COMPETENCE.

Great care is required in the use of multivalued dependencies: in our opinion it
is better to use tree dependencies which are equivalent but which explicity
describe the set of attributes involved.

2.6   Inclusion dependencies

The following is the most general form of an inclusion dependency:
RR $\subseteq$ RS where RR and RS are two relations.
It means that every entity of RR is also an entity of RS. Of course, it requires
that $RR^+ = RS^+$.

Such dependencies have received attention in the literature (CASANOVA-FAGIN-
PAPADIMITRIOU82; MITCHELL83; ABITEBOUL85; HUONG87). The different types of
inclusion dependency derive from the nature of the relations RR and RS: these
relations can in fact designate relations in the model or relations obtained by
joining of relations in the model, perhaps followed by a projection. These
dependencies are generalisable to all relational expressions.

Example (research laboratory)
A researcher identifies by his name (RESNAME) belongs to a research
laboratory identified by its initials (LABO). A researcher writes several articles
identified by their number (NOART). The domains (DOM) of each of these
articles must be research domains of his laboratory. These are the relations:

ARTICLE(RESNAME NOART)   with key: RESNAME NOART,
LABORATORY(RESNAME LABO)   with key: RESNAME,
DOM-ART(NOART DOM)   with key: NOART DOM,
DOM-LABO(LABO DOM)   with key: LABO DOM.

This is a referential dependency:
ARTICLE[RESNAME] ⊆ LABORATORY[RESNAME].

This is an inclusion dependency:
(ARTICLE * DOM-ART)[RESNAME DOM] ⊆
(LABORATORY * DOM-LABO)[RESNAME DOM].

2.6.1   Referential dependencies

RR and RS are projections of simple relations on a key KRS of RS belonging
to RS^+ and RR^+. Inclusion dependency is then called referential dependency:
RR[KRS] ⊆ RS[KRS].

2.6.2   Special inclusion dependencies

We are chiefly interested in inclusion dependencies that allow for RR or for
RS a relation in the model that is perhaps projected on one or other of its keys.
This limitation leads to the creation of new relations: we believe that this
method is important for an understanding of the model.

So for the preceding example we will create a new relation formed on
RESNAME DOM which is defined as:
(LABORATORY * DOM-LABO)[RESNAME DOM],
or as: (ARTICLE * DOM-ART)[RESNAME DOM],
or with a predicate less than the first and greater than the second.

In this example, an association between a researcher res and a research domain
d has as its "natural" sense the fact that d is one of the research domains of res.
We choose the predicate for the new relation that we call COMPETENCE.
The preceding inclusion dependency is transformed into two inclusion
dependencies:

(ARTICLE * DOM-ART)[RESNAME DOM] ⊆ COMPETENCE and
COMPETENCE ⊆ (LABORATORY * DOM-LABO)[RESNAME DOM].

These inclusion dependencies are of a special type; the first is called a
reference dependency and the second a *relative dependency*.
The new relation COMPETENCE is described as *multifunctional* (2.10.1).

2.6.3   Reference dependencies (rd)

Take two decompositions $D = \{R_1...R_n\}$ of R and $D' = \{R_1'...R_m'\}$ of R'. The reference dependency D: D' only exists if $R'^+ \subseteq R^+$.
It means that: $R[R'^+] \subseteq R'$.

Notation
D designates a decomposition of R, $D_1\, D_2\, D_3\, D_4\, D'$ are partial decompositions.

Properties of reference dependencies
The proofs of these properties are obvious.
(rd1) Reflexivity
If D' is an included decomposition of D then D -: D'.

(rd2) Union
If D -: D_1 and D -: D_2 are two reference dependencies and if $D_1\, D_2$ is a decomposition, then D -: $D_1\, D_2$.

(rd3) Transitivity
If D -: D' and D' -: D" then D -: D".

(rd4) Pseudo-transitivity
If D_1 -: D_2 and $D_2\, D_3$ -: D_4 are two reference dependencies and if $D_1\, D_3$ is a decomposition, then $D_1\, D_3$ -: D_4 is a new reference dependency.

(rd5) Decomposition
If D_{22} is an included decomposition of D_2, D_1 -: D_2 involves D_1 -: D_{22}.

(rd6) Projection
If D_{11} is an included decomposition of D_1 and if $D_2^+ \subseteq D_{11}^+$, then D_1 -: D_2 involves D_{11} -: D_2 .

Proof
$\forall r_2 \in R_{11}[D_2^+]\, \exists\, r_{11} \in R_{11}$ such that $r_{11}.D_2^+ = r_2$. Since D_{11} is an included decomposition of D_1 and because of the completeness property, there is an entity r_1 of R_1 such that $r_1.R_{11}^+ = r_{11}$. Because of the reference dependency D_1 -: D_2 , there is an entity r_2' of D_2 such that $r_1.D_2^+ = r_2'$.
Since $r_1.R_2^+ = r_{11}.R_2^+$, $r_2 = r_2'$.

2.6.4 Relative dependencies (div)

Take two decompositions $D = \{R_1...R_n\}$ of R and $D' = \{R_1'...R_m'\}$ of R'. The relative dependency $D +: D'$ only exists if $R'^+ \subseteq R^+$.
It means that $R' \subseteq R[R'^+]$.

Properties of relative dependencies
(div1) Reflexivity
If D' is an included decomposition of D then $D +: D'$.

Proof
$D = (R_1...R_{n-1} S_1...S_j...S_p)$: decomposition of R.
$D_n = (S_1...S_j...S_p)$: decomposition of R_n.
By the group property (jd5) we obtain:
$R[R_n^+] = R_n$. Thus $D +: D'$.

(div2) Isotony
If $D_1 +: D_{11}$ and $D_2 +: D_{22}$,
and if $(D_1 \ D_2)$ and $(D_{11} \ D_{22})$ form decompositions,
and if the hinge $(R_1 \ R_2)^+$ is included in (or equal to) that of $(R_{11} \ R_{22})^+$, then
$D_1 D_2 +: D_{11} D_{22}$ is another relative dependency.

Proof
$\forall \ r_{1122} \in R_{1122}, \exists \ r_{11}$ of R_{11} and r_{22} of R_{22} such that:
$r_{11} = r_{1122}.R_{11}^+$ and $r_{22} = r_{1122}.R_{22}^+$,
because $(D_{11} \cup D_{22})$ is a decomposition of R_{1122}.
Because of the two relative dependencies, there is r_1 of R_1 and r_2 of R_2 such that: $r_1.R_{11}^+ = r_{11}$ and $r_2.R_{22}^+ = r_{22}$.
r_1 and r_2 are compatible because the hinge of R_1 and of R_2 is included in that of R_{11} and of R_{22}. $r_{12} = (r_1 * r_2)$ is an entity of R_{12} because $(D_1 \cup D_2)$ is a decomposition of it; r_{12} verifies by construction $r_{12}.R_{1122}^+ = r_{1122}$.

Example
The following is an example where the inclusion property of hinges is not verified:

$D_1 : S(ABE)$ $D_{11} : V(AB)$
$D_2 : T(ACE)$ $D_{22} : U(AC)$.

S(ABE)	V(AB)	T(ACE)	U(AC)
a b e	a b	a c e	a c
a b'e'	a b'	a c'e'	a c'

S*T	V*U
a b c e	a b c
a b'c'e'	a b'c
	a b c'
	a b'c'

Although $V \subseteq S[AB]$ and $U \subseteq T[AC]$,
V*U is not contained in (S*T)[ABC].

(div3) Transitivity
If D_1 +: D_2 and D_2 +: D_3 are two relative dependencies then D_1 +: D_3 is also one.
The proof is obvious.

(div4) Pseudo-transitivity
If D_1 +: D_2 and D_2 D_3 +: D_3,
if $D_1 D_3$ is a decomposition,
if $(R_1 R_3)^+$ is included in (or equal to) $(R_2 R_3)^+$,
then $D_1 D_3$ +: D_4.

Proof
It is sufficient to apply the property of isotony to the relative dependencies
D_1 +: D_2 and D_3 +: D_3 to obtain $D_1 D_3$ +: $D_2 D_3$; by transitivity, we obtain
$D_1 D_3$ +: D_4.

Example where the condition relating to the hinges is not verified
Take the following relative dependencies:
$R_1(ABC)$ +: $R_2(AC)$,
$(R_2(AC) R_3(BCE))$ +: $R_4(AE)$,
$(R_1 R_3)^+ = BC$ and $(R_2 R_3)^+ = C$,
$(R_1 R_3)^+$ is not included in $(R_2 R_3)^+$.

R_1	R_2	R_3	R_4
a b c	a c	b c e	a e
a b c'	a'c'	b c'e'	a'e'
a'b'c'		b'c e	

$R_1 * R_3$

a b c e

a b c'e'

a'b'c'e

$(R_1 * R_3)[R_4^+]$ does not contain R_4.

(div5) Decomposition

D_{22} is an included decomposition of D_2.

If $D_1 +: D_2$ then $D_1 +: D_{22}$.

Proof

By reflexivity we have $D_2 +: D_{22}$ and by transitivity $D_1 +: D_{22}$.

(div6) Projection

D_{11} is an included decomposition of D_1 and D_2^+ is included in D_{11}^+.

If $D_1 +: D_2$ then $D_{11} +: D_2$.

The proof is obvious.

2.6.5 Join-projection dependencies

Take two decompositions $D = \{R_1...R_n\}$ and $D' = \{R_1'...R_m'\}$. The join-projection dependency $D =: D'$ only exists if $R'^+ \subseteq R^+$.

It means that $R' = R[R'^+]$.

A join-projection dependency is a special case of relative dependency and reference dependency.

Properties of join-projection dependencies

They derive from the properties of relative and reference dependencies.

(jpd1) Reflexivity

If D' is a partial decomposition D then $D =: D'$.

(jpd2) Isotony

If $D_1 =: D_{11}$ and $D_2 =: D_{22}$,

if $(D_1\ D_2)$ and $(D_{11}\ D_{22})$ form decompositions,

if the hinge $(R_1\ R_2)^+$ is included in $(R_{11}\ R_{22})^+$ or is equal to it,

then $D_1\ D_2 =: D_{11}\ D_{22}$.

(jpd3) Transitivity
If $D_1 =: D_2$ and $D_2 =: D_3$ then $D_1 =: D_3$.

(jpd4) Pseudo-transitivity
If $D_1 =: D_2$ and $D_2 D_3 =: D_4$ are two join-projection dependencies,
if $D_1 D_3$ is a decomposition,
if $(R_1 R_3)^+$ is included in $(R_2 R_3)^+$,
then $D_1 D_3 =: D_4$.

(jpd5) Decomposition
D_{22} being a partial decomposition of D_2 ,
if $D_1 =: D_2$ then $D_1 =: D_{22}$.

(jpd6) Projection
D_{11} being a partial decomposition of D_1 and $D_2^+ \subseteq D_{11}^+$,
if $D_1 =: D_2$ then $D_{11} =: D_2$.

2.7   Relation cycles

The set of relations $\{R_1 R_2 ...R_n\}$ forms a *proper relations cycle* if:
n is greater than 2;
and each attribute of each relation belongs to at least one other of these relations;
and each relation permits common attributes with at least two other relations;
and none of these relations contains the set of attributes of another relation.

The set of relations $\{S_1 S_2 ...S_n\}$ forms a *relations cycle* if:
S^+ designates the set of attributes belonging to at least two of these relations, the set of relations $R_i = S_i [S_i^+ \cap S^+]$ forms a proper relations cycle.

The set of relations $\{S_1 S_2 ...S_n\}$ forms an *atomic relations cycle* if they form a cycle and if none of its subsets forms one.

Example
$S_1(ABDX), S_2(BCDY), S_3(CAZ)$ form a relations cycle.
The relations $S_1 S_2 S_3$ form a relations cycle whose set of attributes is:
$S^+ = ABDC$. The relations $S_1[ABD], S_2[BCD], S_3[CA]$ form a proper relations cycle.

Relations cycles are very important in the study of a model because they show the existence of several possible associations between the same attributes. Thus in the preceding example, an association between attributes ABD can be obtained in two ways: $S_1[ABD]$ and $(S_2 * S_3)[ABD]$.

Are these two associations *independent*? Or is there an integrity rule?

In our view, the designer has the responsibility of answering such a question and we will show how the inclusion dependencies allow him to do so.

THEOREM (id)

If $R_1 R_2...R_n$ form a proper relations cycle and if there is the reference dependency $R_1 R_2...R_{n-1}$ -: R_n , then all the following relative dependencies exist:

if $\{R_1...R_{k-1} R_{k+1}...R_n\}$ form a decomposition,
then $\forall k \in (2,...,n-1)$ $R_1...R_{k-1} R_{k+1}...R_n$ +: R_k,
and if $\{R_2...R_n\}$ forms a decomposition, then $R_2...R_{n-1}R_n$ +: R_1 .

Proof
$\forall r_1 \in R_1 \exists (r_2...r_{n-1}) \in R_2*...R_{n-1}$ are mutually compatible with r_1 to form an entity $r = (r_1*r_2...*r_{n-1})$ of $(R_1*...R_{n-1})$ according to the completeness property applied to the decomposition $\{R_1...R_{n-1}\}$.

Because $R_1 R_2...R_{n-1}$ -: R_n , there is an entity r_n of R_n such that $r.R_n^+ = r_n$. By construction, $(r_2..r_i..r_n)$ are compatible (for $i = 2...n$) and there is $r' = r_2*...*r_n$ an entity of $R_2*...*R_n$ and $r'.R_1^+ = r_1$.

Therefore $R_2...R_n$ +: R_1 if $(R_2...R_n)$ forms a decomposition.

Corollary (id)
If $R_1,R_2...R_n$ form a proper relations cycle and if the following reference dependencies are verified:
         a) $R_1R_2...R_{n-1}$ -: R_n
         b) $R_2...R_{n-1} R_n$ -: R_1
then the following join-projection dependencies are also verified:
         c) $R_1R_2...R_{n-1}$ =: R_n
         d) $R_2...R_{n-1} R_n$ =: R_1 .

Proof

By the preceding theorem, we derive from a): e) $R_2...R_{n-1} R_n$ +: R_1 ; from b) and from e) we derive d) by definition of the join-projection dependency.

When faced with a cycle, the designer tries first to reveal all the join-projection dependencies and the reference dependencies; if he finds at least one, his work is finished according to theorem (id). Otherwise, he tries to reveal the relative dependencies.

He thus determines all the inclusion dependencies and the mutual interdependence of the relations entities of the cycle.

The inclusion dependencies are by no means the only integrity rules that may exist between the relations that form a cycle. But they do permit a serious study of a difficult problem.

The CONTEST example at the end of this chapter illustrates an application of the preceding theorem.

Theorem (v)

$\{R_1 R_2...R_n\}$ forms a decomposition D of R,
if $\{R_2...R_n\}$ is another decomposition of R, then there exists the join-projection dependency: $R_2...R_n$ =: R_1 .
The reciprocal is verified.

Proof

a) Since $R_2*...* R_n = R$ and $R[R_1^+] = R_1$ because D is a decomposition, $R_2...R_n$ =: R_1 is verified.

b) The reciprocal derives from the generalised reflexivity property (jd7).

Corollary (v)

If $R_2...R_n$ -: R_1 or $R_2...R_n$ +: R_1 exists, then relations $R_1 R_2...R_n$ cannot form a decomposition of relation R.

This corollary is very useful in the determination of contexts: since the preceding relations $R_1 R_2...R_n$ do not form a decomposition of a relation, they cannot belong to the same context (see 2.10.2).

2.8 Other integrity rules

Integrity rules can take various forms and *it is not possible for us to present an exhaustive procedure* that will enable one to find all the integrity rules of a model. Nevertheless, we will sketch out a procedure that will allow the designer to ask himself the right questions in order to extend his knowledge of the field of application and reveal integrity rules. This procedure applies to each space, one after the other.

a) *Case of relations with several keys*
Take a relation R allowing several keys K_1, K_2 ...

Take a relation S such that S^+ contains one or more keys to R.
We need to know whether the key(s) to R contained in S^+ is well chosen in order to ensure the associations between the entities of S and those of R.

So in the CONTEST example (2.10.4) at the end of this chapter, there are two particular relations:
RESULTS (EXAMINER MARK ADDRESS-TITLE) and
SUBJECTS (ADDRESS-TITLE CANDIDATE TOPIC HALF-DAY FINAL-
            MARK)
Explained briefly, these relations mean that a candidate taking an oral test in a given topic, gives an address during one half-day in front of examiners, each of whom awards a mark; he obtains a final mark for this address.
RESULTS allows one key: EXAMINER ADDRESS-TITLE,
SUBJECTS allows three keys: ADDRESS-TITLE,
                             CANDIDATE TOPIC,
                             CANDIDATE HALF-DAY.

The given model contains an integrity rule that is deceptively subtle: every examiner's mark can only be recorded if the address title is known.
Since the SUBJECTS relation has several keys, we might have imagined another relation instead of RESULTS:
        RES (EXAMINER MARK CANDIDATE TOPIC), or even
        RES (EXAMINER MARK CANDIDATE HALF-DAY).

If we were to choose RES in preference to RESULTS, we would then have to have the candidate and the topic in order to record an examiner's mark.

b) *Attributes belonging to several relations having a common domain*

The designer must be aware that such a situation is analogous to that of a relation cycle.

In the CONTEST example later, we introduce an example of such a situation with the attributes MARK and FINAL-MARK having the same domain MARK.

Attributes that express dates, or time intervals, are frequent examples of such types of attribute.

c) *Attributes expressing measurements*

Often, the integrity rules concern sums of measurements. For example, the sum of the totals of command lines (COMMAND-LINE relation) must be equal to the total of the command (COMMAND relation) in the case of the following relations:

COMMAND (NOCD TOTAL NBLN):
a command is designated by a number (NOCD); its total (TOTAL) is assigned to it, together with the number of command lines that go to make it up:

COMMAND-LINE (NOCD NPRODUCT TOTALLN):
there is a command line for each product for each command which contains the value of the product quantity ordered (TOTALLN).

d) *Attributes expressing counting*

In the previous example, the number of command lines (NBLN) in the COMMAND relation for a product is equal to the number of command lines (COMMAND-LINE relation) of this command.

e) *Attributes expressing a state or class criterion*

Generally, there are integrity rules that express conditions to ensure that an entity has a particular value for such a attribute.

So, in the workshop example, the model has identified MACHINE-AVAILABILITY and OCCUPATION.

MACHINE-AVAILABILITY is formed from the attributes MHN (machine number), HN (hour in the week), MHAVAIL (machine availability which allows as values 'available', 'occupied', 'being serviced').

OCCUPATION is formed in particular from attributes PN (product number), BN (batch number), HN and MHN, and assigned to a batch, the machine that will produce it and the production time.

Attribute MHAVAIL expresses a state and it involves the following integrity rule: no batch can be produced by a machine that is being serviced.

2.9 Table of ir ranges

2.9.1 Range of each ir

The range of each ir has to be determined; that is, the modification primitives that are to be subject to verification of the ir must be indicated. These primitives relate to every base relation: *create* an entity (c), *delete* an entity (d), *update* the value taken by an entity for an attribute (u), query entities (q).

The following integrity rules are assumed to be verified:
- intrinsic functional dependencies of a base relation;
- attribute domains: the value taken by an entity for an attribute belongs to the domain of the attribute;
- referential dependencies between two relations R and S when a key KS to one (S) is included in the set of attributes of the other: at the level of instances stored in the database at the same time, it is assumed that condition iR[KS] $\subseteq$ iS[KS] is always verified.

We will therefore not specify the range of the above integrity rules.

2.9.2 Table of ranges

We will construct a table of ir ranges: each column k corresponds to an integrity rule ir_k. Each row j corresponds to a relation R_j of the model. Each location marking the intersection of column k and row j contains the primitives for altering relation R_j which must be operated on by a verification algorithm of ir_k.
Section 2.10.4 contains the range table of integrity rules for the CONTEST example.

Such a table allows these different primitives to be realised and later facilitates applications programming without requiring verification of the integrity rules if this programming makes use of these primitives. Another advantage is when the integrity rules have to be changed as the database environment evolves: whether an integrity rule is altered, deleted or introduced, the user knows exactly which primitives have to be changed; in addition, in the majority of cases the application programs will not have to be changed. If the action to be taken in the event of non-verification of an integrity rule depends on the context of the application program, the latter can undergo changes if the integrity rule is changed. We describe such a way of realising a set of applications programs for a database as the *normal architecture* of a database.

2.10   Conclusions

We will now show how the study of integrity rules is introduced into the modelling process and how, in our opinion, it helps the designer to understand better the field of application.

The model process has already introduced several relations that we call basic relations. The designer can continue his analysis of these basic relations, using in particular different dependencies, and thus enrich the model.

First we present two very important features in the analysis of a model:
- the *independence* of some data compared with other data, and as a corollary the interdependence of some data: this will be expressed by means of inclusion dependencies;
- the determination of sets of basic relations; each forms a decomposition of a relation, called a *space*. We illustrate the importance of this concept by an example.

Then we present a working canvas for the designer to enable him to analyse a model and possibly alter and enrich it. We conclude by presenting a *complete example*, CONTEST.

2.10.1   Independence: multifunctional relation

We will use the CONTRACT relation (NOCONTRACT EMPLOYEE CLIENT SUBJECT DURATION STARTDATE RESPONSIBILITY) from example DD in section 2.4.2. A contract is let for a task involving a single subject.

CONTRACT [EMPLOYEE SUBJECT] allows an employee e to be assigned to a subject s if this employee e is engaged in at least one contract whose work subject is s. Pursuing the analysis further, it can be seen that an employee can only work on a contract if he is competent in the subject of the contract. The employee's competences are defined *independently* of the contracts in which he participates.

There is therefore a new relation COMPETENCE (EMPLOYEE SUBJECT) which links an employee and a subject if he is competent in this subject, together with a new integrity rule: CONTRACT -: COMPETENCE.

The method described below suggests that the designer analyse every base relation R: if the entities linked to a projection of R on some of its attributes, for example A and B, can be known *independently* of the entities of R, then it is important to consider them as entities of a new relation S(AB) verifying R -: S.

Such a new relation is described as *multifunctional*.

Of course, this study can be generalised to the relations obtained by the join of basic relations. These multifunctional relations in fact generalise the concept of functional dependency as we mentioned in section 2.4.2. In particular, they can emerge rapidly in the case of the existence of fd: $A \rightarrow B$.

For example, from the relation PROVISION
(PRODUCT SUPPLIER-NAME SUPPLIER-ADDRESS)
with fds: PRODUCT $\rightarrow$ SUPPLIER-NAME
              SUPPLIER-NAME $\rightarrow$ SUPPLIER-ADDRESS,
one can easily construct the relation: SUPPLIER
              (SUPPLIER-NAME SUPPLIER-ADDRESS).

Note
This feature of independence is not expressed by means of multivalued dependencies as we showed in section 2.5.6.

2.10.2 Contexts and spaces

To introduce this feature, we start from a simple fact: relational database systems allow users to interrogate the database themselves using a relatively simple language. This language allows them to join several basic relations and obtain a new relation RC. If from the formal point of view the predicate of this relation is perfectly defined, from the *operational* point of view, the users give a meaning to the linking of attributes that form RC: the pitfall is there as soon as the operational meaning does not correspond to the predicate of RC. We will illustrate this viewpoint with the following example.

Example

Here is an example of such a pitfall faced by users of the following database structure:

	Abbreviation
CHARGE (NOCASE ACCUSEDNAME)	(NC ACCN)
PROSECUTION (NOCASE BARRISTERNAME)	(NC BARN)
DEFENCE (BARRISTERNAME ACCUSEDNAME)	(BARN ACCN)

CHARGE links a case number and an accused's name if the latter has been accused during this case;

PROSECUTION links a case number and a barrister's name if the latter has pleaded during the case;

DEFENCE links a barrister's name and an accused's name if this barrister has defended this accused.

We want to find the names of all the barristers who have defended scapegoat during the case number 969.
This question relates to relation CASE (NC ACCN BARN) having as predicate: during case number cn, the person named accn is accused and the barrister named barn pleads in his defence.

A user familiar with database querying languages could formulate the question in one of the following ways:

(1) (CHARGE*PROSECUTION) [ACCN = scapegoat, CN = 969],
(2) (PROSECUTION*DEFENCE) [ACCN = scapegoat, CN = 969],
(3) (DEFENCE*CHARGE) [ACCN = scapegoat, CN = 969],
(4) (DEFENCE*CHARGE*PROSECUTION) [ACCN = scapegoat, CN = 969].

What should one think about these formulations? Are they equivalent? Are they correct? Each in fact assumes a decomposition of the relation CASE.

Thus formulation (1) assumes that {CHARGE PROSECUTION} is a decomposition of CASE; now if there are several accused in the same case, the barristers do not normally defend all the accused, they generally defend only one accused. Therefore {CHARGE PROSECUTION} is not a decomposition of CASE and formulation (1) is incorrect.

Below is an example of real facts that will show that *none of the four formulations is correct.*

CASE

NC	ACCN	BARN
969	scapegoat	allrisksinsurance
969	lucky-luke	dalton
001	scapegoat	deadloss
969	mania	deadloss

The instances that are stored in the database are therefore:

CHARGE	NC	ACCN
	969	scapegoat
	969	lucky-luke
	001	scapegoat
	969	mania

PROSECUTION	NC	BARN
	969	allrisksinsurance
	969	dalton
	001	deadloss
	969	deadloss

DEFENCE	BARN	ACCN
	allrisksinsurance	scapegoat
	dalton	lucky-luke
	deadloss	scapegoat
	deadloss	mania

From the previous formulations, we find the following significant incorrect responses:

In (1)	969	scapegoat	dalton
In (2)	969	scapegoat	deadloss
In (3)	969	scapegoat	deadloss
In (4)	969	scapegoat	deadloss

The relation CASE cannot be decomposed as the example shows.

If in fact users of the database want to know the barristers who have defended a particular accused during a particular case, the designer must introduce the relation CASE in the model.

An *operational relation* is a relation in which the set of attributes is the union of attributes from several basic relations and for which the predicate has a natural, known and unambiguous meaning for users.

To determine whether a predicate has a known meaning that is unambiguous and natural for users, it is best to ask them by providing the set of attributes of the relation and asking them the meaning that they give to their association; if the replies are noticeably in agreement, the relation is taken to be operational.

In our view the task of modelling should provide a list of operational relations that users will need. The model will be complete with regard to this set if every operational relation can be expressed by a relational expression of basic relations.

A *context* is an operational relation OR obtained by the joining of some basic relations the set of which forms a decomposition of OR.

A *space* or a space relation SR of a database is a context which is maximal in the sense in which no other set of basic relations can be added to the one that forms SR to obtain a new context.

A *context* of a space relation SR corresponds to a partial decomposition of SR.

The pitfall revealed by the previous data structure arises from the fact that the relation CASE which is an operational relation is not a space relation. The model is not complete. This structure contains three space relations: CHARGE, PROSECUTION and DEFENCE.

It is this type of pitfall that we are trying to *reveal* and we believe that it is the responsibility of database designers to *clear away* such traps from a data structure. To do this, they must show the space relations and contexts of a data structure. Within these users can formulate their queries without running so many risks as before.

The establishment of an SR space or a context C requires the designer to pay due attention to the property $SR[R_k^+] = R_k$ or $C[R_k^+] = R_k$. He can make use of properties of (fd-jd2), extension (jd2) augmentation (jd3) substitution (jd6). But the establishment of a space cannot be reduced to a simple application of mathematical properties: it requires the designer to reflect on the data to determine if the relation is operational or not.

2.10.3   Framework for the analysis of a model

This framework does not presume to be exhaustive.

a) Find all the fds defined in each basic relation and determine their keys.
Find all multifunctional relations of every basic relation, and find their keys.
Add the multifunctional relations to the basic relations.
b) For every relations cycle, examine if there is an interdependency between their associations. Determine in particular the reference dependencies, the relative dependencies and the join-projection dependencies.

c) Reveal the contexts and spaces.

d) Find the fds defined on several basic relations.

Find the multifunctional relations that are not defined from a single basic relation and find their keys.

Add these new relations to the basic relations.

For as long as there are new relation cycles, repeat points b) c) d).

We will show in the following CONTEST example how the designer might proceed.

2.10.4   Example CONTEST

We are concerned with the organisation of a contest in which all the tests are orals. The contest covers several topics.

Each topic is assigned to a scale which provides weightings.

A test in a topic takes place in a room during a half-day and several candidates are examined during the same test.

Each candidate gives an address as the test in a topic in front of a certain number of examiners all qualified in this topic.

Each examiner gives a mark for each address that he hears.

The candidate's final mark in a topic is the average of the examiners' marks.

MARK and FINAL-MARK have the same domain which is of type ordered word. The domains of the other attributes are of type word.

The following is the model already obtained:

TOPIC-LIST (TOPIC SCALE)
Each topic has a scale assigned to it.

PROGRAMME (TOPIC HALF-DAY ROOM)
The programme p = (t, hd, r) designates a test in the topic occurring during the half-day hd in room r.

SUBJECTS (ADDRESS-TITLE TOPIC CANDIDATE HALF-DAY FINAL-MARK)
The entity of SUBJECTS s = (at, t, c, hd, fm) designates the address title at, which the candidate c has given as the test in the topic t, during the half-day hd; fm gives the final mark.

RESULT (EXAMINER ADDRESS-TITLE MARK)
The entity of RESULTS r = (e, at, m) designates the mark m given by the examiner e for the address title at.

2.10.4.1   Continuing the task of modelling

a) *Finding fds and keys to relations*

The designer looks for all the functional dependencies of a relation: with this aim in mind he forms all the fd schemas that it is possible to generate using attributes of the relation; for each of them he must decide whether or not it corresponds to an fd defined on the relation by analysing the field of application.

This task, which can be irksome, is relieved by the fact that it is simply a question of finding a base for the set of fds: thus if AB → C is an fd of the relation, there is no need to find out whether ABD → C is also one. Similarly if C → D and D → E are two fds defined on the relation, we then know that C → E is too: it is no effort for the designer to find it.

Considering a relation R we write C → D to mean that the fd C → D is defined on R, and we write C not → D to mean that the fd C → D is not defined on R.

This part can easily be computerised. We illustrate it using questions.

The designer can derive the keys to the relations from these results.

TOPICS-LIST (TOPIC SCALE)

Can one assign several scales to a topic?
     Answer: no.
Can one assign several topics to a scale?
     Answer: yes.
TOPICS-LIST has a single key: TOPIC

PROGRAMME (TOPIC HALF-DAY ROOM)

1.   Do the tests of a topic always take place in the same room?
        Answer: no.
2.   Do the tests of a topic always take place during the same half-day?
        Answer: no.
3.   Do the tests of a topic always take place in the same room during a half-day?
        Answer: yes.
4.   Is a room the test place of a topic for at most one half-day?
        Answer: no.
5.   Is a half-day given over to the tests of a single topic?
        Answer; no.

6. During a half-day, do the tests all take place in the same room?
    Answer: no.
7. Are the tests which take place in the same room during the same half-day on the same topic?
    Answer: yes.
8. Is a room the test place of a single topic?
    Answer: no.

These answers allow the following set of fds to be determined:

1. TOPIC   no → ROOM,
2. TOPIC   no → HALF-DAY,
3. TOPIC HALF-DAY   → ROOM,
4. TOPIC ROOM   no → HALF-DAY,
5. HALF-DAY   no → TOPIC,
6. HALF-DAY   no → ROOM,
7. HALF-DAY ROOM   → TOPIC,
8. ROOM   no → TOPIC.

The keys to PROGRAMME are therefore: TOPIC HALF-DAY
                                    and   ROOM HALF-DAY.

TOPICS (ADDRESS-TITLE TOPIC CANDIDATE HALF-DAY FINAL-MARK)

1. Can a candidate make several addresses to take the test in a topic?
    Answer: no.
2. Are there several candidates for a topic?
    Answer: yes.
3. Can a candidate take tests in several topics?
    Answer: yes.

4. Can a candidate give the same address title for tests in different topics?
    Answer: no.
5. Can an address title be given by several candidates in the framework of a test?
    Answer: no.
6. Can an address title be given in the framework of distinct topics?
    Answer: no.
7. Does a candidate receive several final marks for a topic?
    Answer: no.
8. Are there several final marks for a topic?
    Answer: yes.

9. Does each candidate receive the same final mark for all the topics for which he takes the test?
    Answer: no.
10. During the same half-day, are there several candidates which can take the test in a topic?
    Answer: yes.
11. Can an address take place on several half-days?
    Answer: no.
12. Can a candidate take several tests during the same half-day?
    Answer: no.

These answers allow the following set of fds to be established:

1. CANDIDATE TOPIC		→	ADDRESS-TITLE,
2. TOPIC	no	→	CANDIDATE,
3. CANDIDATE	no	→	TOPIC,
4. CANDIDATE ADDRESS-TITLE		→	TOPIC,
5. ADDRESS-TITLE TOPIC		→	CANDIDATE,
6. ADDRESS-TITLE		→	TOPIC,
7. CANDIDATE, TOPIC		→	FINAL-MARK,
8. TOPIC	no	→	FINAL-MARK,
9. CANDIDATE	no	→	FINAL-MARK,
10. TOPIC HALF-DAY	no	→	CANDIDATE,
11. ADDRESS-TITLE		→	HALF-DAY,
12. CANDIDATE HALF-DAY		→	TOPIC.

The keys to the relation SUBJECTS are: ADDRESS-TITLE,
                                        TOPIC CANDIDATE,
                                        CANDIDATE HALF-DAY.

RESULTS (EXAMINER ADDRESS-TITLE MARK)
Can an address receive several marks?
    Answer: yes.
Can an examiner give several marks?
    Answer: yes.
Can an examiner give several marks to the same address?
    Answer: no.
Can an examiner give the same mark once only?
    Answer: no.

The key to RESULTS is therefore: EXAMINER ADDRESS-TITLE.

For relations that allows several keys, the designer indicates at least one mandatory key. If TOPIC HALF-DAY is a mandatory key to PROGRAMME, this means that the values taken by each entity of PROGRAMME for TOPIC and HALF-DAY must be known.

b) *Finding multi-functional relations (mfr)*

So if in PROGRAMME there is the mfr (TOPIC ROOM), then it means that the tests in a topic take place in a predefined list of rooms and a room receives the tests of a predefined list of topics.
We assume that this is not the case for the organisation of this contest. Otherwise, it would have been necessary to create this new relation (TOPIC ROOM).

If from SUBJECTS there is the mfr (CANDIDATE HALF-DAY) then it means that a candidate takes his tests in the half-days belonging to a list established separately from other data: we assume that that is not the case. Similarly, we assume that the mfr (TOPIC HALF-DAY) does not exist.
If there is the mfr (TOPIC CANDIDATE) defined in SUBJECTS, it means that independently of address titles, final marks, half-days, we can establish the list of candidates who must take a test in this topic: we assume that this is the case. We need a relation formed on CANDIDATE TOPIC; this already exists because CANDIDATE TOPIC is a key to the relation SUBJECTS.
One way of taking this fact into account is to make this key to SUBJECTS mandatory. Thus the creation of an entity of SUBJECTS amounts to creating a association between a topic and a candidate, without perhaps knowing the address title, the mark and the half-day which can be added to it later.

c) *Cycle analysis*

Our proposition provides no reasoning that would allow the designer to discover the underlying integrity rule applying to a cycle when it exists. It simply places him before a particular situation that might be a potential source of an ir.

An analysis of the relations cycle PROGRAMME SUBJECTS reveals the referential dependency which is assumed to be verified (2.9.1):
PROGRAMME[TOPIC HALF-DAY] +: SUBJECTS[TOPIC HALF-DAY].
This is not very interesting and we consider only cycles with more than two relations.

An analysis of the cycle RESULTS SUBJECTS leads to the following ir MARK (as domain) (2.8.b): the final mark of an address is the average of the marks given for this address by the examiners. It is expressed algorithmically as follows:

(IR1) $\forall$ s $\in$ SUBJECTS[FINAL-MARK $\neq$ Nil]
s.FINAL-MARK =
     average(RESULTS[MARK][ADDRESS TITLE = s.ADDRESS-TITLE]).

d) *Revealing spaces*

The designer shows the spaces by extracting the join dependencies. These are obtained by trial and error.

We will try to find a space EXAM a decomposition of which is formed from the set of the four basic relations. The predicate of this space is easily derived from the predicates of these relations: an examiner (e) assigns a mark (m) to an address (a) of a candidate (c) during a half-day (hd) in a room (r) for the test in a topic (t) having a scale (s), the candidate having a final mark (fm) for this test.

The projection of EXAM on the set of attributes of each of the four basic relations is certainly identical to this basic relation. In this relation are defined the functional dependencies defined in each of the four basic relations. By successive application of property (fd-jd2):

EXAM = LIST-TOPICS $*$ EXAM[EXAM$^+$ - SCALE]
= LIST-TOPICS $*$ PROGRAMME $*$ EXAM[EXAM$^+$ - {SCALE ROOM}]
= LIST-TOPICS $*$ PROGRAMME $*$ SUBJECTS $*$ RESULTS.
EXAM is thus a space allowing the set of basic relations as decomposition.

By application of (jd8) and since LIST-TOPICS is an extremity, we obtain the following partial spaces:

C_1 = PROGRAMME $*$ SUBJECTS $*$ RESULTS,
C_2 = SUBJECTS $*$ RESULTS,
C_3 = LIST-TOPICS $*$ PROGRAMME $*$ SUBJECTS,
C_4 = LIST-TOPICS $*$ PROGRAMME.

e) *Non-intrinsic fds of spaces*

The designer studies the fds of the space EXAM which have not yet been revealed and tries to discover any possible multifunctional relations defined from EXAM.
The designer must look for them in those relations obtained by projection of EXAM on attributes belonging to several basic relations.

EXAM [CANDIDATE ROOM].
If a mfr exists, then each candidate is assigned to rooms independently of other data. We assume that this is incorrect.

EXAM [EXAMINER ROOM].
The same reasoning leads us not to record a mfr (EXAMINER ROOM).

EXAM [EXAMINER TOPIC].
The mfr JURY (EXAMINER TOPIC) exists in EXAM: it assigns an examiner to those topics in which he is qualified. It means that an examiner can only mark tests in topics for which he is qualified.
This ir can then be written according to the reference dependency as:
RESULTS SUBJECTS-: JURY.

EXAM [EXAMINER CANDIDATE].
The mfr EC(EXAMINER CANDIDATE) does not exist because each candidate is not assigned to examiners independently of other data (for instance TOPIC).

EXAM [EXAMINER HALF-DAY].
The mfr AVAILABILITY (EXAMINER HALF-DAY) is defined from EXAM: it allows an examiner (e) to be assigned to a half-day (hd) on which he is available. It means that an examiner can only participate at tests of exams on those half-days when he is available.
This ir is then written as a reference dependency:
RESULTS SUBJECTS-: AVAILABILITY.

Five new cycle relations are introduced:

(c1) JURY-SUBJECTS-RESULTS;
(c2) AVAILABILITY-SUBJECTS-RESULTS;
(c3) AVAILABILITY-PROGRAMME-JURY;
(c4) AVAILABILITY-SUBJECTS-JURY;
(c5) JURY-AVAILABILITY-SUBJECTS-RESULTS.

The bringing of these cycles into effect is done simply by beginning with the set of relations and reducing it in proportion in order to analyse systematically whether a subset of relations forms a cycle or not.

The set of relations does not form a cycle because of the relation TOPIC-LIST. JURY-AVAILABILITY-SUBJECTS-PROGRAMME-RESULTS cannot form a cycle around the attributes common to at least two relations: {JURY HALF-DAY TOPIC ADDRESS-TITLE}; in fact PROGRAMME then projects on HALF-DAY TOPIC which is contained in the projection of SUBJECTS on HALF-DAY TOPIC ADDRESS-TITLE.

(c5) JURY-AVAILABILITY-SUBJECTS-RESULTS forms a cycle around the attributes {JURY HALF-DAY TOPIC ADDRESS-TITLE}. This cycle is not atomic because cycles c1, c2 and c4 can be formed.

f) *Finding new spaces*

Since new relations and new cycles have just been introduced during the preceding phase, the designer will record the following new spaces:
EXAM = PROGRAMME * LIST-TOPICS * SUBJECTS * RESULTS;
POSSIBILITIES = AVAILABILITY * JURY;
POSSIBLE-TIMETABLE = AVAILABILITY * RESULTS.

g) *Analysis of new relations cycles*

(c1) By construction EXAM-: JURY.
Since SUBJECTS RESULTS is a context, we obtain:
SUBJECTS RESULTS-: JURY (property rd6).
Theorem (id) on page 59 shows us that the possible relative dependencies linked with this cycle derive from this reference dependency and that there cannot be other reference dependencies.

(c2) By construction EXAM-: AVAILABILITY.
In the same way we obtain:
SUBJECTS RESULTS-: AVAILABILITY.

(c3) JURY * PROGRAMME provides the potential examiners and half- days for taking the tests in a topic.
JURY * AVAILABILITY provides the possible half-days for an examiner and the topics in which he is qualified.
AVAILABILITY * PROGRAMME provides the available examiners and the topics handled on a given half-day.
The last relation cannot be considered to be a partial space.
JURY AVAILABILITY +: PROGRAMME [HALF-DAY TOPIC] is an integrity rule; it is the only inclusion dependency linked with this cycle.

(c4) AVAILABILITY JURY +: SUBJECTS [HALF-DAY TOPIC].

(c5) From SUBJECTS RESULTS-: AVAILABILITY and from SUBJECTS RESULTS -: JURY, we obtain by union (rd2) SUBJECTS RESULTS-: JURY AVAILABILITY.

2.10.4.2 Range of different integrity rules

(MFR1) Multifunctional relation (CANDIDATE TOPIC).
The underlying ir is embedded in the structure because TOPIC CANDIDATE is a mandatory key to SUBJECTS.

(MFR2) RESULTS SUBJECTS-: JURY:
range: c(RESULTS), c(SUBJECTS), s(JURY).

(MFR3) RESULTS SUBJECTS-: AVAILABILITY:
range: c(RESULTS), c(SUBJECTS), s(AVAILABILITY), u(SUBJECTS [HALF-DAY]).

(DIV1) JURY AVAILABILITY +: PROGRAMME:
range c(PROGRAMME), s(JURY), s(AVAILABILITY).

(IR1) This ir is concerned with the calculation of the final mark. Its range: u(RESULTS [MARK]), u(SUBJECTS [FINAL-MARK]): prohibited, s(RESULTS), c(RESULTS).

These results can be summarised in the following table: the columns correspond to the integrity rules, the rows to the relations. At the intersection of a row and a column appear the primitive names for that relation row, for the execution of which the ir of the column has to be verified.

Table of ir ranges

Relations\IR	MRF2	MFR3	DIV1	IR1
LIST-TOPICS				
PROGRAMMES			c	
SUBJECTS	c	c uHALF-DAY		uFINAL-MARK
JURY	s		s	
RESULTS	c	c		c s uMARK
AVAILABILITY		s	s	

Note
The reader is invited to extend the example by considering now the fd:
EXAMINER HALF-DAY $\rightarrow$ TOPIC and the fact that an address takes place in
front of all qualified examiners for the given address.

2.10.5   Conclusions

We trust that we will have convinced the reader that integrity rules are not
merely interesting because they guarantee a certain coherence in the database:
in this simple role, they play the part of ensuring that the designer and/or the
user undertakes to protect himself from certain false steps. But allowing them
that quality alone would be to underrate their value.

By expressing non-variables in the field of applications, they are very useful to
the designer in the difficult process of modelling the field of application. We
have presented in this chapter particular situations that an alert designer can
uncover in the model that he is building. It is for him to tease out the integrity
rule(s) that can underlie such situations. As applications analyst he is not
merely playing a "passive" role, accepting data that users wish to entrust to
him, he is also playing an "active" role where these special situations enable
him to ask pertinent questions in order to understand the field of application
and realise the database. Not only does the search for integrity rules facilitate
this active role, it also provides the designer-analyst with a guide to prevent
him from becoming an activist.

It is by such a study of special cases that the designer will be led to modify his
model: in the CONTEST example, this led to the construction of two new
relations.

If the search for integrity rules is very important in the modelling process, it is
equally important for the general architecture of applications programming: we
have shown the *normal architecture* of a database which involves the
definition and realisation of modification primitives in the database that verify
all the integrity rules. Application programs are then written using these
primitives without regard for the verification of integrity rules; indeed they
often resist any subsequent modifications to the integrity rules.

In part 3, we will show how the integrity rules, and notably the functional
dependencies, have an important role in the determination of a quality database
structure; in that case, there is an important requirement to avoid data
redundancy.

2.11 Appendix

2.11.1 Simplified keys algorithm

There are several algorithms for finding keys to a relation, such as those of (FADOUS-FORSYTH75), (LUCCHESI-ORSBORN76), (KUNDU85). We will outline here the principle for finding the keys to a relation.

Take a relation R provided with a set of functional dependencies F.

The *outflow* of a set of attributes X in F, described as outflow (X), is the set of attributes A of R such that there exists the fd $X \rightarrow A$ in the closure of F^{**}.

The definition of a key to a relation R can then be expressed as follows: a set K of attributes of R is a key to R if and only if:

outflow(K) = R^+, and $\forall K' \subseteq K$ outflow(K") $\neq R^+$.

The algorithm for finding keys to a relation examines the set of parts of R^+ and calculates the outflow of each:

if it is not equal to R^+, it cannot form a key;

conversely, if it is equal to R^+, it is a key only if it contains no part whose outflow has the value R^+.

This non-optimised algorithm is described below; it uses the functions Parts(X), outflow(X), min(XYZ) which are also described. We have written these algorithms using the set operations and the operation of assigning an element to a set $(:\in)$ (ABRIAL74).

Keys(R,F) contains in the end the set of keys to relation R provided with the set of fds F. C defines a variable that may contain a set of attribute sets of R.

    C := ∅

for each K ∈ Parts(R^+) do:

        if outflow(K) = R^+ then K :∈ C endif

    repeat

    Keys := min(C).

Parts(X) provides the set of all parts of X. P is a variable that may contain a set of the attributes sets of R.

    P := ∅

    {∅} :∈ P   (an element of P is the empty set)

    for each A ∈ X do

        for each Y ∈ P do

        Y ∪ {A} :∈ P

        repeat

    repeat

    Parts(X) := P.

outflow(X) calculates the outflow of X in F.

o defines a variable that may contain a set of attributes of R.

    o := X; F' := F;

    new := true (new is a boolean that takes the value false as soon as no new attribute can be added to the outflow of X)

    while new do

        new := false

        for each f ∈ F' do

            if l(f) ⊆ o then r(f) :∈ o; new := true; F' := F' - {f} endif

        repeat

    repeat

    outflow(x) := o.

min(XYZ) provides the minimal non-empty sets in relation to inclusion contained in XYZ.

2.11.2   Optimising the keys algorithm

2.11.2.1   Sources and wells

We do not want to introduce here the sophisticated optimisations of the preceding algorithm; we will simply use a property linked to the fds to limit the number of Parts of R^+ that have to be considered.

An attribute is a *source* in F if it does not belong to any right fd part of F.

It is a *well* in F if it does not belong to any left fd part of F and if it is not a source.

It may be shown that every key to R contains all the sources of R and that it contains no well. The set of parts of R^+ to be considered is then reduced to only those parts of R^+ containing all the sources and containing no wells.

2.11.2.2   Extending the definition of a well

It is possible to extend the definition of a well in the following recursive way:

an attribute of R is a *well* in F if it is not a source and if

it does not belong to any left fd part of F, or all the fds of which it constitutes one of the left part attributes allow wells as right part.

The set of wells becomes larger and thus the set of parts of R^+ to be considered becomes less.

The set of sources and that of wells depends on the covering of F: they are maximal if the complete base F* is used.

2.11.3 Example

We take the CONTEST example from 2.10.4.

2.11.3.1 PROGRAMME relation

PROGRAMME(TOPIC HALF-DAY ROOM)
Programme p. = (t, hd, r) designates a test in the topic t that takes place on half-day in room r. The list of fds found is:

TOPIC HALF-DAY $\rightarrow$ ROOM,
HALF-DAY ROOM $\rightarrow$ TOPIC.

HALF-DAY is a source; there is no well.
Since the outflow of HALF-DAY only contains HALF-DAY, the keys to PROGRAMME are therefore: TOPIC HALF-DAY,
and ROOM HALF-DAY.

2.11.3.2 SUBJECTS relation

SUBJECTS(ADDRESS-TITLE TOPIC CANDIDATE HALF-DAY FINAL-MARK)
The entity of SUBJECTS s = (at, t, c, hd, fm) designates the address title at, that the candidate c has given in order to take the test in the topic t, during the half-day hd; fm gives the final mark.
This is the list of the fds obtained:

1. CANDIDATE TOPIC $\rightarrow$ ADDRESS-TITLE,
2. CANDIDATE ADDRESS-TITLE $\rightarrow$ TOPIC,
3. ADDRESS-TITLE TOPIC $\rightarrow$ CANDIDATE,
4. ADDRESS-TITLE $\rightarrow$ TOPIC,
5. CANDIDATE TOPIC $\rightarrow$ FINAL-MARK,
6. ADDRESS-TITLE $\rightarrow$ HALF-DAY,
7. CANDIDATE HALF-DAY $\rightarrow$ TOPIC.

There are no sources: FINAL-MARK is a well and cannot therefore belong to any key.
The following parts of the set of attributes need to be considered:
{ADDRESS-TITLE TOPIC CANDIDATE HALF-DAY}.

The outflow of ADDRESS-TITLE contains first TOPIC, HALF-DAY (4,6); then it contains CANDIDATE (3); then it contains FINAL-MARK (5). It thus contains all the attributes of SUBJECTS. ADDRESS-TITLE, being formed from a single attribute, is therefore a key to SUBJECTS.

The outflows of TOPIC, CANDIDATE, and HALF-DAY do not contain other attributes: they do not form keys.

The outflow of CANDIDATE TOPIC contains ADDRESS-TITLE (1): it thus contains all the attributes of SUBJECTS. It is a key because neither CANDIDATE nor HALF-DAY alone forms a key.

The outflow of TOPIC HALF-DAY contains no other attribute. It is not a key. If we add another attribute to it, we obtain a set of attributes that contains a key. We cannot therefore find other keys to SUBJECTS.

These are the keys to the relation SUBJECTS: ADDRESS-TITLE,
                                              CANDIDATE TOPIC,
                                              CANDIDATE HALF-DAY.

PART 2

TRANSFORMATIONS

3 Introduction and access paths graph

The aim of the design process for a database is to provide a database management system with the data that is necessary to manage that database. If the design problem can be posed by reference to a particular database management system, we shall give results that will be independent of a DBMS and indeed independent of the use of any specific DBMS. Our point of view stems from a paradigm that is fundamental: a DBMS does not have a finality in itself; on the contrary there is a kind of joint between the world of data use that it manages and the information world in which this data is stored. Furthermore, taking a particular DBMS implies the removal of any opportunity of criticising the connection that it makes and therefore locks any study of the database design into the logic of a DBMS. Our aim is to show designs or mechanisms that seem to us to be fundamental to this connection, and thereby criticise the connection currently proposed by DBMSs in order to try to discover the basic problems linked with the design of a logical data structure.

In this second part of the book, we shall present a heuristic that transforms a relational model into a database structure. Because our approach aims to be as independent of available DBMSs as possible, we shall define an abstract DBMS model for the design of a data structure: this model, which we shall call an *access paths graph* APG, takes account of all aspects of the majority of DBMSs so far as the definition of a data structure is concerned.

Part 2 describes the different difficulties encountered during the database design process, once the choice of model has been made. There are three levels:

a) transformation of a relational data model into a particular access paths graph that we shall call the raw access paths graph and denote by APGr in order to distinguish it from other APG;
b) choice of an access path graph from the APG class centred around the previously obtained APGr;

c) transformation of the chosen APG into a internal data structure with the specification of all the selected access and storage internal methods.

Before embarking on the subject proper, we should provide answers to the following questions posed in the introduction to Part 2:

- Why does the model adopted for the phase studied in Part 1 not provide the final result of the design process?
- What are the conditions to be respected in order to ensure that the final data structure remains faithful to the initial data model? How can this concept of faithfulness be defined?

We shall then introduce the APGs as the conclusion to Part 2.

3.1   Choice of an internal data model

We understand an internal data model to be a data model that allows data storage to be represented in the database. We shall illustrate this simple concept by an example that uses a relational data model as the internal data model.

3.1.1   Example

COURSE(NAMECOURSE NBHCOURSE)
This relation links the name of a course with the weekly number of hours for the course; the key of COURSE is NAMECOURSE.

LECTURER(NAMELECT ORGANISM)
This relation links the name of a lecturer with the organism in which he works; its key is NAMELECT.

LECTURE(NAMELECT NAMECOURSE NBWEEK)
A lecturer (NAMELECT) is linked to a course (NAMECOURSE) because he gives a lecture in this course for so many weeks (NBWEEK). The key of LECTURE is made up of NAMELECT NAMECOURSE.

PLANNING(HALL NOH NODAY NAMELECT NAMECOURSE)
A hall (HALL) is booked for a lecture (NAMELECT NAMECOURSE) for a particular time (NOH) on a particular day (NODAY) of the week.
A key for PLANNING is made up of HALL NOH NOD.

3.1.2   Relational data model used as internal data model

If the relational data model serves as internal data model, the foregoing database is quite simply established in the following way: each relation has a memory area; each entity relation has a corresponding record in the area. Given below is an example of the entities of these relations:

COURSE

(NAMECOURSE	NBHCOURSE)
Databases	3
Software design	3
Architecture	3
Graphics & communication	3
Expert systems	3
Information systems	3
Compilers	3

LECTURER

(NAMELECT	ORGANISM)
Dobbs	LONDON
Peters	KENT
Hammond	KENT
Atkins	BRISTOL
Bond	BRISTOL
Kettle	BRISTOL
Lane	KENT
Curtis	KENT
Stead	BRISTOL
Moss	BRISTOL
Brown	LEEDS
Hughes	LEEDS
Talbot	KENT
Smith	BRISTOL
Court	BRISTOL
Knight	LEICESTER

Transformations

LECTURE

NAMELECT	NAMECOURSE	NBWEEK
Atkins	Databases	14
Dobbs	Databases	14
Curtis	Information systems	14
Hammond	Architecture	14
Kettle	Databases	14
Hughes	Databases	14
Peters	Expert systems	28
Lane	Compilers	14
Talbot	Information systems	14
Brown	Information systems	14
Moss	Software design	28
Stead	Programming	28
Smith	Software design	28
Court	Information systems	14
Knight	Databases	14

PLANNING

HALL	NOH	NODAY	NAMELECT	NAMECOURSE
148	1	1	Lane	Compilers
002	1	2	Brown	Information systems
B110	1	1	Curtis	Information systems
148	2	1	Lane	Compilers

The great advantage of this method of storage is to avoid the need for pointers to store the associations between several entities of different relations.

So, to obtain the organism of the lecturer working in hall B110 on Monday (NODAY = 1) at 08.00 hours (NOH = 1) it is only necessary to look for his name in PLANNING (Curtis) and examine the corresponding entity in LECTURER to find KENT.

This association could have been achieved by simply consulting the values taken by the entities and by the use of the key access mechanism that enables an entity to be reached through the value it has for a key.

The elimination of pointers without doubt removes a burden from the database; it also improves efficiency and reliability. Thus the relational data model is a serious candidate to be the internal data model.

3.1.3 Towards an internal data model

Though promising, the relational data model cannot be an appropriate internal data model. It is incomplete for this role. This point of view will be justified in the following discussion of several special cases using the previous example.

a) If we look for the organism of the lecturer named Jones, the DBMS can only find the corresponding entity by sequentially examining the entities of LECTURER.

b) If the database course is deleted, there can no longer be lectures on this course and halls assigned to a lecture relating to this course. To execute these two operations, the DBMS must be able to determine the entities of LECTURE and PLANNING taking the value Databases for NAMECOURSE. With the current modelling taken as model of the data information, the DBMS must sequentially examine all the entities of LECTURE and PLANNING.

c) If a LECTURE entity is removed (for example (Lane Compilers 14)), the DBMS must free the halls reserved for this lecture (HALL = 148 NOH = 1 NOD = 1) and (HALL = 148 NOH = 2 NOD = 1). The DMBS can only find all of them by a sequential examination of PLANNING.

d) If we look for all the associations between a lecturer and a course, we obtain the complete answer by interrogating LECTURE only if the DBMS works exactly as we have described in c); otherwise the answer will again have to be found in PLANNING.

e) These three special but frequently occurring cases prevent us from choosing the relational data model as the internal data model. It therefore seems necessary to have an internal data model that takes access paths into account. So in the preceding example we shall consider the access paths allowing the assignment to an entity of CONFERENCE of all the entities of PLANNING relating to this conference: the DBMS will then easily be able to execute the process envisaged in c). Later, we shall study how to establish these access paths: by indices, pointers and tables to obtain the internal structure. In particular, we assume that there is an internal device (*access key mechanism*) that allows the entity relation to be found that has a particular value for the key. This device can be a hash code, B-tree, sequential index, etc. This internal data model is called the *access paths graph* (APG). It is based substantially on the work of (ABRIAL74).

Following are the reasons that lead us to transform a relational data model into an access paths graph and then into an internal data structure.

3.2   Accuracy of an internal structure

The following transformations must take account of the conditions that stem from the meaning of the initial model in order to ensure that the final internal structure accurately represents the initial model.

a) The initial model has been established by observation of the field of application and this model highlights data that must be capable of being stored in the database in the form of entity relations of the model. The final internal structure must allow storage of these entities and only these entities. This condition is called *preservation of the contents.*

b) A model contains basic relations from which we can define space relations. Implicitly, and that is our interpretation, a model requires that the basic entity relations and space relations should be easily accessible in the final database. We call this condition *preservation of access.*

c) In the chapter on decomposition we have shown that in general there are several decompositions of the same relation. Also, the model that is transformed into an internal data structure has normally been chosen from others because it allows efficient validation of the integrity rules. The final internal structure must preserve this property. We call this condition the *preservation of efficiency.*

If the transformation process of a data model into an internal data structure fulfils these three conditions, we describe it as accurate and say that the *final structure is true to the initial model.* During our presentation of this transformation process we shall provide more details on these criteria.

3.3   Access paths graph

We use the concept of an access paths graph as an abstract tool that allows representation of the decomposition of both a space relation and an internal data structure. Our approach is similar to (HAINAUT86).

3.3.1   Review of definitions of graph theory

As we shall be working with graphs, we shall briefly review the definitions of those concepts of graph theory that we shall be using. These are taken from (BERGE70) with the exception of those of basin and outflow.

A graph $G = (X,U)$ is the couple made up of:
a set of nodes $X = \{x_1 x_2 ... x_n\}$,
a family $U = \{u_1 u_2 ... u_m\}$ of elements of the cartesian product XxX, in which one element (x,y) may appear several times.
A graph is *simple* if one element of the family U only appears once.
If the graph is not oriented, one element $u = (x,y)$ of the family U is called an *edge* whose x and y are the extremities.
If the graph is oriented, one element $u = (x,y)$ of the family U is called an arc whose x is the initial extremity and whose y is the terminal extremity. An arc is a particular edge. Two arcs (or edges) are *adjacent* if they have at least one common extremity.

A *chain* is a sequence $ch = (u_1, u_2, ..., u_q)$ of arcs (or edges) of G such that each arc in the sequence has an extremity in common with the preceding arc, and the other extremity in common with the next arc.
ch is then said to be a chain linking N_1 , the extremity of u_1 which is not common with u_2 *and N_q* , the extremity of u_q which is not common with the preceding edge. N_1 and N_q are the extremities of the chain.
A chain is *simple* if it does not meet the same node twice; it is *elementary* if it does not use the same arc twice.

A *path* $ch = (u_1, u_2, ..., u_p)$ is a chain formed of arcs, where for every arc u_i (with $i < p$) the terminal extremity of u_i coincides with the initial extremity of u_{i+1} .
N_1 being the initial extremity of u_1, and N_p the terminal extremity of u_p, there is said to be a *path from N_1 to N_p*. N_1 and N_p are respectively the initial and terminal extremities of the path.

A *cycle* is a chain $ch = (u_1, u_2, ..., u_p)$ such that:
the same edge (arc) does not appear twice in the sequence,
the two nodes at the extremities of the chain coincide.
A *circuit* is a cycle formed by a path.

Two chains are *different* if they contain no edge in common.
In a graph $G(N,U)$, *a basin of N_1* is a set of elements of U: $E = \{u_1, u_2, ..., u_n\}$ such that:
these elements are edges,
and one of them accepts N_1 as extremity,
and for each extremity of these edges N_i , there is a chain linking N_1 and N_i , formed from elements of E.

In a graph G(N,U), a *outflow from node N_1* is a set of elements of
U: $E = \{u_1, u_2,...,u_n\}$ such that:
these elements are arcs,
and one of them accepts N_1 as initial extremity,
and for each extremity N_i of these arcs, there is a path from N_1 to N_i made up
of elements of E.
This is a restricted form of the outflows examined in (REYNAUD75).
The extremities of the elements of a basin of N_1 (or of an outflow of N_1) are
the nodes of the basin (or of the outflow).

3.3.2   Definitions linked to an access paths graph

An *access paths graph* APG(NO,U,REL,Fa,f,g,h,i,j) is a graph defined in the
following way:

NO	the set of nodes in the graph;
$U \subseteq NOxNO$	the set of arcs;
REL	the set of relations;
Fa	the set of access paths;
$f:NO \rightarrow REL$	f is a one-to-one mapping defined everywhere;
$g:U \rightarrow REL$	g is a mapping defined everywhere;
$h:U \rightarrow Fa$	h is a one-to-one mapping;
$i:Fa \rightarrow NxNxN$	N designates the set containing integers and an unknown value described as -;
	i is a mapping defined everywhere;
$j:NO \rightarrow \{0,1\}$	a node no is an entry node if j(no) = 1.

The following condition is verified: $f(NO) \cup g(NO) = REL$.

Note
The term *access path* used in particular in (ABRIAL74) designates an *arc* of an
APG in the terminology of graphs.

Additional definitions
A *node relation* NR is a relation such that there is a node no of the APG that
verifies NR = f(no). An *arc relation* AR is a relation such that there is an arc a
that verifies AR = g(a).
There are at most two arcs a and a' that belong to $g^{-1}(AR)$: they are then
described as *reciprocal*. The *access paths* of two reciprocal arcs a and a':h(a)
and h(a') are also described as *reciprocal*: the initial extremity of one is the
terminal extremity of the other and reciprocally.

The relation of an access path ch is the relation $g(h^{-1}(ch))$.

A relation ER is an *entry relation* if and only if there is a node no that verifies $h(no) = ER$ and $j(no) = 1$.

Interpretation of an APG

An arc a_{ij} directed from the node of R_i to the node of R_j corresponds to an access path $f_{ij} = h(a_{ij})$ and signifies that to each entity of R_i may correspond a set of entities of R_j called $f_{ij}(r_i)$. To each arc a_{ij} is assigned a relation $g(a_{ij}) = R_{ij}(K_iK_j)$ (arc relation) formed on a key K_i of R_i and a key K_j of R_j.

Each arc is informed with the help of application i which assigns three parameters to it:

cardmin provides the minimum number of entities of $f_{ij}(r_i)$ for each entity r_i of R_i (minimum cardinality);

cardmax provides the maximum number (maximum cardinality);

card80 provides the minimum number such that for 80% of the entities r_i of R_i the cardinality of $f_{ij}(r_i)$ is less than card80. Card80 is only of interest if cardmax is greater than 1. The example in the next section shows its usefulness.

If for an access path directed from relation R_i to relation R_j the maximum cardinality is 1, then the key of the relation R_{ij} is a key K_i of R_i and there is a functional dependency $K_i \rightarrow K_j$; if, moreover, the minimum cardinality is 1, then there is an referential dependency between R_i and R_j.

If the relation ER is an entry relation, the final database will contain an information device that will allow the entities of ER to be reached directly through the values that they take for the attributes of a key of ER.

Definition of a raw access paths graph

A *raw access paths graph* APG_r is an access paths graph where all the nodes are entry nodes and where all the arcs allow their reciprocal arcs.

In addition, all the node relations of an APG_r must have keys that are distinct from one another.

3.3.3   Example of an APG

The following access paths graph is a raw access path graph.

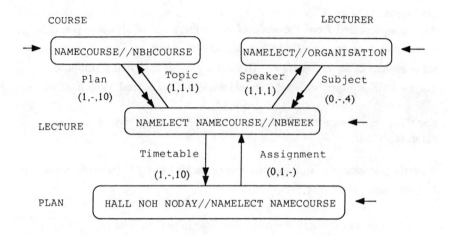

Figure 3.1 Example of an access paths graph

Graphic conventions

An edge that corresponds to an access path of cardmax equal to 1 is marked with a single arrow, whereas if the cardmax is greater than 1, it is shown with two arrows.
The entry nodes are shown by arrows.

If the relation of a node allows several keys, as for example R (ABCX) of keys AB and AC, we indicate this in the following manner in the access paths graph:

R(AB/AC//X)

The keys are separated from one another by a slash and they are separated from the attributes of R that do not belong to any key by a double slash.

Commentary

Subject is an access path that allows a lecturer to be assigned to the lectures that he gives; from the parameters of the subject, it is known that a lecturer can give no lecture (cardmin = 0), and 80% of lecturers give at most four lectures (card80 = 4). The maximum number of lectures of a lecturer is unknown. Of course, this parameter (card80) may be a rough estimate. It allows Subject to be implemented by means of a table of dimension 4 and an overflow zone that will not be used in 80% of cases.

Speaker and Subject are two reciprocal access paths and they are assigned to a relation formed on NAMELECT and COURSENAME.

When an APG contains two reciprocal access paths f_{ij} and f_{ji}, it contains redundancy: the entities of the arc relation R_{ij} are in fact taken into acount twice, once from f_{ij} and the other time from f_{ji}.

Thus, in the example the fact that Brown gives a lecture for the Information Systems course will on the one hand be taken in account through the access path Subject and on the other through the access path speaker.

3.4   Relation graph

A relation graph is a simplification of a raw access paths graph. This simplification replaces the reciprocal arcs with a single edge (or arc) and makes no differences between the entry relations and the others. It will allow us to separate into two parts the numerous problems to be solved when transforming a model into an access paths graph:

- those that concern conceptual aspects and which are solved when the model is transformed into a relation graph,
- and those which concern the facilities for data access that have to be provided for future processing and future interrogation, and which are resolved when a relation graph is transformed into an access paths graph.

3.4.1   Definition

A *relation graph* RG(NR,UR,RELR,fr,gr,kr) is a graph defined in the following way:

NR	the set of nodes;
UR $\subseteq$ NRxNR	the set of edges or arcs;
RELR	the set of relations;
fr:NR $\rightarrow$ RELR	fr is a one-to-one mapping defined everywhere;
gr:UR $\rightarrow$ RELR	gr is a one-to-one mapping defined everywhere;
kr:UR $\rightarrow$ {0,1}	kr is a mapping defined everywhere;
	u is an arc if and only if kr(u) = 0.

The following condition is verified: fr(NR) $\cup$ gr(NR)) = RELR.

Interpretation of a relation graph

If there is an arc a directed from node N_1 towards node N_2, then the relations $R_1 = fr(N_1)$ and $R_2 = fr(N_2)$ are such that the fd $KR_1 \rightarrow KR_2$ exists: gr(a) is formed on the key attributes of the two relations, and allows as keys the keys of R_1.

If there is an edge a' between two nodes N_1 and N_2, then the relation gr(a') is formed on the key attributes of $R_1 = fr(N_1)$ and of $R_2 = fr(N_2)$, and its keys are neither those of R_1 nor those of R_2.

Relations such as gr(a) and gr(a') are *edge relations*. The other relations of REL are *node relations*.

A *directed relation graph* is a relation graph that only contains arcs. Thus each element of UR verifies that kr(u) = 0.

3.4.2   Transformation of a relation graph into a raw access paths graph and reciprocally

(a) Following is the transformation of a raw access paths graph $APG_r(NO,U,REL,Fa,f,g,h,i,j)$ into a relation graph RG(NR,UR,RELR,fr,gr,kr):

NR =NO,
RELR =REL,
fr = f.

To each pair (a,a') of reciprocal arcs of U, there corresponds an element (ur) of UR such that:
gr(ur) = g(a) (which is equal to g(a'));

kr(ur) = 1 if the cardmax parameters of a and a' are greater than 1 (ur is then not an arc);
kr(ur) = 0 otherwise (ur is an arc);

ur = a   if ur is not an arc or if the cardmax parameter of a is equal to 1;
            else ur = a'.

(b) Following is the reciprocal transformation of a RG into an APG_r:

NO = NR,
REL = RELR,
f = fr.

To each element ur = (N_1,N_2) of UR is assigned a pair of reciprocal arcs of U:
a = (N_1,N_2) and a' = (N_2,N_1) such that:
g(a) = gr(ur);   g(a') = gr(ur).

If kr(ur) = 0 then the cardmax parameters of h(a) and h(a') are greater than 1;
otherwise the cardmax parameter of h(a) is equal to 1 and that of h(a') is
greater than 1. The designer is responsible for specifying the parameters
cardmin, cardmax and card80.

For all the nodes no of NO, j(no) = 1.

Example
Here is the relation graph that corresponds to the raw access paths graph of the
previous example:

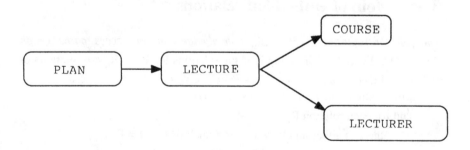

Figure 3.2 Example of a relation graph

3.4.3   Functional cycle in a relation graph

A functional cycle in a relation graph is formed by two paths whose extremities
are identical and which allow no arc in common. The initial extremity of these
paths is the *source* node of the functional cycle; the terminal extremity of these
paths is the *well* node of the functional cycle.

Example of a functional cycle: RP

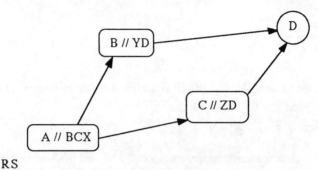

RS

Figure 3.3 Example of a functional cycle

The study of functional cycles appears to us to be very important (chapter 8). It is linked with the discovery of potential contradictions in the database: an entity in the source must be linked with the same entity in the well via the two paths of the cycle.

In the example, **a** must be assigned to the same **d** via **b** and **c**. The algorithm that transforms a decomposition into a relation graph (chapter 4) will reveal them.

3.5   Join of embedded relations

The join of relations $R_1, R_2, ..., R_n$ is embedded in an access paths graph APG(NO,U,Fa,f,g,h,i,j) *if and only if the relations $R_1, R_2, ..., R_n$ are relations of* RELR, *and there is an outflow E in APG all of whose elements u verify:*

    $g(u)$ is one of the relations $R_i (i \in \{1...n\})$,

    and for each relation R_i

        there is either an element u of E such that $g(u) = R_i$,

        or there is a node no of E such that $f(no) = R_i$.

The join of relations $R_1, R_2, ..., R_n$ is embedded in a relation graph RG(NR,UR,RELR,fr,gr,kr) *if and only if:*

the relations $R_1, R_2, ..., R_n$ are relations of RELR,

and there is a basin E in RG all of whose elements u verify:

    $gr(u)$ is one of the relations $R_i (i \in \{1...n\})$,

    and for each relation R_i:

        either there is an element u of E such that $gr(u) = R_i$,

        or there is a node nr of E such that $fr(nr) = R_i$.

Interpretation

If the join of relations $R_1, R_2, ..., R_n$ is embedded in an APG, there is then a node E, whose source is for example node NS.

From relation RS assigned to this node, it is possible to execute the following algorithm to obtain the entities of the join of the relations $R_1, R_2, ..., R_n$: for each entity rs of RS, traverse the access paths assigned to the elements of E and so obtain all the entities of the relations $R_1, R_2, ..., R_n$ that are compatible with rs.

There is thus a simple and effective algorithm for obtaining entities of the join of the relations $R_1, R_2, ..., R_n$ in the APG. This algorithm will be applicable in the future database built from this APG. This is the sense in which we describe this join as embedded.

Property

Take a relation graph RG and a raw access paths graph APG_r which are transformed one into the other as described in section 3.4.2. If a decomposition of relations is embedded in one, it is also in the other.

The proof is obvious.

A space SR is said to be *embedded* in an APG or in an RG if the join of the relations $\{R_1...R_n\}$ which form it, is embedded in this APG or in this RG.

In chapter 5 we transform a decomposition $\{R_1, R_2, ..., R_n\}$ of a relation R into an internal data structure in which the join of the relations $R_1, R_2, ..., R_n$ is embedded.

Example

Take the relations $R_1(AX), R_{12}(AB), R_2(BY), R_{23}(BC)$ and $R_3(CZ)$ and we examine the join of the relations: $ER = R_1 * R_{12} * R_2 * R_{23} * R_3$ for the following three APGs:

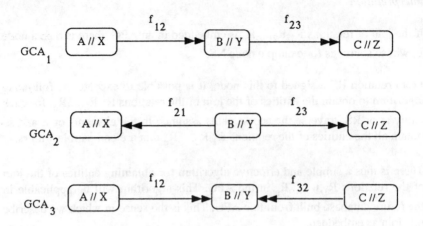

Figure 3.4 APG and join of relations

This join is embedded in APG_1 (outflow f_{12} f_{23} leaving from node 1) and in APG_2 (outflow f_{21} f_{23} from node 2). On the other hand, it is not in APG_3.

3.6   Plan of the second part

Following are the different levels of the design process for databases that we propose:
- transformation of an initial relational data model into a relation graph and then into the corresponding raw access paths graph;
- choice of an access paths graph from those that it is possible to obtain from the preceding raw APG;
- determination of an internal data structure indicating the information method chosen for the embedding of each access path.
Such transformations guarantee that the final internal structure is faithful to the initial model if:
- the node and edge relations of the final APG cover the relations of the initial model; thus they preserve the contents of the database;
- the space relations are embedded in the final APG; thus they preserve the access to the entities;
- the integrity rules integrated with the model, like the functional dependencies intrinsic to the relations, and the join dependencies defined on the relations, can easily be verified in the context of the final information structure.

4 Transformation of a decomposition into a relation graph

There are several graphical methods of representing a set of relations that form a decomposition (ZANIOLO76, MAIER83) especially from hypergraphs (BERGE70). We will propose another which we called a *relation graph* in chapter 3.

This representation is only an intermediate stage towards obtaining an information data structure: it will allow information problems to be tackled step by step. The transformation of a compact decomposition D into a relation graph RG will be a faithful transformation in the sense of section 3.2. Complex situations can then be studied in part 3 of the book.

We will present the algorithm that ensures the transformation of a compact decomposition into a relation graph in the first section in a fairly informal way; we will illustrate it by means of an example from a previous chapter; we will then describe it formally in an appendix to the chapter, and we will show by means of some simple examples the use of different parts of the algorithm.
In section 4.2 we invite the designer to criticise the relation graph obtained by the algorithm, by questioning the use of all the joins of relations embedded in the relation graph.

4.1   Relation graph of a decomposition

4.1.1   Presentation of the algorithm

We introduce the transformation algorithm for a decomposition D of a space relation SR into a relation graph RG, without all the details that are included in the appendix to the chapter. It extends our own work (LEONARD83) and that of (LUONG86). It consists of 6 stages:

E1. Compact decomposition of an initial decomposition
The first stage transforms the initial decomposition D into a compact
decomposition (definition in 4.4.1) where:
all the relations having a common key are grouped into one relation, and each
hinge between the relations has its own relation.

The second condition becomes complex in certain situations that are studied in
the appendix.

E2. Nodes of the relation graph
Each relation R of the compact decomposition is assigned to a node of RG.

E3. Arcs of the relation graph
If a relation R_i contains in its attributes a key of relation R_j, then there must be
in RG a path that goes from the node of R_i to the node of R_j.
$DEP(R_i)$ designates the set of the relations R_j whose key attributes are key
attributes of R_i; $INF(R_i)$ designates the set of the relations R_j whose at least one
key belongs to set of R_i attributes.
We classify as not useful the arcs which would link relation R_i to relation R_j if
there is a relation R_k of $INF(R_i)$ (respectively $DEP(R_i)$) whose set of key
attributes   contains   that   of R_j;   NOTUSEFUL(R_i)   (respectively
NOTUSEDEP(R_i)) is that set of relations.
$MINFD(R_i) = (INF(R_i) - NOTUSEFUL(R_i)) \lor (DEP(R_i) - NOTUSEDEP(R_i))$.
In the appendix we explain that there are other possible ways of defining the
non-useful arcs and we indicate why we have adopted this approach.

E4. House-keeping nodes
This is a minor detail that we discuss in the appendix.

E5. Refining relations assigned to nodes
It may be necessary to delete some relation attributes; this stage is described in
the appendix. This stage is optional.

E6. Determining edges (B-edges)
Take a node N_{ij} (relation R_{ij}) joined only to two nodes $N_i(R_i)$ and $N_j(R_j)$ by
arcs leaving N_{ij}, whose relation is formed from the set of the key-attributes of
R_i and R_j and whose keys are each formed by the union of a key of R_i and one
of R_j.
It is replaced by an edge joining nodes N_i and N_j; the arcs joining N_{ij} to N_i and
to N_j are deleted.

Note

If one only wants to find a **directed relation graph** from a decomposition, all that is required is to omit stage E6.

4.1.2 Example: Machine workshop

4.1.2.1 Compact decomposition

Following are the relations which form a decomposition of the relation WORKSHOP (1.5):

WORKMAN(NOV NOMOV).	Key:	NOV.
ACTIVITY(NOV NH ACTIVE).	Key:	NOV NH.
MACHINE(NMH FUNCTION).	Key:	NMH.
AVAIL-MACHINE(NMH NH AVAILMH).	Key:	NMH NH.
PRODUCT(NP QMINFAB).	Key:	NP.
BATCH(NP NBATCH NBH NMH).	Key:	NP NBATCH.
M-P(NMP QMP).	Key:	NMP.
APPR(NP NMP QMINMP).	Key:	NP NMP.
SKILL(NOV NMH).	Key:	NOV NMH.
USAGE(NP FUNCTION).	Key:	NP.

TIME-TABLE(NH NP NBATCH NOV NMH)
Keys: NH NP NBATCH,
        NH NMH,
        NH NOV.

This decomposition is not compact because there are relations that have the same key:

on the one hand	TIME-TABLE and ACTIVITY (key NOV NH),
and	TIME-TABLE and AVAIL-MACHINE (key NMH NH),
on the other hand	USAGE and PRODUCT (key NP).

These relations must be grouped respectively into:
TIME-TABLE'(NH NP NBATCH NOV NMH ACTIVE AVAILMH), and
PRODUCT'(NP QMINFAB FUNCTION).

This decomposition is not yet compact because there is a hinge FUNCTION between the relations PRODUCT and MACHINE which is not key of any relation in the decomposition: a new relation FUNCTION must be created that allows only one attribute FUNCTION to make the decomposition compact.

The hinge of the relations TIME-TABLE and BATCH: NP NBATCH NMH is a complex one. The key to this hinge is NP NBATCH; as this is key to a relation of the decomposition (BATCH), there is no need to create a new relation.

But one should not stop here; one needs to consider the attributes of the hinge that do not belong to the key to the hinge NMH (see 4.4.1) and carry out the same study. Here there is no need to create a new relation because NMH is key of a relation (MACHINE).

All the other hinges are keys to other relations: for example, the hinge of APPR and of BATCH is NP which is key of PRODUCT.

This method of proceeding reveals the functional cycles contained in the decomposition and sources of potential contradictions (chapter 8).

The decomposition formed by the relations WORKMAN TIME-TABLE' MACHINE PRODUCT' BATCH M-P APPR SKILL FUNCTION is compact.

4.1.2.2 Arcs and nodes of the RG (stages E2, E3)

INF(TIME-TABLE')   =   {WORKMAN MACHINE PRODUCT' BATCH SKILL},

NOTUSEFUL(TIME-TABLE') =   {WORKMAN MACHINE PRODUCT'}

MINFD(TIME-TABLE')   =   {BATCH SKILL}.

The keys of relations WORKMAN MACHINE PRODUCT' BATCH SKILL are attributes of the relation TIME-TABLE' and so these relations form INF(TIME-TABLE'). WORKMAN belongs to NOTUSEFUL(TIME-TABLE') because its key NOV is contained in that of SKILL.

Thus a workman is assigned to a machine in TIME-TABLE' only if he is competent to operate it. This rule derives from the fact that the first relations form a decomposition of WORKSHOP; thus

TIME-TABLE'[NOV NMH] = SKILL.

INF(WORKMAN) = ∅.

INF(SKILL) = {WORKMAN MACHINE},

　　NOTUSEFUL(SKILL) = ∅,

　　MINFD(SKILL) = {WORKMAN MACHINE}.

INF(MACHINE) = {FUNCTION},

　　NOTUSEFUL(MACHINE) = ∅,

　　MINFD(MACHINE) = {FUNCTION}.

INF(BATCH) = {PRODUCT' MACHINE},

　　NOTUSEFUL(BATCH) = ∅,

　　MINFD(BATCH) = {PRODUCT' MACHINE}.

INF(PRODUCT') = {FUNCTION},
    NOTUSEFUL(PRODUCT') = $\varnothing$,
    MINFD(PRODUCT') = {FUNCTION}.
INF(APPR) = {M-P PRODUCT'},
    NOTUSEFUL(APPR) = $\varnothing$,
    MINFD(APPR) = {M-P PRODUCT'}.
INF(M-P) = $\varnothing$.
INF(FUNCTION) = $\varnothing$.

The relation graph is shown in figure 4.1.
The sixth stage does not modify this relation graph. No node can be transformed into an edge. APPR contains an attribute QMINMP which is not a key-attribute, and SKILL is joined to three nodes.

Note
The functional cycle between TIME-TABLE' BATCH SKILL and MACHINE is relative to the possible contradictions between the machine assigned to a batch at a given time in TIME-TABLE' and the machine which is to manufacture this batch according to BATCH.

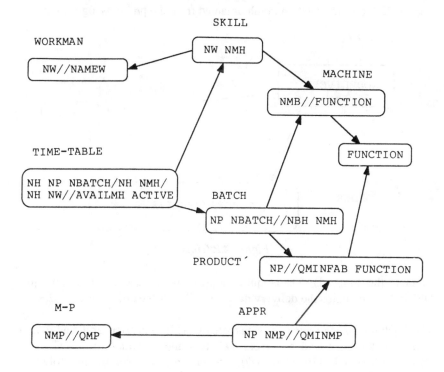

Figure 4.1 Production workshop

4.2   Use of hinges

With the use of a compact decomposition we systematically construct all the possible hinges between these relations. However, some of these may be non-useful because they are never used to produce the join of two instances. We will give an example which appears to be very important.

These hinges result from a mistake in the initial model: two attributes have the same name whereas in fact they designate data that is semantically different even they are represented by attributes that have the same domain.

Example
DELIVERY(NDELIVERY DATE NOORDER)
A delivery is known by its number; the date of delivery is recorded, as well as the order that originated it.

ORDER(NOORDER DATE NOCLIENT)
An order is known by its number: its date of receipt is recorded, as well as the number of the client who ordered it.
Figure 4.2 shows the relation graph obtained from the previous algorithm:

DELIVERY

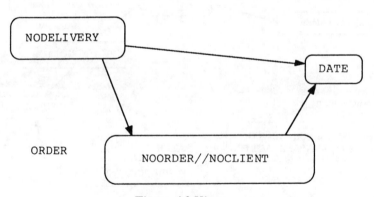

Figure 4.2 Hinge

In fact, the hinge DATE is quite non-useful because it allows no join: DELIVERY contains the delivery date and ORDER the order date.

The database designer must appreciate that this hinge is not useful, and that the initial model may lead to errors (what is the meaning of DATE when DELIVERY * ORDER is made?); he will rapidly propose the following modification:

DELIVERY(NDELIVERY DATE-DELIVERY NOORDER);
ORDER(NOORDER DATE-ORDER NOCLIENT);

DATE-DELIVERY and DATE-ORDER have the same domain: DATE.

4.3 Conclusions

The design of databases requires in addition:
– on the one hand the transformation of the relation graph obtained in a data information structure: this is the purpose of the following chapter in this part;
– on the other hand the choice of the initial compact decomposition: in part three, we advocate the use of a compact decomposition which guarantees the equivalence of all keys of each of its relations: we call this a *completely homogeneous decomposition.*

To avoid overcomplicating this second part, we will anticipate the results of section 8.10. These will allow us to guarantee that the transformation of a compact decomposition D of a relation RE into a relation graph RG using our algorithm

– preserves the contents of the database: the relations of D are all to be found in the relations that can be extracted from RG;
– preserves access: if D is compact and homogenous, we will show that RG is connected and the join of the relations of D is embedded in RG;
– preserves efficiency: the intrinsic fds to the relations of D are also intrinsic to the relations of RELR of RG. Their verification will be just as efficient in the case of D as in that of RG.

Thus the relation graph RG is faithful to the decomposition D in the sense of the previous chapter (3.2).

4.4 Appendix

We now present our algorithm for transforming a decomposition D of a space relation SR into a relation graph RG (NR, UR, RELR, fr, gr, kr).

4.4.1   Compact decomposition

Definition
A decomposition $D = \{R_1, R_2, ..., R_n\}$ of a relation SR is compact if and only if:
- there are no two relations R_i and R_j such that their keys K_i, K_j are equivalent, that is verify $K_i \rightarrow K_j$ and $K_j \rightarrow K_i$,
- and for each distinct pair of relations R_i and R_j of D:

if $R_{ij}^+ = R_i^+ \wedge R_j^+$ is not empty, there is a relation of D: R' which allows the same keys as the relation $R_{ij} = SR[R_{ij}^+]$ and which contains the attributes of R_{ij}^+ (R' being able to be equal to R_{ij});

if $RR_{ij}^+ = R_{ij}^+ - KR_{ij}^+$ is not empty, then there is a relation of D: RR' which allows the same keys as the relation $RR_{ij} = SR[RR_{ij}^+]$ and which contains the attributes of R_{ij}^+ (RR' being able to be equal to RR_{ij}).

Interpretation
The relations R' and RR' are relative to the hinge of the relations R_i and R_j; their presence in the compact decomposition will allow the join of the relations R_i and R_j is possible in the final database.

Examples
(1.1) Take a relation SR(ABC) which is decomposed according to $R_1(BA)$ and $R_2(CA)$ from respective keys B and C. The placement of the hinge node $R_{12}(A)$ allows relation SR to be embedded in the relation graph (figure 4.3).

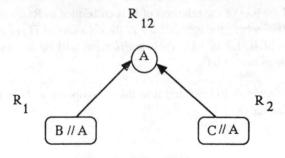

Figure 4.3 Use of hinges

(1.2) Take the relation SR(SABC) which decomposes into the relations: $R_1(SAB)$, $R_2(AC)$, $R_3(BC)$ which allows each a single key formed by the attributes in italics.
To make this decomposition compact, the relation $R_4(C)$ must be added. Figure 4.4 shows a functional cycle in the relation graph.

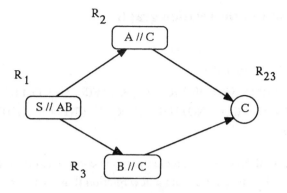

Figure 4.4 Hinge and functional cycle (1)

(1.3) Take another relation SR(ABCX) which is decomposed as follows:
R_1(ABCX) which allows two keys: AB and BC
and R_2(CA) which allows C as unique key.

To make this decomposition compact, the relation R_3(A) must be added to it. In fact the hinge between R_1 and R_2 is formed from CA whose key is C; this leaves A which is the key of no relation and which brings about this new relation. The introduction of this new relation causes a cycle to appear in the RG (see 8.9). Property 6 shows the importance of this functional cycle; it shows up the risks of contradictions between R_1[CA] and R_2(CA).

Figure 4.5 shows the relation graph.

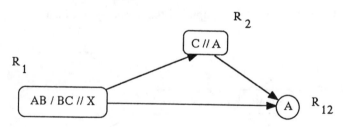

Figure 4.5 Hinge and functional cycle (2)

4.4.2   Nodes of the relation graph

RELR of the relation graph RG is equal to the set of relations that form this compact decomposition.
A node NO is assigned to each relation R of RELR and fr(NO) = R.

4.4.3 Arcs of the relation graph

For each R_i assigned to a node, determine:

$INF(R_i) = \{R_j, R_i^+ \supset KR_j\}$,

$NOTUSEFUL(R_i) = \{R_j \in INF(R_i), \exists R_h \in INF(R_i) \text{ such that } KR_h^+ \supset KR_j^+\}$

$MINFD(R_i) = (INF(R_i) - NOTUSEFUL(R_i)) \vee (INF(R_i) - NOTUSEDEP(R_i))$
(stage E3.1);

For each R_j of $MINFD(R_i)$ a directed graph is constructed from the node of R_i to the node of R_j (stage E3.2); and a new relation R' is created from

$RELR: R' = SR[KR_i^+ \cup KR_j^+]$ (stage E3.3).

We thus obtain a new arc u of RG:
$u = (fr^{-1}(R_i), fr^{-1}(R_j)) \in UR$ and $kr(u) = 0$ and $gr(u) = R'$.

4.4.3.1 Different possible solutions

Take the relation SR(SABXYZ) which decomposes as follows:
$R_1(SAB)$, $R_2(ABX)$, $R_3(AY)$ and $R_4(BZ)$ of respective keys S, AB, A and B.
$INF(R_1) = \{R_2, R_3, R_4\}$.
R_3 does not belong to $MINFD(R_1)$ because R_2 exists in $INF(R_1)$ such that $KR_2^+ (=AB)$ contains $KR_3^+ (=A)$.

Figure 4.6 shows the relation graph RG that is finally obtained.

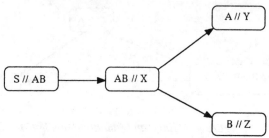

Figure 4.6 Solution proposed for the arcs

This is our proposal. It has an advantage:$iSR[AB] = iR_2[AB]$; one only has to consult the entities of iR_2 to obtain all the entities of $iSR[AB]$. It has one disadvantage. If we want to store the fact (sa) in the database, we will only be able to do so if we know (sb) and we will then store (sab).

This problem belongs in a more general framework that we will examine by proposing the complementary association mechanism in chapter 10.3.
It is possible to imagine two other solutions. Figures 4.7 and 4.8 show the relation graphs RG1 and RG2 for these.

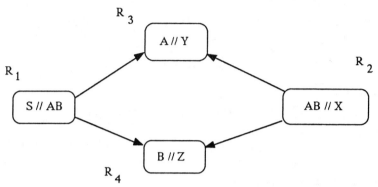

Figure 4.7 A second solution for the arcs

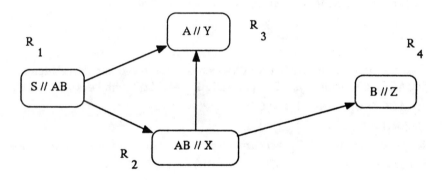

Figure 4.8 A third solution for the arcs

The second solution (figure 4.7) has a major disadvantage:
$iSR[AB] = iR_1[AB] \cup iR_2[AB]$. A complex algorithm must be used to obtain a complete answer to a question relating to $iSR[AB]$.
The third solution (figure 4.8) contains redundancy on $SR[SA]$. These disadvantages lead us to prefer the first solution corresponding to RG (figure 4.6).

4.4.3.2   Example illustrating the solution we propose

Take the relation $SR(ABCXYZ)$ which is decomposed in a compact manner according to the relations $R_1(ABCX)$, $R_2(BCY)$, $R_3(CZ)$ with the respective keys ABC, BC and C. INF(R_1) = {R_2, R_3}.

R_3 does not belong to MINFD(R_1) because the set of key attributes of R_2(=BC) contains that of R_3(=C). MINFD(R_1) = {R_2}.

Figure 4.9 shows the relation graph that is finally obtained.

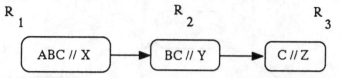

Figure 4.9 Arcs and inclusion of keys (1)

The arc joining R_1 and R_3 appears not useful because if an entity r_1 exists then there must be an entity r_2 such that $r_2.BC = r_1.BC$; if r_2 exists then there must be an entity r_3 such that $r_2.C = r_3.C$.

So if r_1 exists, there is r_3 such that $r_1.C = r_3.C$.

The arc joining R_1 to R_3 then appears deductible from the other two.

4.4.3.3   Further example

Take the relation **SR**(ABCDEXYZ) which is decomposed into the relations: R_1(ABCDEX) with keys CDE and ADE, R_2(ABCDY) with keys AD and CD, R_3(ABCZ) with keys AB and C.

INF(R_1) = {R_2, R_3}.

R_3 belongs to MINFD(R_1) because the set of attribute keys of R_2 (=ACD) does not contain that of R_3 (=ABC). MINFD(R_1) = {R_2, R_3}.

Figure 4.10 shows the relation graph that is finally obtained.

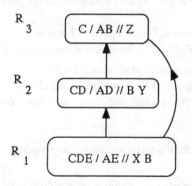

Figure 4.10 Arcs and inclusion of keys (2)

Here the arc joining R_1 to R_3 appears useful because it shows the functional cycle subjacent to the decomposition and a problem of contradiction relating to the verification of the fd $C \rightarrow AB$ for example (chapter 8).

4.4.4 House-keeping nodes (optional)

We delete every node N_1 of RG such that

- its relation R_i allows a unique key KR_i equal to R_i^+,
- and N_i is joined to a single node N_j by an arc directed from N_j to N_i.

This allows the elimination of useless nodes which may have been constructed during the second stage and which arise from hinges between relations: it serves one practical purpose. There follows an example of its use.

Take the relation SR(SABCDXYZ) which is decomposed in compact fashion as follows:

R_1(SABCDX) with key S, R_2(ABCDZ) with keys AD and BD,

R_3(ABCY) with keys A and BC, and R_{12} = SR[C].

Figure 4.11 shows the relation graph obtained at the end of the third stage.

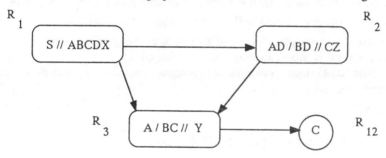

Figure 4.11 Non-useful node

By applying the fourth stage the node of R_{12} is deleted, together with the arc joining R_3 to R_{12}.

4.4.5 Refining the relations assigned to nodes

(5.1) For each node N_i (of R_i):

for each $R_j \in$ MINFD(R_i),

$KR_j^{'+} := KR_j^+ - \{A \in (KR_i^{'+} \cap KR_j^+)\}$

(5.2) $R_i^{'+} := R_i^+ - \{\cup KR_j^{'+}\}$ (for $\forall R_j \in$ MINFD(R_i)).

This new relation $R'_i = SR[R'^+_i]$ is assigned to node N_i.

Of course, all the key attributes must be preserved.

We will show the advantage of this stage using the previous example.

Figure 4.12 shows how the algorithm of the fifth stage transforms the previous relation graph.

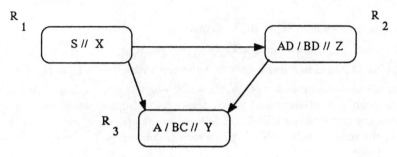

Figure 4.12 Refining a relation

The attributes ABCD have disappeared from the node of R_1 because if we wish to store an entity (sabcdx), it is sufficient to store an entity $r_1 = (sx)$ in iR_1 , $r_2 = (abd\text{-})$ in iR_2 , $r_3 = (abc\text{-})$ in iR_3 and to assign r_1 to r_2 and r_1 to r_3.

We will see in chapter 5 how to embed such assignments. One possibility among several is simply to store the entity (sabcdx).

The fifth stage thus preserves the possible choices for embedding these assignments.

4.4.6   Determining edges (B-edges)

Take a node N_{ij} (relation R_{ij}) joined only to two nodes N_i (R_i) and N_j (R_j) by two arcs, $u = (N_{ij}, N_i)$ and $u' = (N_{ij}, N_j)$, and which verifies:

$KR^+_{ij} = R^+_{ij}$ and $KR^+_{ij} = KR^+_i \cup KR^+_j$,

each key of R_{ij} is formed from the union of one key of R_i and one key of Rj.

It is replaced by an edge $u'' = (N_i, N_j)$, $kr(u'') = 0$ and $gr(u'') = R_{ij}$ joining nodes N_i and N_j; the arcs joining N_{ij} to N_i and to N_j are deleted.

Here is an example that shows the role of this stage. Take the relation $SR(ABXY)$ with compact decomposition into the relations:

$R_1(AB)$ with key AB, $R_2(AX)$ with key A, $R_3(BY)$ with key B.

Figure 4.13 shows the relation graph obtained after the first five stages.

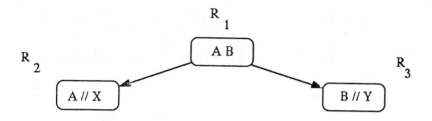

Figure 4.13 B-edge situation

The sixth stage considers that in fact an entity of R_1 allows an assignment to be made between an entity of R_2 and an entity of R_3.

One way of embedding such an assignment (as we will examine in chapter 5) is to store the entities of R_1 . But there are other possibilities.

So, in order to preserve the choices for embedding, this sixth stage transforms this relation graph into the form shown in figure 4.14.

Figure 4.14 B-edge

5 From a relation graph to an internal data structure

The aim of this chapter is to show the transformation of a relation graph into an internal data structure.

We will first transform the graph into a raw access paths graph (APG) using the quite simple algorithm already described. We will then analyse this access paths graph using the results obtained from the activity analysis. The problems encountered are notably of the following nature:

a) Are all the access paths useful?

b) What are the indexes that need to be added?

c) What is the redundancy that it is important to introduce?

d) What are the relations assigned to nodes that it is advisable to decompose into several relations with the same or with equivalent keys?

We will show some important results that must be contained in an activity analysis in order to define an internal structure from a raw APG.

The answers to these questions also depend on the database management system used; some systems embed automatically all the reciprocal access paths. In that case the designer no longer has to concern himself with question a). Such DBMSs work directly from the raw access paths graph.

The designer specifies the names of the access paths finally decided upon, together with the parameters.

It is then a question of transforming the chosen APG into an internal structure written in the terms of the selected DBMS. We will, however, examine a more general situation independent of a DBMS which gives the elements of the answer to the following question:

e) How are access paths embedded?

Some DBMSs impose their own method for storing access paths and then the database designer does not need to concern himself with this question.

Even if some of these points may appear irrelevant for some DBMSs, they may make one appreciate the quality of the artificial intelligence that DBMSs contain.

The subject matter of this chapter is by no means exhaustively treated, because of the great variety of possible methods used for embedding. (HAINAUT86) (KINKELSTEIN SCHKOLNICK TIBERIO88) contain more detailed examination of this subject. At the same time, we put forward a transformation (as described in section 3.2) of the initial relation graph into an internal data structure.

5.1   Choice of an access paths graph

All the previous discussion (chapter 4) has led to the development of a raw access paths graph. We will now try to provide a guide for the designer in choosing the most appropriate internal data structure for the database for which he is responsible. As already mentioned, some DBMSs offer the designer little choice at this level. Without taking sides on whether such an approach is well conceived or indeed on the opposite approach (allowing the designer a completely free hand), we will leave this matter aside, in order to concentrate on explaining the problems associated with this stage.

For us, the possible choices for the designer at this level concern:

- the possibility of not embedding reciprocal access paths corresponding to the relation T:

If an access path is one-to-one or zero-to-one, and given the ease of embedding such an access path, it seems hair-splitting to interest oneself in its possible uselessness (except in special cases which of course confirm the rule!). This leaves the case of multivalued access paths. The following sections examine the conditions in which they may be considered to be non-useful.

However, in his haste to eliminate multivalued access paths, the designer must ensure that there is an outflow in the APG for each space, in order to preserve access for the entities of that space. In this way the APG will remain faithful (3.2) to the initial model.

- the choice of entry relations

The fact that relation R is an entry relation means that it will be possible to reach directly an entity r of iR by knowing the value that it takes for a key. Generally, to make such an access possible, quite sophisticated techniques are required (DATE75,DELOBEL-ADIBA82), such as sequential indexing, hash code, B-trees. But if use of the database is only of interest to entities of iR by scanning through them all in sequence or reaching them from the entities of other relations via access paths, why retain such a costly access for R? In this case the designer no longer considers R as the entry relation.

- inverting a relation of a node or index of a relation

This is the classic case. Our approach has greatly favoured access to the entities of a relation R(AMNO) by knowing the values that they take for a key. But it is certainly quite conventional in using a database to want to access entities of R by knowing the values that they take for attributes that do not form a key to R.

We represent this in an APG by the creation of a new node assigned to the attributes on which the inversion of the relation R bears; this node is joined to the entry point; it is joined to the node of R by a single value access path from the node of R and by a reciprocal multivalued access path.

Figure 5.1 shows an example of inversion of R by MN.

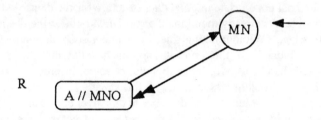

R

Figure 5.1 Inversion of a relation

MN then forms an index of relation R.

- adding redundancy

We will study in part three how to avoid redundancy in databases. It may therefore appear paradoxical here to study how to introduce redundancy. The great difference between the two parts derives from the position of the designer. In part three we seek to guide the designer towards a relation graph containing the minimum of redundancy; above all we seek to avoid situations where the designer would not perceive the redundancy contained in the relation graph.

Here the designer introduces redundancy knowingly. He knows that each redundancy involves coherency controls that are costly in execution and installation time, but that on the other hand a well placed redundancy may make the execution of processes on the database much more efficient.

It is for him to take the decision while remembering that redundancy is penalising in the execution of processes only if it affects data that is often modified.

This addition of redundancy is translated principally in two ways as illustrated in figure 5.2.

One (or more) attribute C is added to a relation R (ABX) with key A; to ensure that this transformation retains the faithfulness of the APG to the initial relation graph, the fd A $\rightarrow$ C must exist; a pair of reciprocal access paths is added in the APG, between two relations R and S whose nodes are joined by a path that does not reduce to a single arc.

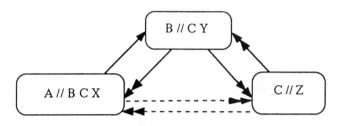

Figure 5.2 Redundancy

The dashed lines shows the redundancy introduced in terms of access paths; the solid lines show that introduced by an attribute.

- node duplication

Take a relation R(AMNOP) to which there is a corresponding node in the APG. The designer may have to decompose this relation R into two (or more) relations R_1 and R_2 that have keys equivalent to those of R, with a non key attribute of R only being found in one of these relations, for example R_1(AMN) and R_2(AOP). The APG then becomes as shown in figure 5.3.

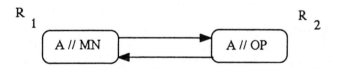

Figure 5.3 Node duplication

The R node is replaced by two nodes assigned to the relations R_1 and R_2 and joined to one another by two reciprocal single value access paths.
A question arises concerning the access paths which left the node of R or arrived at it. A possible answer is to choose one of the two relations, for example R_1 , and connect to its node all these access paths. This crude method can be bettered by a more subtle approach where the designer chooses to which node of R_1 or R_2 to connect the access paths.

Why might a designer wish to duplicate a node? Here are two reasons.

The first concerns the information size of an entity of R. The larger it is, the less likely it is that entities of R will be brought by a single read operation into central memory. Now, some attributes of R may have domains that require much memory space (a postal address, for example), while others require very little (a turnover figure, for example); if in addition the processes that work on the one are often different from those that work on the other, it is sensible to separate the attributes.

Example
CLIENT(NOCLIENT TOMONTH NBORDERS ADDRESS NAME).
ADDRESS and CLIENT NAME are used for processes that send correspondence to clients; these processes are not the same as work on the number of orders from the client (NBORDERS) and his monthly turnover figure (TOMONTH). The designer would be well advised to decompose the relation CLIENT into (NOCLIENT TOMONTH NBORDERS) and (NOCLIENT ADDRESS NAME).

The second reason concerns concurrent access; returning to the previous example if two processes T_1 and T_2 have the respective aims of altering the TOMONTH of client 150386 and of altering the same client's address, they will be in contention if the relation CLIENT is not decomposed: if they both execute at the same time, one must give way to the other. In fact, logically they are not in contention: one is allocated a higher priority than the other, which has to wait. The prior decomposition of CLIENT allows them to execute without being in contention.

5.2 Computing methods of embedding access paths

We will examine three types of edges of a relation graph:

D-edge: directed arc between the nodes of relations R and S, when KR$^+$, the set of key attributes of R, contains KS$^+$: R is then said to be dependent on S.

F-edge: directed arc between the nodes of relations R and S, R not being dependent on S. (There is a functional dependency KR $\rightarrow$ KS.)

B-edge: edge between the nodes of relations R and S (binary edge).

We will introduce the basic data manipulation operations that apply both to the access paths and to the instances of the relations assigned to the nodes; the basic operations are refined depending on the particular edge involved.

Then, for each edge type, we will review briefly different methods for embedding the access paths used in DBMSs; we will compare the efficiency with respect to each of the basic operations, in order to arrive at an algorithm for choosing between these methods.

Finally, we will derive from the choice algorithms some algorithms for measurement: in the design phase of a database it is important to know which parameters it is useful to estimate.

For us, the choices open to the designer at this level revolve around the possibility of not embedding two reciprocal access paths. Take the three relations R(AX), S(BY), T(AB) and the access path graph shown in figure 5.4.

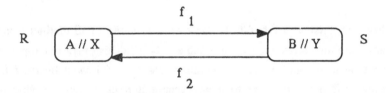

Figure 5.4 Basic APG

f_1 and f_2 are the access paths corresponding to the relation T. Examination of the non-usefulness of one of these two access paths has the value of establishing the redundancy caused by f_1 and f_2 ; for the entity (ab) of T to be stored in the database, we must have both a $\in$ f_2(b) *and* b $\in$ f_1(a). Every update of an entity of T will have to be reflected on these two access paths. So, both for reasons of space saving and efficiency it is advisable only to retain one or other of these access paths. All these operations are supposed to verify the integrity rules that contain it in their range.

5.2.1   Atomic operations for data manipulation

All the operations that we will examine are atomic in the sense that none of them can be executed by a computer by means of other operations, with comparable performance.

To introduce them, we will use the previous three relations R(AX), S(BY) and T(AB) and the previous access paths graph.

5.2.1.1   Atomic operations relating to access paths

Link: this operation has the notation :∈ in (ABRIAL74). r:∈ $f_2(s)$ or a:∈ $f_2(b)$ or
(a,b):∈ iT, for example. This operation allows entities to be created in iT. It
verifies that the entities r and s exist in iR and iS, and that they are not already
linked to one another, and it executes the symmetric operation: s:∈ $f_1(r)$ (when
f_1 exists).

Unlink: this operation has the notation :∉ in (ABRIAL74): r:∉ $f_2(s)$
or a :∉ $f_2(b)$ or (a,b) :∉ iT. It allows the removal of entities in iT. It contains
the verification of the existence of entities r and s in iR and iS and of the link
between them. It executes the symmetric operation s :∉ $f_1(r)$ (when f_1 exists).

Access: $f_2(s)$ allows access to all the entities r of iR, joined to entity s of iS by
the access path f_2 . It verifies the existence of s in iS. We also note $f_2(b)$.

Modify: r:∉ $f_2(s)$ and r:∈ $f_2(s_1)$ where s_1 is an entity of iS distinct from s.
We also note this operation a:∉ $f_2(b)$ and a:∈ $f_2(b_1)$. This operation appears to
be identical to the succession of operations r:∉ $f_2(s)$ followed by r:∈ $f_2(s_1)$;
however, it is not equivalent to them because it requires fewer verification
controls.
Another reason is the following one: the state of the database after the unlink
operation may be incoherent, whereas after the two operations this may not be
the case. This operation verifies that the entities r, s, s_1 and the link between
the entities r and s exist and that there is no link between r and s_1 already in
existence; it executes the symmetric operation: s:∉ $f_1(r)$ and s_1:∈ $f_1(r)$ when f_1
exists.

5.2.1.2   Atomic operations relating to node relations

Create: this operation allows a new entity to be created in an instance of a
relation assigned to a node (for example R). We describe it as r :∈ iR.
This operation verifies that r does not exist already in iR; it verifies any
possible dependency rules if R is a relation that depends upon another.

Example: take the two relations R(AX) (key : A)and V(ACZ) (key : AC), V
being dependent on R. (acz):∈ iV can be executed only if there is an entity r in
iR such that r.A = a.

Delete: this operation allows the deletion of an entity of an instance of a relation assigned to a node (for example R).

We describe as **r :∉ iR**. This operation:

-    verifies that r exists in iR,
-    verifies any referential dependency rules if there are relations that depend on R,
-    executes the unlink operations for all access paths going from r or arriving at r.

Example: take the access paths graph shown in figure 5.5 where the entry point is not shown as it plays no role.

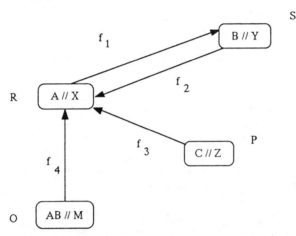

Figure 5.5 Deleting an entity

O is a relation dependent on R.

r = (a,x) :∉ iR contains the following operations after verification of the existence of r in iR:

for all s ∈ f_1(r) *do* r :∉ f_2(s) *repeat*

for all p of iP do

        if r ∈ f_3(p) *then* r :∉ f_3(p) *endif*

repeat

for all o of iO *such that* o.A = a *do* o :∉ iO *repeat*.

Access: this operation allows one to access sequentially all the entities of iR: it is described by **take iR,r**: the new entity read is stored in r, a variable that has been declared of type R.

If in the APG the node of relation R is linked with the entry point by an edge, it is then possible to access an entity of iR by knowing the value that it takes for a key KR; it is described by **r := R[KR=a]**.

Modify: here an entity r of iR is replaced by a new r' such that for every mandatory key KR of R, r.KR = r'.KR. This operation verifies that r belongs to iR and that r' does not belong to it. It is described by r :∉ iR and r' :∈ iR. Here again, as for the modify operation relating to access paths, and for the same reasons, this operation is not identical to the sequence of operations r :∉ iR then r' :∈ iR.

5.2.2   Embedding access paths corresponding to an F-edge

5.2.2a   Introduction

Take the relations R(A X) S(B Y) and T(A B) and their relation graph as shown in figure 5.6 (where B is not written in the node of R as allowed by stage E5 of the algorithm discussed in chapter 4).

Figure 5.6 F-edge

Figure 5.7 shows their access path graphs.

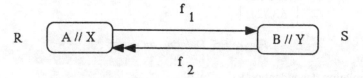

Figure 5.7 F-edge in APG

Where
nR   the number of entities in iR
nS   the number of entities in iS
q   the probability that there is at least one entity of iR linked to an entity of iS
p   the probability that there is at least one entity of iS linked to an entity of iR
nBA   the average number of entities of iR assigned to an entity of iS when there is at least one
nRmax   the maximum number of entities in iR
nSmax   the maximum number of entities in iS
nBAmax   the maximum number of entities of iR assigned to an entity of iS.

5.2.2b   Methods for embedding f_1 and f_2

From the methods often used in DBMSs (especially those that follow the CODASYL norms) we will examine:

for f1:

- *the pointer* (1): a new attribute Ref of R is created, whose domain is the set of addresses of the entities of S: $\forall\ r \in$ R, r.Ref designates the address of the entity s of S such that (r.A, s.B) $\in$ T.
- *duplicating* B: B is added to the set of the attributes of R. Thus each entity of R contains the key to the corresponding entity of S.

for f2:

- *the list* (1): R(A X Foll), S(B Y Tlist).
$\forall\ s \in$ S s.Tlist indicates the first entity of R corresponding to s,
$\forall r \in$ R r.Foll indicates the entity of R that follows r in the list of s.

- *circular list* (2): R(A X Foll Parent), S(B Y Tlist). This is a list where, in addition, the last entity points to the original entity in the list (Parent).

- *double list* (3): R(A X Foll Pre), S(B Y Tlist Finlist).
This is a list in which each entity not only has a pointer indicating the following one (Foll), but also another that indicates the preceding one (Pre). In addition, $\forall\ s \in$ S s.Finlist indicates the final entity in the list of s.

- *circular, double list* (4):
R(A X Foll Pre Parent), S(B Y Tlist Finlist).
This is both a double list and a circular list (see example in 5.4.1).

- *table* (5): R(A X), S(B Y PT).
PT is a table of pointers; s.PT(i) indicates the address of an entity r of R such that (r.A, s.B) $\in$ T.
There are two kinds of embedding of tables: fixed size tables and those with an overflow area (see 5.4.2).

- *inversion* of the relation R by B.
An index B of the relation R(A B X) is constructed; this method is especially useful if this index has already been created in the preceding phase (5.1). It is difficult to compare it with other methods; the logical I/O operations that it requires are as much to do with additional accesses to the indexes as with accesses to the relation entities.

From the computing point of view, these methods may be classified according to their facility of use, the first being the easiest:
- list and fixed size table
- double list and circular list
- table with overflow area.

Thus, to embed T we can
- embed f_1 without embedding $f_2(10)$;
- embed f_2 without embedding f_1 by list (01), circular list (02), double list (03), circular, double list (04), table (05);
- embed f_1 and f_2 ;

solution 11: f_2 is embedded using a list;

solution 13: f_2 is embedded using a double list;

solution 15: f_2 is embedded using a table'.

Solutions 12 (f_2 embedded using a circular list) and 14 (f2 embedded using a circular, double list) are respectively identical to 11 and 13.

5.2.2c   Calculation of number of I/O operations

The operations $(a,x) :\in$ iR or $(b,y) :\in$ iS play no part in our study. On the other hand, we refine the operations for:

- Unlink: we not only consider $s :\notin f_1(r)$ (or $(a,b) :\notin$ iT) but also $\emptyset :\in f_1(r)$ (or $(a,-) :\notin$ iT); in the first case, the database contains an assignment between r and s which must be destroyed; in the second case, the database contains an assignment between r and an unspecified entity of iS, which must be destroyed.

For example, $R(AX)$ designates the relation CAR(NOCAR M) and $S(BY)$ the relation PERSON(NAME ADDRESS)
and $T(AB)$ the relation OWNER(NOCAR NAME);
to establish that car number G856CRU no longer has an owner, may require to know its owner: (G856CRU, James) $:\notin$ iOWNER,
        or not: (G856CRU,-) $:\notin$ iOWNER.

- Modify: the fd $A \rightarrow B$ breaks the symmetry between the relations R and S. We can see by programming the algorithms that on the one hand $(a,b) :\notin$ iT *and* $(a,b_1) :\in$ iT and on the other hand $(a,b) :\notin$ iT and $(a_1,b) :\in$ iT are two operations with different performance. As before, there is a variant of the first operation which is : $(a,-) :\notin$ iT *and* $(a,b_1) :\in$ iT.

Here are three quick examples with the same relations:
(G856CRU, James) :∉ iOWNER and (G856CRU, John) :∈ iOWNER; this operation changes the ownership of the car with number G856CRU: it was James; it becomes John.
(G856CRU,-) :∉ iOWNER and (G865CRU, John) :∈ iOWNER; the car number G856CRU had an owner, it is changed and its new owner is John.
(G856CRU, James) :∉ iOWNER and (D586VAN, James) :∈ iOWNER. James is no longer the owner of car number G856CRU but now owns car number D586VAN.

For the calculation of the efficiency of the different operations in the framework of the 9 embedding methods described, we have enumerated the number of logical read and write operations carried out for the instances iR and iS knowing that an operation modifying an entity counts as a single operation. The tables considered are of fixed size.
The number of I/O operations for each of the 9 solutions and for each of the operations may be found in (LEONARD88).
A solution s_1 is said to be superior to a solution s_2 if for all the basic operations, the number of I/Os necessary to execute s_1 is less than that of s_2 .
This relation is a partial order relation in the set of solutions.
Our results show that: 15>13>04>03,
                15>11>03>02,
15, 05 and 10 could not be compared.

5.2.2d   Selection algorithm

The preceding result does not mean that the choice is restricted only to the solutions 15, 05, 10. In fact, since it is not always possible to embed f_2 by a table of fixed size, another solution must be chosen. The choice is governed by the frequency of basic operations triggered by the processes anticipated. In some cases, some solutions are equivalent; one then chooses the one that is simplest.
We note the frequency of an operation thus: F <operation name> <argument>.
Simplified selection algorithm:
if Fdelete (b,y) $\cong$ 0 and Ff$_2$(b) $\cong$ 0 *then* choose 10
else if the solution to the table is possible *then* choose 15
      else if nBA>7 *then* choose 13
            else choose 11
            endif
      endif
endif.

5.2.3   Embedding access paths corresponding to a D-edge

5.2.3a   Introduction

Take the relations R(*A* B X) (key : AB) S(*A* Y) (key : A) and the relation graph shown in figure 5.8.

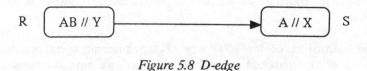

Figure 5.8 D-edge

Take the access paths graph shown in figure 5.9.

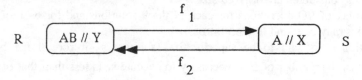

Figure 5.9 D-edge in an access path graph

These are the parameters used:
nR   number of entities of iR
nS   number of entities of iS
q   probability that there exists at least one entity of iR linked to an
           entity of iS
nSR   average number of entities of iR linked to an entity of iS when at
           least one exists
nSRmax   maximum number of entities of iR linked to an entity of iS.

5.2.3b   Computing methods for embedding f_1 and f_2

We will examine:

for f_1 :
access by a value from the domain of A or by a pointer, whose domain is the set of addresses of entities of S and which replaces A in R.

for f_2 :
- the same solutions as in the preceding cases apply, since there is functional dependency, AB → A;

- sequential contiguity (06): it is a question of considering a single file which contains two kinds of records corresponding to the entities of iR and those of iS. The entities of iR relative to the same object *a* of A are stored in sequence after the entity of iS relative to *a*. Coding these values with the keys of A and A,B will allows this difference to be made.

If we know the maximum number nSRmax of entities of R corresponding to an entity of S, this method is the least complex of all the other solutions because it requires no pointer; if not, it requires the control of an overflow area and becomes as complex as the table solution with overflow area.

5.2.3c Calculating the number of operations

We have calculated the number of I/O operations necessary to carry out atomic operations adopting the same conventions as in the preceding section. The atomic operations of link and unlink are triggered by operations carried out on the instances iR and iS since R is dependent on S.
Solution 16 cannot be validly compared with the others by our method because the I/Os are made predominantly through sequential traverses.
The number of I/O operations executed by the atomic operations for the different solutions are to be found in (LEONARD88).

5.2.3d Selection algorithm

We use the same conventions as before.
if $Ff_2(a) \cong 0$ and $Fdelete(a,x) \cong 0$ *then* choose 10
else if- the solution to the table is possible
    then choose 15
    else choose 13
    endif
endif.

5.2.4 Embedding access paths corresponding to a B-edge

5.2.4a Introduction

Take the relations R(*A* X) (key : A) S(*B* Y) (key : B) and T(*A* B) (key : AB) and their relation graph (figure 5.10).

Figure 5.10 B-edge

Take their access paths graph (figure 5.11).

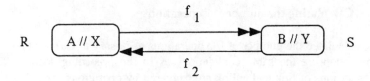

Figure 5.11 B-edge in an access paths graph

The notation is:

nR   number of entities in iR
nS   number of entities in iS
p   probability that there is at least one entitiy i of iT such that t.A = a
q   probability that there is at least one entity t of iT such that t.B = b
nAB   average number of entities of iT such that t.A = a knowing that there
            is at least one
nBA   average number of entities of iT such that t.B = b knowing that there
            is at least one.

5.2.4b   Computing methods for embedding f₁ and f₂

f_1 and f_2 play symmetrical roles: each method applicable for one is valid for
the other. Of the possible methods, we will examine:

- the correspondence table
In this case another relation TABLE-R-S is created whose attributes are only
pointers and whose entities make a correspondence between the entities of R
and those of S. TABLE-R- S is dependent on R and S.

This method is the one used especially in CODASYL DBMSs. The two access
paths f_1 and f_2 are then embedded as shown in figure 5.12.

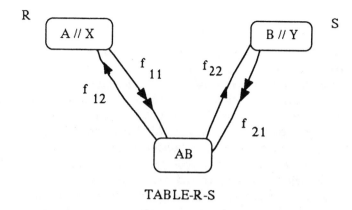

TABLE-R-S

Figure 5.12 Correspondence table

It is here a question of embedding four access paths relative to the two dependency edges.

From the solutions discussed in the preceding section, solution 13 is the one obtained:

- it is more efficient than 11 in the majority of cases
- 16 cannot be applied for the two dependency edges
- 15 gives rise to a more direct embedding of f_1 and f_2 by table and is examined subsequently.

We therefore consider the relations:

$R(A$ X Ahead)
$S(B$ Y Bhead)
TABLE-R-S$(NO$ Afoll Apre Aparent Bfoll Bpre Bparent) where:
    NO is a number identifying the entities of TABLE-R-S
    Ahead,Afoll,Apre serve to embed f_{11} (duplicated list)
    Bhead,Bfoll,Bpre serve to embed f_{21} (duplicated list)
    Aparent serves to embed f_{12} (pointer)
    Bparent serves to embed f_{22} (pointer).

- the table
if we embed f_1 by table, the relations become:
$R(A$ X PTA) and $S(B$ Y) where PTA is in fact a table of pointers.
r.PTA(i) indicates the address of an entity of S, such as $(r.A, s.B) \in iT$.

There are two kinds of table: those of fixed size and those with an overflow area (see 5.4.2).

- the multilist

if we embed f_1 by multilist, the relations become:

R(A X Ahead Atpos) and S(B Y Afoll Apos) where r.Ahead gives the address of the first entity s of S in the list of r.A;

but because an entity s may belong to several lists, it is also necessary to indicate in r.Atpos the position i of the list of r.A in tables Afoll and Apos: s.Afoll(i) indicates the address of the entity s' that follows in the list; s.Apos(i) indicates the position of this list in tables Afoll and Apos of s'.

If the number of objects a of A corresponding to an object b of B does not have a maximum, then it is necessary to provide an overflow area as in the case of a table. As the table is a simpler and more efficient solution, the multilist solution may not be adopted in this case. Furthermore, we are only considering fixed size multilists, that is, those whose tables Afoll and Apos are of fixed size (see 5.4.3).

- the table (f_1) and the multilist (f_2) (or vice versa):

the relations become: R(A X PTA Bfoll) and S(B Y Bhead).

We can then agree that:

$\forall$ r $\in$ R if r.PTA(j) = b then r.Bfoll(j) is relative to the list of b.

Finally, to embed T we can choose between:

the correspondence table (33)

embedding f_1 and f_2 with tables (11)

embedding f_1 with a table, f_2 with a multilist (12)

and inversely (21)

embedding f_1 with a table without embedding f_2 (10)

and inversely (01)

embedding f_1 with a multilist without embedding f_2 (20)

and inversely (02).

The solution involving the embedding of f_1 and f_2 using multilists cannot be adopted: it assumes in effect that nABmax and nBAmax are known; but then 11 is simpler to implement and leads to a lower number of I/O operations.

From the computing point of view, we can classify these methods according to their ease of implementation:

10 and 01	a fixed size table
11	with fixed size tables
20 and 02	a multilist
12 and 21	a fixed size table and a fixed size multilist
33	a correspondence table
10, 01, 11	a variable size table.

5.2.4c Calculation of the number of operations

We have calculated the number of I/O operations necessary to carry out atomic operations in the case of the 8 solutions proposed, adopting the same convention as in section 5.2.2d.

The table which gives the number of I/O operations necessary for each solution and for each basic operation is given in (LEONARD88).

Taking the same definition as in section 5.2.2d for the superiority of one solution over another, we find that: 11>33, 11>12, 11>20.

5.2.4d Selection algorithm

If the solution of the fixed table for f_1 is possible
and *if* the solution of the fixed table for f_2 is possible *then*
            choose 11
elseif   the solution of the fixed table for f_1 is possible
           and $Ff_2(b) \cong 0$ and $Fdelete(b,y) \cong 0$
           then   choose 10
elseif   the solution of the fixed table for f_2 is possible
           and $Ff_1(a) \cong 0$ and $Fdelete(a,x) \cong 0$
           then   choose 01
else
           if the solution of the fixed table for f_1 is possible *then*
                if $Ff_1(a) \cong 0$ and $Fdelete(a,x) \cong 0$ then choose 02
                elseif choose 12
                endif
           elseif the solution of the fixed table for f_2 is possible *then*
                if $Ff_2(b) \cong 0$ and $Fdelete(b,y) \cong 0$ then choose 20
                else choose 21
                endif
           else choose 33
           endif
endif.

5.2.5   Relevance of these results

The whole of this study has identified criteria for the choice of methods for embedding access paths. These are based on the number of I/O operations that result from the use of these access paths and the method of their embedding.

These results have their limitations. In particular, they do not take account of integrity rules other than the functional dependencies intrinsic to the relations. Nevertheless these results underline the importance of the data processing frequency to make rigorous selections. If we can easily admit that all the single value access paths (those that assign one entity to at most one other entity) will be embedded because their embedding is easy, the main problem concerns the multivalued access paths which assign one entity to several entities (f_2 for example): these may give rise to complex embedding. The need to retain them in the database depends on two frequencies $Ff_2(s)$ and $Fdelete(s)$.

It is therefore necessary for the analysis of the processes to estimate these frequencies by summing the expected uses of the two atomic operations $f_2(s)$ and $delete(s)$. In our opinion, it is a question of balancing the frequencies of use, on the one hand by the operating system conditions which trigger them (interactive, time lapse, batch processing), and on the other hand by the importance of these processes; some may only be executed quite rarely, but may still require very fast response when they are required.
It is this study that enables the designer to know if an access path is useful or not (see 5.1).

5.3 Conclusions

We have just drawn up a list of the possible choices that one faces in transforming a raw access paths graph into an internal data structure.

These choices concern first the access paths graph:

Which are the access paths to be retained?
How is redundancy to be introduced?
Which are the indexes that should be provided?
Which are the relations that it is desirable to decompose?

These are the results of the analysis of the data processes foreseen, which allow the designer to answer such questions. We have specified the parameters that must be estimated from such an analysis: in particular the traverse frequency of a multivalued access path and the frequency of entity removal from the original relations of the multivalued access paths.
The designer specifies the names of the access paths adopted and their parameters, then these choices concern the internal method used to embed each of the access paths adopted.

The transformation that we propose, of a raw APG into an internal data structure, is not an algorithm: it is only a guide that limits the possible modifications so that the transformation remains faithful in the sense of section 3.2. That is:

- it preserves the contents since the relations of nodes and edges of the APG are found in the final APG even if a node relation has been decomposed;

- it preserves access since in the final APG there is still at least one outflow corresponding to a decomposition of a space relation: this precaution is taken when access paths are eliminated;

- it preserves efficiency: the intrinsic fds of the relations of the APG_r are identical to those of the final APG.

5.4   Appendix

5.4.1   Example of a circular double list

Take the relations $R(AX)$, $S(BY)$, $T(AB)$ and the following instances:

iR	iS	iT
$a_1 x_1$	$b_1 y_1$	$a_1 -$
$a_2 x_2$	$b_2 y_2$	$a_2 b_2$
$a_3 x_3$	$b_3 y_3$	$a_3 b_1$
$a_4 x_4$		$a_4 b_2$
$a_5 x_5$		$a_5 b_2$

Only access path f_2 is embedded using a circular double list: instances iR and iS are then:

iR						iS				
Rank	A	X	Next	Pre	Parent	Rank	B	Y	Tlist	Finlist
1	a_1	x_1	Nul	Nul	Nul	1	b_1	y_1	3	3
2	a_2	x_2	4	Nil	Nil	2	b_2	y_2	2	5
3	a_3	x_3	Nil	Nil	1	3	b_3	y_3	Nul	Nul
4	a_4	x_4	5	2	Nil					
5	a_5	x_5	Nil	4	2					

Nul means "belongs to no list"; Nil means "is the last entity in a list" for Next, "is the first entity in the list" for Pre, "is not the last entity in the list" for Parent.

5.4.2   Embedding an access path by table

Take the relations $R(A\ X)$, $S(B\ Y)$, $T(A\ B)$ of an access paths graph as shown in figure 5.13.

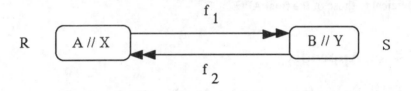

Figure 5.13 Table

We consider f_2 to be a multivalued access path. It can assign an entity of iS to several entities of iR. Take nBAmax to be the maximum cardinality of $f_2(s)$ for each entity s of S. According to the semantics of relations, this parameter may be known or unknown. For example, a library rule may limit the number of simultaneous borrowings (relation T) of books (relation R) to a subscriber (relation S) to 5: nBAmax = 5. On the other hand, the maximum number of journeys (relation R) that an explorer (relations S) may have been able to undertake (relation T) in his lifetime, makes little sense.

If nBAmax is known, then it is possible to embed f_2 with a fixed dimension table equal to nBAmax; each entity s of iS takes values not only for the attributes B and Y but also for a table F_2 of pointers indicating the addresses of the entities of iR that are assigned to it by s.

This solution is very easy to embed; but it cannot be space saving. In fact, all the entities of iS are not necessarily assigned to nBAmax entities of iR; the set of locations occupied by the pointers is only filled in the proportion of qnBA/nBAmax. This ratio should not be too far from 1 if nBAmax is large enough, to ensure that not too much space is wasted. If this is the case, we say that *"the fixed table solution is possible"*.

Otherwise, it is possible to turn to tables with overflow areas. Then, a table of pointers of size card80 is assigned to each s of iS; for entities assigned to more than card80 entities of iR their tables are extended by overflow areas. For example, if it is difficult to know the maximum number of cars (relation R) that a household may own (relation S), it is conversely easy to know that 80% of households do not have more than 2 cars; the entity relative to a household will contain a table of size 2; a pointer to an overflow area will be useful for those households with more cars.

If it is possible to estimate card80 and if the tables of pointers of this size are sufficiently filled, we say that *"the table solution is possible"*. The fixed table solution is a special case of this.

Note that some DBMSs systematically embed all the multivalued access paths using tables.

5.4.3   Example of a multilist

Take the relations $R(AX)$, $S(BY)$, $T(AB)$ and the following instances:

iR	iS	iT
a_1x_1	b_1y_1	a_2b_1
a_2x_2	b_2y_2	a_2b_3
a_3x_3	b_3y_3	a_2b_4
a_4x_4	b_4y_4	a_3b_4
a_5x_5		a_4b_4
		a_4b_3
		a_3b_2

Only the access path f_1 (of iR towards iS) is embedded.

nBAmax is equal to 3 and f_1 is embedded using a multilist. The instances iR and iS are then:

iR:

Rank	A	X	Ahead	Atpos
1	a_1	x_1	Nul	Nul
2	a_2	x_2	1	1
3	a_3	x_3	4	2
4	a_4	x_4	4	3
5	a_5	x_5	Nul	Nul

iS:

Rank	B	Y	Anext			Apos		
1	b_1	y_1	3	Nul	Nul	2	Nul	Nul
2	b_2	y_2	Nil	Nul	Nul	Nil	Nul	Nul
3	b_3	y_3	Nil	4	Nul	Nil	1	Nul
4	b_4	y_4	Nil	2	3	Nil	1	1

Thus b_4 corresponds to a_4 because a_4.Ahead = 4; b_3 also corresponds to it because a_4.Atpos = 3 and b_4.Anext(3) = 3. No other entity corresponds to it because b_4.Apos(3) = 1 and b_3.Anext(1) = Nil.

PART 3

DECOMPOSITION

OF A RELATION

6 Choosing a relation decomposition

A study of the *decomposition* of a relation involves the difficult problem of the *equivalent representations* of information. We will examine in particular the equivalence between a relation R and a set of relations $\{R_1...R_i...R_n\}$; this equivalence means that any information taken into account in R in the form of an entity, must be able to be taken into account in the set of relations $\{R_1...R_i...R_n\}$ in the form of entities of these relations, and reciprocally. This equivalence is formally constructed first with the help of the *projection* operation for relations which allows an entity of R to be transformed into entities of R_i relations, and second with the *join* operation for relations which allows compatible entities of different R_i relations to be transformed into an entity of R. The relations $\{R_1...R_i...Rn\}$ then form a *decomposition* of the relation R.

We will first show the advantage of storing the entities of R in the database using their projections on R_i^+ rather than storing them themselves, by means of the following example.

Example

Take the commercial structure CS of a consumer products enterprise. This relation is built on 3 attributes: representative name (R), salespoint name (SP), product name (P) with the following predicate: (r sp p) is an entity of CS if the representative r visits the salespoint sp and presents the product p from his catalogue. CS (R SP P) may be decomposed into CS[R SP], CS[R P] because the commercial structure is organised in that way: every representative presents all products in his catalogue at all the salespoints that he visits.

We can store the information according to two structures:

the first according to CS (R SP P) provided with the preceding integrity rule expressed in the form of a join dependency;

the second according to CS1 = CS[R SP] and CS2 = CS[R P].

Using the example of an instance of R, we will show the advantage of the second over the first.

CS	(R	SP	P)
	Frost	Corner	Breeze
	Frost	Cross	Breeze
	Frost	Corner	Fresh
	Frost	Cross	Fresh
	Grant	Angle	Pine

Now if Mr Frost visits salespoint Mall, in the first structure it is necessary to include all the products in Mr Frost's catalogue and then *create* the entities (Frost Mall Breeze) and (Frost Mall Fresh); in the second structure, it is only necessary to create the new entity in CS1: (Frost Mall).

Again, if Mr Frost no longer has the product Breeze in his catalogue, with the first structure all the CS entities relating to Mr Frost and to Breeze will have to be *deleted*; with the second only the entity (Frost Breeze) needs to be deleted from CS2.

If the same method is applied to the case where Mr Grant no longer has the Pine product in his catalogue, with the first structure we will lose the information that Mr Grant visits Angle, whereas this information is retained with the second structure.

Now if the product Fulfil replaces Breeze in Mr Frost's catalogue, with the first structure all the CS entities relating to (Frost Breeze) must be found and *updated* by replacing Breeze with Fulfil; however, with the second structure we only have to replace the entity (Frost Breeze) with (Frost Fulfil) in CS2.

To conclude, the modifying operations (create, delete, update) are greatly assisted with the second structure. On the other hand, the first structure will require programs to verify join dependency that are costly in execution time, whereas with the second structure no verification programs will have to written and the alterations are simply made.

In fact, the decomposition has restricted the *information redundancy*: in the first structure, the fact that Mr Frost's catalogue contains Fresh has to be written several times; in the second, it is only written once.

As this example has shown, one advantage of decomposing a relation R is to avoid data redundancy and the need to maintain the coherence of this redundancy by means of verification programs. To study this advantage in general, we will:

– first show different ways of decomposing a relation R;

– then identify the links that exist between a decomposition of R and the satisfaction of integrity rules defined on R: formally, it is a question of defining the *projection or the extension of an integrity rule;*

– finally compare different decompositions of R relative to the efficiency of the validation of these integrity rules; in particular we will define the *qualities* of a decomposition.

6.1 Decomposing a relation

6.1.1 Definition and properties of a decomposition

A first formulation of the concept of a decomposition may be found in (DELOBEL73).
We will recall some points of section 2.5.1.

DEFINITION

A *decomposition* D of a relation R is a set of relations R_1, R_2,...R_i,...R_n verifying:

a) $R_i = R[R_i^+]$

$$
\text{(b) } R = \overset{n}{\underset{i=1}{*}} R_i
$$

D^+ designates the set of attributes of the R_i relations: $D^+ = R^+$.

A decomposition D of R is *trivial* if it contains a single relation, R itself.

A decomposition D of R is *cleared* if for each relation R_i of D that admits R_i^+ as key there is no relation R_j of D such that $R_i^+ \subseteq R_j^+$.

Example

R(ABCD) and F = {AB → C}.

$R_1 = R[ABC]$, $R_2 = R[ABD]$, $R_3 = R[AB]$.

The decomposition $D' = \{R_1\ R_2\ R_3\}$ is not cleared because of R_3; conversely, the decomposition $D = \{R_1\ R_2\}$ is cleared.

DEFINITION

D' is a *partial decomposition* of decomposition D if D' is included in D, and if D' is a decomposition of $R' = R[D'^+]$.

Note

A relation R cannot be decomposed by means of any division of R^+ as the following example shows: take R(ABC) which accepts this set of entities as closure:

a_1 b_1 c_1

a_1 b_2 c_1

a_1 b_1 c_2

It may not be decomposed according to R[AB] and R[AC] because the join of the closure projections yields the entity $(a_1\ b_2\ c_2)$ which does not belong to the closure.

Property (d) (section 2.5)
If a set of relations $\{R_1 ... R_i ... R_n\}$ verifies the property a) and

the property c) $\bigcup\limits_{i=1}^{n} R_i^+ = R^+$, then it verifies: $R \subseteq \mathop{*}\limits_{i=1}^{n} R_i$.

The properties of decompositions and the properties of join dependencies are closely linked (section 2.5.2).

6.1.2   Instances

Property of completeness (section 2.5.2)
If the relations $R_1...R_i...R_n$ form a decomposition D of relation R, for every instance iR_i of relation R_i there is a set of mutually compatible instances iR_i $iR_2...iR_n$ formed from an instance of each relation of the decomposition.

Property (di) (revision)
If $iR = \mathop{*}\limits_{i=1}^{n} (iR_i)$, then $iR[R_i^+] \subseteq iR_i$ for $(i=1,...,n)$.

Note
This last property applies especially to instances of R_i relations stored in the database at the same time.

Example

Take R(ABC) which decomposes into R_1 = R[AB] and R_2 = R[AC].
iR_1 contains entities (ab) and (a'b').
iR_2 contains entities (ac) and (a"c").
iR contains a single entity (abc).
Then iR[AB] contains only (ab).
In fact (a'b') is not compatible with any entity of iR_2 and therefore does not give rise to any entity of iR; the same goes for (a"c").

We are therefore confronted with the following problem which rightly involves the entities (a'b') and (a"c") of the example. Can there or can there not exist a collection of data iR of R, that is, an instance of R that verifies the ir of R, such that $iR_1 \subseteq iR[R_1^+]$ and $iR_2 \subseteq iR[R_2^+]$?

If yes, iR_1 and iR_2 are collections of data and yield the correct responses to the search for entities contained in the database that relate to R_1 and R_2. If no, the correct responses are on one hand limited to (ab) and on the other to (ac) and are obtained by the join of the instances of iR_1 and of iR_2.

6.1.3   Different methods of relation decomposition

We will recall that the functional dependencies allow a relation to be decomposed.

THEOREM (decfd1)

A relation R(XYZ) provided with the fd $X \rightarrow Y$ is then provided with the jd {R[XY], R[XZ]} and can be decomposed thus:
R = R[XY]*R[XZ].

The proof is contained in section 2.5.4.

THEOREM (decfd2)

A relation R provided with a set of fd $F = \{f1_1 .. f_i ... f_n\}$ can be decomposed in the following way:

K designating a key of R obtained from F by applying the algorithm for obtaining keys given in section 2.11,

f_i^+ designating the attributes of f_i,

$$R = (\overset{n}{\underset{i=1}{*}} R[f_i^+]) * R[K].$$

It is also provided with the jd assigned to this decomposition.

If the relation R[K] prevents the decomposition from being cleared, we can eliminate and obtain a cleared decomposition of R.

The proof is given in the appendix to this chapter 6.4.

Examples

Take R(ABCD) and $F = \{A \rightarrow B; B \rightarrow C; B \rightarrow D\}$, with A the key to R.

The decomposition D obtained is as follows:

R = R[AB]*R[BC]*R[BD]*R[A].

Clearing it, we obtain R = R[AB]*R[BC]*R[BD].

Another decomposition of the same relation R may be obtained by considering only a subset F' of F: F' = {A → B; B → D}.
The key to R in relation to F' is then AC. The decomposition obtained is:
R = R[AC]*R[AB]*R[BD]. It is cleared.

Take S(ABC) and F = {A → C; B → C}, with AB the key to S.
The decomposition obtained is:
R = R[AC]*R[BC]*R[AB]. This decomposition is cleared.

Definition
A decomposition D of R is said to be *functional of origin relation* R_1 if and only if there is at least an order of ranking relations of $D\{R_1...R_i...R_n\}$ such that:

$$\forall i \in (1,n-1)\ K_{i+1} \subseteq \bigcup_{j=1}^{i} R_j^+ \quad \text{where } K_{i+1} \text{ is a key to } R_{i+1}.$$

Property
Every decomposition of R obtained by the successive application of the theorem (decfd1) is a functional decomposition.
The proof is obvious.

Property
Every decomposition of R obtained from a covering of fd F by application of the theorem (decfd2) is a functional decomposition.
The proof is deduced from paragraph c) of the theorem proof (decfd2).

PROPERTY (jd)
If R allows join dependency (jd) $\{R_1...R_n\}$ then $\{R_1...R_n\}$ forms a decomposition of R (section 2.5.1).

6.1.4   Conclusion

A possible algorithm for decomposing a relation R considers functional dependencies and join dependencies defined of R; a first decomposition is obtained from a covering of the fds (theorem decfd2) or from an fd (theorem decfd1) or from a total jd defined on R. The algorithm continues to attempt to decompose the relations forming this first decomposition using partial fds and jds, and so on.
If the relation R is provided with several ... and jd, this algorithm will provide *several possible decompositions* of the relation R. We will now examine the difficult problem of choosing between these decompositions.

6.2 Projection and extension of an integrity rule

The decomposition D of a relation R: $D = \{R_1...R_i...R_n\}$ provides an equivalent representation of R and therefore another possible way of storing the entities of R; these will be stored using their projections in the instances of the different relations of D. The database is thus formed from instances of the relations R_i of D and the instance iR of R becomes virtual in the sense that it is not stored but it can be recalculated by the join of the instances. The basic operations for modifying the database are no longer expressed in terms such as create, delete, update an entity of R but in terms of creating, deleting, updating an entity of R_i.

The problem of the coherence of the database, expressed in terms of integrity rules defined on R, must be expressed in terms of integrity rules defined on the R_i entities; in fact the coherence checks are carried out when an instance of R_i is modified.

DEFINITIONS

The *projection of an integrity rule* ir defined on relation R on the set of attributes S^+ is the integrity rule described as ir[S^+] which is defined on the relation $S = R[S^+]$ and whose predicate is verified by all the instances iS of S such that there is at least one instance iR verifying ir and projecting on S^+ in iS =iR[S^+].

The *extension of an integrity rule* ir defined on relation R to the set of attributes S^+ containing R^+ is the integrity rule described as ext(ir/S^+) which is defined on the relation $S = $ focus (R/S^+) and whose predicate is verified by all instances iS such that iS[R^+] is an instance of R verifying ir.

Theorem
ir being defined on R^+, and ir' on S^+,
ir' = ext(ir/S^+) is equivalent to ir = ir'[R^+].
The proof is obvious.

Property (irfd1) and definition
The projection on S^+ of the functional dependency fd: $X \rightarrow Y$ defined on the relation R is equal to:
a) the trivial integrity rule 1 if X is not included in S^+, and the domain of at least one attribute of $X - S^+$ is unlimited;
b) the trivial integrity rule 1 if $Y \wedge S^+ = \emptyset$;
c) the fd $X \rightarrow W$ where $W = Y \wedge S^+$ if $X \subseteq S^+$.

Proof

a) Take $XS = X \wedge S^+$. Take $XR = X - XS$ which is not empty.

It is sufficient to consider the extension iR of iS such that each entity of iS has a different value from the others for each attribute of XR; this is possible because at least one of their domains is unlimited; iR thus verifies $X \to Y$ and iS verifies the trivial integrity rule.

b) The same reasoning applies by giving to the entities of iR the same value for Y.

c) We will show that $X \to W \le fd[S^+]$, and then that $fd[S^+] \le X \to W$.

c1) $\forall$ iS which verifies $X \to W$, $\forall$ iR an extension of iS to R^+. If iR does not verify $X \to W$, then $\exists r, r' \in iR$ such that $r.X = r'.X$ and $r.W \ne r'.W$.

As $iS = iR[S^+]$, $\exists s, s' \in iS$ such that $s = r.S^+$ and $s' = r'.S^+$.

Thus $s.X = s'.X = r.X$ and $s.W \ne s'.W$.

Therefore iS would not verify $X \to W$, which is impossible.

iR therefore verifies $X \to W$.

We can easily transform iR into iR' by arranging for all the entities of iR' to take the same values for the attributes of $Y - W$. iR' verifies $X \to Y$ and its projection on S^+ is iS. Thus $X \to W \le fd[S^+]$.

c2) Reciprocally:

$\forall$ iS which verifies $fd[S^+]$; by definition there exists an instance iR of R which verifies fd and whose projection on S^+ is iS.

If iS does not verify $X \to W$, then

$\qquad \exists s, s' \in iS$ such that $s.X = s'.X$ and $s.W \ne s'.W$.

As $iS = iR[S^+]$, $\exists r, r' \in iR$ such that $r.S^+ = s$ and $r'.S^+ = s'$.

Then $r.X = r'.X$ and $r.W \ne r'.W$.

So iR would not verify $X \to W$ and would therefore not verify $X \to Y$. This is impossible. iS verifies $X \to W$.

Therefore $fd[S^+] \le X \to W$.

c3) Finally $fd[S^+] = X \to W$.

Property (irfd2) and definition

The extension to S^+ of the fd: $X \to Y$ defined on the relation R (R^+ included in S^+), is equal to the functional dependency $X \to Y$ defined in the relation $S = focus(R/S^+)$.

Proof

X and Y are included in S^+ by construction.

a) If iS verifies $X \rightarrow Y$, then $iR = iS[R^+]$ verifies $X \rightarrow Y$ according to the preceding property.

b) If iS is such that $iR = iS[R^+]$ verifies $X \rightarrow Y$ then

$\forall$ s, s' $\in$ iS such that s.X = s'.X.

Take $r = s.R^+$ and $r' = s'.R^+$. As iR verifies $X \rightarrow Y$, r.Y = r'.Y.

Thus s.Y = s'.Y and iS verifies $X \rightarrow Y$, and ext (fd/S^+) $\leq X \rightarrow Y$.

So $X \rightarrow Y$ = ext(fd/S^+).

DEFINITION

A *set* of integrity rules $I = \{i_1...i_n\}$ defined on R is a new integrity rule i defined on R such that all the instances of R verifying i verify the integrity rules of I:

$$i = i_1 \wedge i_2 \wedge...i_n$$

i is the *characteristic integrity* rule of I.

DEFINITIONS

The *extension* of I to S^+ (R^+ included in S^+) is the extension of the integrity rule $i = i_1 \wedge i_2 \wedge...i_n$.

The *dispersed extension* of I to S^+ (R^+ included in S^+) is the integrity rule ext(I/S^+) = {ext(i_1/S^+), ext(i_2/S^+)...ext(i_n/S^+)}.

The *projection* of I on a set of attributes X is the projection of the integrity rule $i = i_1 \wedge i_2 \wedge...i_n$.

The *dispersed projection* of I on a set of attributes X is the rule $I[X] = \{i_1[X], i_2[X],...i_n[X]\}$.

A set of integrity rules I defined on R^+ is *complete for the projection* if $\forall X \subseteq R^+$ the projection of I on X is equivalent to its dispersed projection on X.

A set of integrity rules defined on R^+ is *complete for the extension* if $\forall X$ containing R^+ the extension of I to X is equivalent to its dispersed extension to X.

A set of integrity rules defined on R^+ is continuous if it is complete for the projection and extension.

Property (irfd3)
Each set of fds F is *complete* for the extension.

Proof
Take $F = \{f_1...f_n\}$ defined on R.

Take f to be the characteristic ir of F. The extension of f to S^+ ($R^+ \subseteq S^+$) is the integrity rule $g = \text{ext}(f/S^+)$; the dispersed extension of F to S^+ is the set G.
According to the property (irfd$_2$) G is a set of fd $\{g_1...g_n\}$ defined on S^+ and expressed in the same way as the fds $f_1...f_n$. Take g' to be the characteristic integrity rule of G.

The equality of g and g' needs to be shown.

a) $\forall$ iS verifying g, iR = iS[R^+]. As iS verifies g, iR verifies f and therefore verifies all the fds f_i; thus iS verifies the fds $g_i = \text{ext}(f_i/S^+)$ and thus g'.

b) $\forall$ iS verifying g', it verifies all the fds $g_i = \text{ext}(f_i/S^+)$; iR = iS[$R^+$] therefore verifies the fds f_i (property irfd$_1$); iR thus verifies f; iS verifies $g = \text{ext}(f/S^+)$ by definition of the extension of integrity rule.

Note that a set of fds F cannot be complete for the projection.

Example
Take R(ABC) and $F = \{A \rightarrow B; B \rightarrow C\}$.
$F[AC] = \varnothing$
If f is the characteristic ir of F then $f[AC] = \{A \rightarrow C\}$.

Property (irfd4)
The complete base of a set of fds F is complete for the projection when the domains of the attributes are unlimited.

Proof
We assume that F is a complete base of fds defined on R^+. Take f to be the characteristic integrity rule of F and $g = f[S^+]$ where $S^+ \subseteq R^+$. Take g' to be the characteristic integrity rule of F[S^+]. That is S = R[S^+].

a) $g \leq g'$?
$\forall$ iS verifying g, there is iR of which iS is the projection on S^+, and which verifies f; thus iR verifies all the f_i. By the definition of projection, iR[S^+] verifies all the $f_i[S^+]$ and thus iS verifies g'.

b) $g' \leq g$?

$\forall$ iS verifying g', iS verifies all the fds $f_i[S^+]$ which are possibly trivial fds (property irfd1).

We will construct an extension iR of iS to R^+ which verifies all the fds f_i; thus iR will verify f and iS g by definition of the projection of an integrity rule.

That is $S^* = \{A, S^+ \to A$ is an fd of $F^{**}\}$.

We will complete the entities of iS in the following way to obtain entities of iR:

- to each entity s of iS there corresponds an entity r of iR such that $r.S^+ = s$;

- $\forall A \in S^* - S^+$: two entities r_a and r_b of iR verify $r_a.A = r_b.A$ if and only if there is X included in S^+ such that $X \to A$ belongs to F and if $r_a.X = r_b.X$;

- $\forall A \in R^+ - S^*$: all the entities of iR take values for A that distinct from one another.

We will prove that *iR, thus formed, verifies F.*

Take $Y \to A$ to be an fd of F and r_a and r_b two entities of iR such that $r_a.Y = r_b.Y$ and $s_a = r_a.S^+$ and $s_b = r_b.S^+$

If the intersection of Y and of $R^+ - S^*$ is not empty, $r_a.Y$ is distinct from $r_b.Y$ by construction. There is no problem.

Unless there is X' included in S^+ such that $X' \to Y$ is an fd of F^{**}. Then there is X included in X' such that $X \to A$ is an fd of F^* (=F).

If A is an attribute of S then $X \to A$ belongs to $F[S^+]$ and iS verifies it:

Thus $s_a.A = s_b.A$ and therefore $r_a.A = r_b.A$.

Otherwise, by construction $r_a.A = r_b.A$ since $s_a.X = s_b.X$.

c) Thus $g' = g$ and the complete base of a set of fd F is complete for the projection.

Property
The *complete base* of a set of fd of F is continuous when the domains of the attributes are unlimited.

Property (irfd5)
If iR_i is an instance of R_i verifying F_i for each $i = \{1...n\}$ then

$$iR = \overset{n}{\underset{i=1}{*}} (iR_i) \text{ is an instance of R verifying } \overset{n}{\underset{i=1}{\cup}} F_i.$$

This is a generalisation of the property (irfd2).

Conclusion

The decomposition schema no longer only maps a relation R with a set of relations $R_1 .. R_i ... R_n$ but a *relational structure* (R,I) formed from the relation R and from the set of integrity rules I defined on R with a set of relation structures $\{(R_1,I_1)...(R_i,I_i)...(R_n,I_n)\}$ where R_i is the projection of R on R_i^+ and I_i is the projection of I on R_i^+. In the following section we will be concerned with the different qualities that a decomposition of a relation R may have compared with the integrity rules defined on R.

6.3 Qualities of a decomposition

As we remarked at the end of section 6.1, a relation R may allow several decompositions; we will attempt to compare them in the course of this chapter, and with this in mind we will identify the *qualities* that a decomposition may possess. The whole of our study will take *functional dependencies* as the *sole integrity rules* of relation R and will extract formal results. At the end of this section we will extend the study to the case of a relation R provided with integrity rules that are not all functional dependencies.

6.3.1 Local and global database coherencies: open decomposition

We will assume that each relation R_i of the decomposition has available a mechanism for the verification of the fd of F_i. Thus any modification of an instance iR_i verifying F_i transforms it into another instance verifying F_i (*local coherence*).

We now need to know if the join of the different instances iR_i is an instance of R verifying F (*global coherence*).

Take $iR = \overset{n}{\underset{j=1}{*}} iR_j$; iR verifies $\overset{n}{\underset{i=1}{\cup}} F_i$ (property irfd4).

By construction $\overset{n}{\underset{i=1}{\cup}} F_i \subseteq F^*$.

DEFINITION

iR verifies F only if $(\bigcup_{i=1}^{n} F_i)^{**} = F^{**}$.

In this case the decomposition is said to be *open*: the local coherences are sufficient to guarantee global coherence.

Otherwise there are fds of: $F^{**} - (\bigcup_{i=1}^{n} F_i)^{**}$

which are not verified by the local coherence verification mechanisms. Global coherence verification mechanisms have to be established in order to verify them.

Of course, the simplest solution is to choose an open decomposition.

Property

A decomposition obtained by application of the theorem (decfd2) is open if and only if it is constructed from a cover of the set of fds defined on R.

The proof is obvious.

Example

Take R(FLIGHT PLANE PILOT) with predicate (flight plane pilot) to be an entity of R if this flight is assured by this plane which is piloted by this pilot.

There are two fds:

FLIGHT $\rightarrow$ PLANE : a flight is assured by a single plane;

PLANE $\rightarrow$ PILOT : a plane is piloted by a single pilot;

and by transitivity we deduce FLIGHT $\rightarrow$ PILOT.

These three fds form the complete base.

According to the theorem (decfd1) and using the fd FLIGHT $\rightarrow$ PLANE, we obtain the following decomposition:

R = R[FLIGHT PLANE] * R[FLIGHT PILOT].

Here R_1 = R[FLIGHT PLANE] and F_1 : FLIGHT $\rightarrow$ PLANE,

and R_2 = R[FLIGHT PILOT] and F_2: FLIGHT $\rightarrow$ PILOT.

$F^* - (F_1 \cup F_2)^* = \{PLANE \rightarrow PILOT\}$.

The local coherence is insufficient to guarantee the global coherence, as the following example shows:

iR$_1$ FLIGHT PLANE   iR$_2$ FLIGHT   PILOT
        SR999   X366   SR999   Smith
        AF001   X366   AF001   Jones

These two instances are locally coherent but iR is not coherent because it does not verify PLANE → PILOT:

iR   FLIGHT PLANE PILOT
          SR999   X366   Smith
          AF001   X366   Jones

Thus a modification of iR$_1$ (with regard to iR$_2$) must not only verify F$_1$ (with regard to F$_2$) but also the fd PLANE → PILOT taking into account the entities of iR$_2$ (with regard to iR$_1$).

6.3.2   Fds embedded in the structure: smooth decomposition

We will assume that for each instance iR$_i$ a computing device guarantees that two entities may not take the same values for each of the keys K$_i$ of R$_i$. This device is conventional in file control systems when R$_i$ has a single key. In this case, all the fds of type K$_i$ → A$_i$ (A$_i$ being an attribute of R$_i$) are verified by this device and there is no need to concern ourselves with their verification. We can say that these fds are *embedded* in the structure.

A relation R$_i$ is in the *third normal Boyce Codd Kent form* (BCKNF) if all the elementary fds defined on R$_i$ are of the form K$_i$ → A$_i$ where K$_i$ is a key of R$_i$ and A$_i$ is an attribute of R$_i$.

In the relations in BCKNF, the basic fds are embedded in the structure. So one will attempt to decompose a relation R in a set of relations in BCKNF. There is therefore a special type of decomposition called a *smooth* decomposition which is an open decomposition formed from relations in BCKNF.

Unfortunately, there is not a smooth decomposition for every relation, as our example shows:

Take R(ABC) with the following fds: AB → C and C → B.

This set is the complete base of the fds defined on R. The keys to R are AB and AC.

The decomposition R = R[AC]*R[CB] is not open: the fd AB → C is not defined in any of the decomposition relations. Relation R itself is not in

BCKNF because of the fd C → B. There is no smooth decomposition for this relation.

Note that for every *non-smooth* decomposition there is at least one fd of F* that requires a specific coherence verification.

Property
Each decomposition D formed of relations in BCKNF by application of the theorem (decfd2) has always been able to be formed from a *base* of F. As the following example shows, it may be constructed from a set of fds that is not a base.

Example
Take R(ABCD), F = {AB → C; A → D; D → B}.
R is decomposed according to F: the key to R is A;
R = R[ABC] * R[AD] * R[DB].
These three relations are in BCKNF.
But F is not a base.
The complete base is: F* = {A → B; A → C; A → D; D → B}.
The previous decomposition can also be obtained from this base.

Note that a base does not always lead to a decomposition in BCKNF.

Example
Take R(ABC) provided with F* = {AB → C; C → B}
The keys to R are AB and AC;
R is decomposed into R_i = R[ABC] and R_2 = R[CB].
R_1 is not in BCKNF.

6.3.3 Risky functional dependencies: guaranteed safe decomposition

The departure point for our examination centres on the *obtaining of all the entities of the relation R[X]* (X included in R+) from instances of the relations R_i of the decomposition of R. The only algorithm currently allowed first requires all the instances of the relations R_i to be joined and thus obtain the instance of R, and then project it on X.

This rudimentary algorithm has three main disadvantages:
– it is extremely slow, since even the join of only two instances is generally a costly operation in terms of execution time;

– it is extremely dangerous; in fact, if a user wishes to obtain all the instances of R_i, he must first form the instance iR by join then project it on R_i^+. A user would never think of using such an algorithm when he has available to him a simple command to extract the instance iR_i if he uses a database system.

– it loses data: in fact if $iR = \overset{n}{\underset{i=1}{*}} (iR_i)$

then $(iR) [R_i^+] \subseteq iR_i$ (property (di)).

Example
INVENTORY (EQUIPMENT ROOM BUILDING DEPARTMENT).
(e r b d) is an entity of INVENTORY if the equipment e is located in the room r and if it belongs to the department d whose offices are located in the building b.
This is the set F of the fds defined in INVENTORY:
f_1 EQUIPMENT $\rightarrow$ ROOM,

f_2: EQUIPMENT $\rightarrow$ DEPARTMENT,

f_3: ROOM $\rightarrow$ BUILDING,

f_4: DEPARTMENT $\rightarrow$ BUILDING.

INVENTORY accepts a single key: EQUIPMENT.

To apply the theorem (decfd2), INVENTORY can be decomposed according to the following relations:
R_1 = R[EQUIPMENT ROOM],

R_2 = R[EQUIPMENT DEPARTMENT],

R_3 = R[ROOM BUILDING],

R_4 = R[DEPARTMENT BUILDING].

The complete base of F: F* is formed from f_1 f_2 f_3 f_4
and f_5: EQUIPMENT $\rightarrow$ BUILDING.
These are the sets of fds defined on the R_i:
$F_1 = \{f_1\}$, $F_2 = \{f_2\}$, $F_3 = \{f_3\}$, $F_4 = \{f_4\}$.

This decomposition is open since it has been obtained from a cover of F.
It is smooth because all the relations R_i are in BCKNF.
The join of the instances of the relations R_i provides an instance of R verifying F without specific verification of the global coherence.

Here is an example:

EQUIPMENT	ROOM	EQUIPMENT	DEPARTMENT
vx78001	311	vx78001	chem
mac015	c304	mac015	eng
mbi001	u100	mbi001	university
cry001	a500	cry001	phy

ROOM	BUILDING	DEPARTMENT	BUILDING
1311	lake	chem	lake
c304	bright	eng	bright
u100	uni2	phy	central
a500	expo		

a) If we want to obtain the room where the vx78001 is located, the only algorithm that we have at the moment is rudimentary: it makes the join of the instances of the relations R_1 R_2 R_3 and R_4, then selects the entity relating to vx78001 and finally obtains the value of this entity as room L311. It is a long algorithm!

b) However, if we accept that the user seeks the room containing a piece of equipment directly in the instance of R_1, we certainly obtain a quick result but one that is a little unreliable. It is accurate for vx78001 but it is marred by a *contradiction* for cry001 and thereby even becomes *dangerous*: in fact this piece of equipment is on the one hand assigned to the expo building which contains room a500 and on the other to building central where its owner department phy is located. Now, a piece of equipment must be assigned to a single building. There is therefore a contradiction that may just as well arise from the entities (cry001 phy), (a500 expo), (phy central) as from entity (cry001 a500). At least one of these is false. So in our opinion, the reply "the room for cry001 is a500" obtained from R_1 is dangerous; it is not acceptable.

On the other hand, the rudimentary algorithm constructs the following iR:

vx78001	1311	chem	lake
mac015	c304	eng	bright

There is no room for the cry001 equipment.

c) Although the basic algorithm eliminates contradictions through the construction of iR, it can also cause information to be lost. So, in the previous example it loses the room for equipment mbi001 even though there is no contradiction associated with it.

To avoid use of this rudimentary algorithm, the database must verify the following simple principle: "entities of $R[R_i^+]$ are entities of iR_i"

To this end, none of the entities r_i of iR_i can be in *contradiction* with an entity obtained by joining the entities of other instances.

There must therefore not be any entity fd: f: $X \rightarrow A$ that is defined at the same time on R_i and on a partial decomposition not containing R_i. Thus the basic concept is one of *risky functional dependency*.

DEFINITION (LUONG86)

A functional dependency f is a *risky functional dependency* in D if and only if there are two partial functional decompositions D_1 and D_2 of D such that:

$f^+ \subseteq D_1^+$ and $f^+ \subseteq D_2^+$,

and there may be an instance of the base such that:

$iD_1[f^+] \cup iD_2[f^+]$ does not verify f_1 even though $iD_1[f^+]$ and $iD_2[f^+]$ verify f separately.

Example

In the proposed decomposition of INVENTORY,

f_3: ROOM $\rightarrow$ BUILDING is a risky fd:

   $D_1 = \{R_3\}$ and $D_2 = \{R_1 \, R_2 \, R_4\}$.

f_4: DEPARTMENT $\rightarrow$ BUILDING is another:

   $D_1 = \{R_4\}$ and $D_2 = \{R_1 \, R_2 \, R_3\}$.

So, even if the fds are verified at the level of each of the relations of D, this does not change the fact that $(iD_1[f^+] \cup iD_2[f^+])$ may not verify f_1:

iD_1 and iD_2 then contain *contradictions* in the sense that the value x of X can be assigned to the value a of A in iD_1 while it is assigned to the value a' in iD_2.

So *risky fds* are *sources of contradictions*.

Property

The functional decompositions obtained from a covering of F by application of the theorem (decfd2) allow all redundant fds like risky fds.

Proof

Take C to be a covering of F.

Take f_1 to be a redundant fd of C : then $C' = C-f_1$ is also a covering of F.

Take D, with respect to D', to be the decomposition of R obtained from C (with respect to C') by application of the theorem (decfd2). D contains a relation R_1

constructed from f_1. D' does not contain R_1 and D' is a partial decomposition of D. As f_1 can be generated from C', f_1^+ is included in D'^+.

Thus f_1 is a risky functional dependency where the two decompositions involved are $D_1 = R_1$ and $D_2 = D'$.

Safe decomposition

If a user wishes to extract from the database the entities of $R[R_i^+]$, he must be able very simply to extract the instance iR_i of R_i and thus obtain a reliable and complete result.

Unfortunately, the decomposition of R constructed from a non-redundant covering does not always provide a complete response to this problem as the INVENTORY relation example shows; the fds f_1, f_2, f_3, f_4 form the non-redundant elementary closure of F. However, we have shown that the database constructed according to this decomposition may contain contradictions.

We will therefore examine the decompositions that allow the preceding fundamental problem to be resolved. The entities of $R[R_i^+]$ are those of iR_i and iR_i contains them all. We refer to such decompositions as *safe decompositions*.

6.3.4   Synthesis and generalisation

6.3.4a   Synthesis of results concerning a relation R provided only with fds as integrity rules

The *open* property of a decomposition ensures the global coherence of the database simply from the local coherences. It requires that the fds defined in each of the relations form a *covering of F*. We will therefore consider the decompositions of R obtained by application of theorem (decfd2).

BCKNF relations facilitate control of the verification of their fds. We will therefore attempt to obtain decompositions formed from relations in BCKNF: we will then consider decompositions of R obtained from an elementary closure of F by application of theorem (decfd2).

Risky fds are sources of contradictions and they prevent the use of a simple database extraction algorithm. Redundant fds in a database are risky fds for the decomposition constructed from that database. We consider the decompositions of R obtained from a *non-redundant elementary closure of F* by application of theorem (decfd2). Such a decomposition is called a *direct decomposition* of R.

A direct decomposition is the solution normally proposed (DELOBEL-CASEY73) (BERNSTEIN76) (ADIBA-DELOBEL-LEONARD76) (FLORY82).

But as the INVENTORY example shows, a direct decomposition is by no means safe. This is why we will propose another solution in the following chapter.

6.3.4b   Generalisation

The open quality of a decomposition means that the verification of the integrity rules defined on the relations R_i is sufficient to guarantee the coherence of:

$$iR = \overset{n}{\underset{i=1}{*}} (iR_i) \text{ with respect to the integrity rules of } R.$$

In the general case, the difficulty in obtaining formal results arises in our opinion from the need to express the projection and the extension of any integrity rule; in the case of the fds, the projection and the extension are simply expressed using an fd, which simplifies the verification of the instances iR_i.

The results that we have in the case of the fds are obtained thanks to our knowledge of a complete and valid system for deriving fds.

The concept of *an integrity rule embedded in a structure* is just as important; an ir is embedded in a structure if its verification is not based on any specific program. A join dependency can be embedded in a structure as the commercial structure of Chapter 1 shows.

The concept of *safe decomposition* is important again. Here we need to know if iR_i contains only entities of $R[R_i^+]$ and if iR_i contains them all. Both of these conditions must be fulfilled for the user to obtain a reliable and complete result when he seeks the entities of $R[R_i^+]$ in iR_i without making the join of all the instances. In many cases, this property is essential.

If the decomposition is not safe, it must be made so by triggering special programs when modifying the database. The decomposition is then said to be *guaranteed safe*. We will examine this problem in Chapter 7.

6.4　Appendix

THEOREM (decfd2)

A relation R provided with a set of fd $F = \{f_1...f_i...f_n\}$ allows the following join dependency (jd):

K designates a key to R which is built from F

f_i^+ designates the attributes of f_i.

$$R = (\overset{n}{\underset{i=1}{*}} R[f_i^+]) * R[K].$$

Proof

In this proof, we only work with relation instances as there is no risk of ambiguity; we denote them as R_1, R_i and not iR_1, iR_i for simplicity.

a) As $\forall A \in R^+$, $K \to A$ belongs to F^{**}; therefore $K \to A$ can be generated by the fds of F.

Thus $$R^+ \subseteq \overset{n}{\underset{i=1}{\cup}} f_i^+ \cup K$$

As by construction the reciprocal is verified, we thus have

$$R^+ = \overset{n}{\underset{i=1}{\cup}} f_i^+ \cup K$$

b) Take $R_i = R[f_i^+]$ and $RK = R[K]$. According to the initial property (d) we know that at the relations level and also equally at the instances level we have:

$$R \subseteq (\overset{n}{\underset{i=1}{*}} R_i) * R_k.$$

It is sufficient to demonstrate the reciprocal.

c) To continue the proof to point d), we will construct sets of fd F_0 $F_1...F_n$ that verify the properties c1, c2 and c3.

Take $K_0 = K^+$ (set of attributes keys to R or only a key of R)

$F_0 = \{f \in F/f: X \to A \text{ and } X \subseteq K_0\}$;

$T_0 = \{A \in R^+ - K_0 / \exists f: X \to A \text{ and } f \in F_0\};$
$K_1 = K_0 \cup T_0.$

And by recurrence: $F_j = \{f \in F/f: X \to A \text{ and } X \subseteq K_j\};$
$T_j = \{A \in R^+ - K_j / \exists f: X \to A \text{ and } f \in F_j\};$
$K_{j+1} = K_j \cup T_j.$

(c1) There is a rank m such that $K_m = K_{m+1}$.
In fact, the sequence of the K_j is increasing and bounded (by R^+): it therefore stabilises.

(c2) T_j is empty if and only if $R^+ = K_j$.
In fact, if $R^+ = K_j$ then T_j is empty by construction.
Reciprocally: if K_j is strictly included in R^+, T_j is not empty.
In fact, therefore $A \in R^+ - K_j$, $K_j \to A$ belongs to F^{**} because K_j contains a key to R^+.

Take $K' \to A$ of F^* and $K' \subseteq K_j$.
There is a generation in F of $K' \to A$, according to the generation theorem (see section 8.3.1), after a generation tree $(f_1 \, f_2...f_p)$ where f_p is of type $X_p \to A_p$ with $A_p = A$ and where $f_1: X_1 \to A_1$ verifies that X_1 is included in K' and thus in K_j.
If A_i is not an attribute of K_j, the proof that T_j is not empty is employed.
Otherwise $K_1' = A_1 \cup K'$.

By recurrence, we assume that all the attributes $A_1...A_{e-1}$ belong to K_j and that $f_e: X_e \to A_e$ belong to T_j $(e < p)$.
X_e is included in K_{e-1}' and thus in K_j. If A_e is not an attribute of K_j then T_j is not empty; if not, we form $K_e' = A_e \cup K_{e-1}'$ which is included in K_j. Gradually we find an attribute A_s (perhaps $s = p$ and then $A = A_p$) not belonging to K_j. Thus T_j is not empty.

(c3) T_m is empty because $R^+ = K_m$.

d) $\quad \forall \, rr \in (\displaystyle\mathop{*}_{i=1}^{n} R[f_i^+] * R[K]), \exists \, rr_0 \in R[K]: rr.K = rr_0,$

$\forall\, i \in (1,n)\; \exists\, rr_i \in R[f_i^+]\!: rr.f_i^+ = rr_i.$

As the instances $R[f_i^+]$ and $R[K]$ are projections,

$\exists\, r_0' \in R\!: r_0'.K^+ = rr_0,\; \forall\, i \in (1,n)\; \exists\, r_i' \in R\!:r_i'.f_i^+ = rr_i.$

We will show that $r_0' = rr$ and thus that rr is an entity of R.

The reasoning is based on the fact that the entities $r_0'...r_i'...r_n'$ cannot take values independently from one another because the fds $f_1...f_n$ are verified in R.

- $\forall\, f_i\!: X_i \rightarrow A_i \in F_0,\; X_i \subseteq K^+$ by construction.

Then $r_0'.X_i = rr_0.X_i = rr.X_i = rr_i.X_i = r_i'.X_i.$
As f_i is verified in R, $r_0'.A_i = r_i'.A_i = rr.A_i.$

It is sufficient to apply this same reasoning for the different sets $F_1...F_{m-1}$ in order to conclude that:

$\forall\, A \in R^+\; r_0'.A = rr.A$ and thus rr is an entity of R.

7   Choice criteria for a functional decomposition

7.1   Introduction

We have two criticisms of direct decompositions of a relation which are obtained from a non-redundant base of fds (see section 6.3.4a): first that they privilege keys implicitly, and second that they do not provide a safe decomposition as result. Our aim is to improve these results.

7.1.1   Case of relations having several keys

In the case of a relation having several keys, there are generally several non-redundant bases of fds; one of these serves the construction of a direct decomposition and privileges one of the relation keys. The designers do not directly choose the privileged key: in fact they choose a non-redundant base. We should like to propose a design method that places designers before a clear choice: they will be able to privilege keys, if they wish, when the design process is sufficiently advanced.

We will illustrate our viewpoint with the following examples.

a) *Example ASSIGNMENT*

Take the relation **ASSIGNMENT** (Machine Hour Product Noemp Place) with predicate: at this hour h (Hour) today employee number no (Noemp) operates machine m (Machine) for the production of product p (Product) at place pl (Place).

a = (m h p no pl) is then an entity of ASSIGNMENT, that is, an assignment.

The functional dependencies defined on ASSIGNMENT are:

Machine	Hour	$\rightarrow$	Product	Noemp	Place
Noemp	Hour	$\rightarrow$	Product	Machine	Place
Product	Hour	$\rightarrow$	Noemp	Machine	Place

The relation ASSIGNMENT allows 3 keys: Machine Hour; Noemp Hour; Product Hour.

For us (m h), (no h), (p h) are three distinct, but equivalent ways of designing an assignment. If no assignment can exist without knowing the employee and the hour concerned, the key Noemp Hour is mandatory.

b) *Example SUPERVISION* (extension of the previous example)

Take **R** (Machine Hour Product Noemp Place Nocontr Namecontr) to be the relation that assigns to controller number (Nocontr) its name (Namecontr) and assigns to this number and to a given hour an assignment formed from a machine, a product, an employee number and a place.
R is provided with the following fds:

Nocontr		$\rightarrow$	Namecontr,		
Nocontr	Hour	$\rightarrow$	Machine	Product	Noemp,
Machine	Hour	$\rightarrow$	Product	Noemp	Place,
Product	Hour	$\rightarrow$	Machine	Noemp	Place,
Noemp	Hour	$\rightarrow$	Machine	Product	Place.

The following is a possible decomposition of R:
R = ASSIGNMENT * CONTROLLER * SUPERVISION
where   ASSIGNMENT   = R [Machine Hour Product Noemp Place],
            CONTROLLER   = R [Nocontr Namecontr],
            SUPERVISION   = R [Nocontr Hour Machine Product Noemp].
This decomposition preserves the equivalent role of the three keys to ASSIGNMENT.

c) Obtaining a direct decomposition leads in the ASSIGNMENT example to the designer being required to choose a non-redundant base from the following three, in particular:

F1 = FC $\cup$ (Noemp Hour	$\rightarrow$	Place),	
F2 = FC $\cup$ (Machine Hour	$\rightarrow$	Place),	
F3 = FC $\cup$ (Product Hour	$\rightarrow$	Place),	

with FC = {Noemp Hour	$\rightarrow$	Machine;	
Machine Hour	$\rightarrow$	Product;	
Product Hour	$\rightarrow$	Noemp}.	

If the designers choose the non-redundant base F1, they must understand that it will be possible to store the place of an assignment only if the employee number of this assignment is known. Thus the key Noemp Hour is privileged.

Since the correspondence between the choice of a non-redundant base and that of a privileged key is not apparent, we prefer to respect the equivalence of keys at this stage of the design process.

7.1.2   A direct decomposition may not be guaranteed safe

In the example of the relation INVENTORY, we considered the direct decomposition of INVENTORY. Figure 7.1 shows the corresponding relation graph.

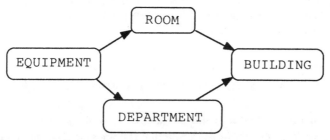

Figure 7.1 Direct decomposition not guaranteed safe

We have shown (section 6.3.3) that in order to interrogate this database it is necessary to join the instances of relations R_1 R_2 R_3 R_4 if we want to obtain results that are not flawed with contradictions.

One direct decomposition is not safe because of the fds ROOM $\rightarrow$ BUILDING and DEPARTMENT $\rightarrow$ BUILDING which are risky fds without however being redundant.

We will suggest mechanisms that guarantee the decompositions to be safe. They will allow "natural" responses to be made to users' questions: so, for example, for every question referring to R_4 = INVENTORY [DEPARTMENT BUILDING] it will be sufficient to interrogate instance iR_4 without first having to make the join of the instances iR_1, iR_2, iR_3 and iR_4.

7.1.3   Our objective

Our objective is:
- to show relation decompositions that do not privilege any key among several keys to a relation. These will be examined in Chapter 8;
- to specify computing mechanisms that *guarantee* that decompositions are safe.
In the following sections we will outline a first specification for these

mechanisms. In a subsequent chapter (10.3) we will broaden the functions of these mechanisms.

7.1.4   The hypothesis for our study

(h0) Every decomposition considered never has two relations having the same key. The only integrity rules taken into consideration are intrinsic fds.

(h1) Every question to the database is relative to a relation R' obtained by join of relations $R_1...R_m$ forming a partial functional decomposition (section 6.1.3) of R.

(h2) Each relation R_i of D is provided with a mechanism called a *key mechanism* which verifies for each instance iR_i the intrinsic fds of R_i.

(h3) The "natural" method for using a database is on the one hand to consult a single relation R_i of D rather than to join the relations of D, in the case where the query only refers to R_i (h31).
On the other hand, if the query refers to attributes that form one or more keys to R_i, the "natural" method for interrogating the database only considers R_i without consulting the other relations (h32).

Example INVENTORY
INVENTORY (EQUIPMENT ROOM DEPARTMENT BUILDING) is a relation that decomposes according to the relations:
R_{12} (*EQUIPMENT* ROOM DEPARTMENT),
R_3 (*ROOM* BUILDING),
R_4 (*DEPARTMENT* BUILDING).
The preceding hypotheses are expressed thus:
(h1) We are not interested in any query concerning the relation $R_{34} = R_3 * R_4$ because the decomposition (R_3 , R_4) is not functional.
(h2) The keys mechanism guarantees for example that in iR_3 there are not two entities relative to the same room.
(h31) If we want to find the building in which the offices of a department are located, we will seek the answer in R_4 without needing relations R_{12} R_3 which form a functional decomposition.
(h32) If we want to find all the rooms considered in the database, we consult R_3 and not R_{12}.

NOTATION

D is a decomposition of R formed from the relations R_1, R_2,...,R_n. In the whole of the chapter we adopt the following convention: T is a relation of D, K is a key to T, f: $K \rightarrow A$ is an fd defined on T which is non-trivial.

7.2   Problems encountered

DEFINITION

A decomposition D_1 is *concerned* by Y (Y being included in R^+) if D_1 is a partial functional decomposition that allows Y in D_1^+.

7.2.1   (pb1) Completeness of keys

A decomposition D_1, concerned by K, *does not overflow for K* if for every instance of the database, $iD_1[K] \subseteq iT[K]$.

Lemma (1):
A decomposition D_1, concerned by K, does not overflow for K if and only if it contains T.

Proof:
The condition is sufficient: if D_1 contains T, then $iD_1[T^+] \subseteq iT$ (property (di) section 1.2) and thus $iD_1[K] \subseteq iT[K]$.
Reciprocally:
If T is not a relation of D_1, there is an instance of the database such that:
– the instances of the relations not belonging to D_1 are empty;
– the instances of the relations belonging to D_1 all contain a single entity taking the value 1 for each attribute.

For each instance, the intrinsic fds are verified since there is at most one entity per instance. Here $iD_1[K]$ is not included in $iT[K]$.

Note
If there exists a decomposition D_1 overflowing for K then obtaining $iR[K]$ requires making for instance $iD_1[K] \cup iT[K]$: this method is the opposite of the "natural" method of using the database (h32).

7.2.2   (pb2) Completeness of entities

A decomposition D_1 concerned by AK does not overflow for AK (or for f: K $\rightarrow$ A) if for each instance of the database,
$iD_1[AK] \subseteq iT[AK]$.

Lemma (2):
A decomposition D_1 concerned by AK does not overflow for AK if and only if it contains T.
The proof is identical to that of the preceding lemma.

Note
If there is a decomposition D_1 overflowing for AK then obtaining iR[AK] requires making $iD_1[AK] \cup iT[AK]$. This method is the opposite of the 'natural' method for using the database (h31, h32).

7.2.3   (pb3) Validity of a partial functional decomposition D'

D'^+ contains KA.
D' verifies f: K $\rightarrow$ A if and only if for every instance of the database, iD' verifies f.
If D' contains T, D' verifies f because iD'[KA] is contained (property (di)) in iT[KA] which verifies f by application of the keys mechanism (h2).
In contrast, if D' does not contain T, D' does not verify f in the general case as the following example shows.

Examples:
R = (*S*KB) * (*K*A) * (*B*A)   (decomposition D of R)
D' = {(*S*KB), (*B*A)},
with the fds S $\rightarrow$ KB, K $\rightarrow$ A, B $\rightarrow$ A.
D' does not verify K $\rightarrow$ A because there are the following instances of the relations of D:

s k b	k a	b a
s' k b'	k a	b' a'

In contrast, take: R = (BCADZ) * (*B*E) * (*E*C*A).
The first relation T has two keys BC and AD; the second one has one key B; the third one has one key EC.

D' = {(*BE*), (*ECA*)} does not contain T.
However D' verifies f: BC → A since it verifies B → E and EC → A.

7.2.4 (pb4) Compatibility of partial functional decompositions for an fd

Two partial functional decompositions D_1 and D_2 concerned by f are *compatible for f* if and only if for every instance of the database, $iD_1[f^+] \cup iD_2\{f^+\}$ verifies f. Otherwise, they are *incompatible for f*, even if $iD_1[f^+]$ and $iD_2[f^+]$ verify f separately.

Lemma (3):
Every partial functional decomposition D_1 concerned by f is compatible with T for f if and only if D_1 contains T.

Proof:

If D_1 contains T, then $iD_1[KA]$ is included in iT[KA] (property (di)) and thus $iD_1[KA] \cup iT[KA]$ is equal to iT[KA] and verifies f.
Reciprocally:
If T is not a relation of D_1, it is possible to consider the next instance in the database:
– all instances of the relations of D not belonging to D_1 are empty, except that of T;
– T contains a single entity that takes the value 1 for all its attributes except for A where it takes the value 0;
– the instance of each relation of D_1 contains a single entity taking the value 1 for each attribute.

The intrinsic fds are verified in each instance because each contains one entity at most.
– $iD_1[f^+]$ contains only one entity taking the value 1 for the attributes of K and the value 1 for A;
– $iT[f^+]$ contains only one entity taking the value 1 for the attributes of K and the value 0 for A;
– $iD_1[f^+] \cup iT[f^+]$ does not verify f. This is impossible by hypothesis. T therefore belongs to D_1.

7.3   Structural elements

DEFINITION

A decomposition D_1 is *minimal* for Y (respectively for f) if and only if it is a partial functional decomposition of D concerned by Y (respectively by f) and the removal of a relation of D_1 leads to a set of relations that either is no longer a partial functional decomposition of D, or remains a partial functional decomposition but is no longer concerned by Y (respectively by f).

Property (1):
If D_1 overflows for K and if D_{11} is included in D_1 and is concerned by K, then D_{11} overflows for K.

Proof:
Since if D_{11} is included in D_1, $iD_1[K] \subseteq iD_{11}[K]$ and thus if $iD_1[K]$ is not contained in $iT[K]$, the same applies for $iD_{11}[K]$.

DEFINITION

K is a *linear risk key* if all the minimum decompositions for K that overflow for K are reduced to a single relation. It is a *cyclic risk key* otherwise.

Property (2):
If D_1 overflows for AK and if D_{11} is included in D_1 and is concerned by AK, then D_{11} overflows for AK.
The proof is established in the same way as for the preceding property.

Property (3):
If D_1 does not verify f then every decomposition D_{11} included in D_1 and concerned by f does not verify f.

Proof:
$D_1[KA] \subseteq D_{11}[KA]$ according to property (di).
If $D_1[KA]$ does not verify f, there is an instance of the database such that $iD_1[KA]$ does not verify f and then the instance of D_{11} does not verify f.
D_{11} does not verify f.

Property (4):
If two decompositions D_1 and D_2 are incompatible for f, then all decompositions D_{11} included in D_1, and D_{22} included in D_2, concerned by f, are incompatible for f.

Proof:

As D_1 and D_2 are incompatible for f, there are two instances iD_1 and iD_2 such that $iD_1[f^+] \cup iD_2[f^+]$ does not verify f.

Take iD_{11} and iD_{22} to be the instances of D_{11} and D_{22} that have served to construct iD_1 and iD_2 respectively.

According to property (di), $iD_1[f^+] \subseteq iD_{11}[f^+]$ and $iD_2[f^+] \subseteq iD_{22}[f^+]$.

Thus $iD_{11}[f^+] \cup iD_{22}[f^+]$ contains $iD_1[f^+] \cup iD_2[f^+]$ and does not verify f.

Property (5):

f is a *risky* fd (6.3.3) if and only if there are two minimal decompositions for f that are incompatible for f.

Proof

The condition is *sufficient* if two such decompositions exist; f is a risky dependence by definition.

Reciprocally:

If f is a risky fd, there are two partial decompositions D_1 and D_2 that are incompatible for f. There is a minimum decomposition for f included in each of them: D_{11} and D_{22}; according to the preceding property D_{11} and D_{22} are incompatible for f and cannot therefore be identical.

Theorem (1)

f is a risky fd if and only if there is a minimal decomposition D_1 for f that is incompatible with T for f.

Proof

The condition is sufficient because of the definition of a risky fd.

It is necessary: according to the preceding property, f is risky if and only if there are two minimal decompositions D_1 and D_2 for f_1 incompatible for f. T is a minimal decomposition for f_1. If D_1 and T are compatible for f_1 then according to lemma 3, T is an element of D_1; as D_1 is minimal, D_1 reduces to T. T and D_2 are then incompatible for f by hypothesis.

Otherwise, D_1 and T are incompatible for f.

DEFINITIONS

An fd is a *cyclic risk* fd if and only if there are two minimal decompositions for f that are incompatible for f, of which at least one is not reduced to a single relation of D.

An fd is a *linear risk* fd if and only if each pair of two minimal and incompatible decompositions for f is in fact formed from two relations of D.

7.4   A solution: mechanisms for completeness of keys and entities

To ensure the "natural" use of the database, one must guarantee (h3) that:
– every decomposition D_1 concerned by each key K of T and overflowing for K verifies that for every instance of the base $iD_1[K] \subseteq iT[K]$.
– every decomposition D_2 concerned by KA overflowing for KA verifies that for every instance of the base $iD_2[KA] \subseteq iT[KA]$.

According to the preceding structural properties relating on the one hand to the completeness of keys and on the other hand to the completeness of entities, it is in fact sufficient to guarantee that:
– every minimal decomposition D_1 for K verifies that for every instance in the base $iD_1[K] \subseteq iT[K]$.
– every minimal decomposition D_2 for KA verifies that for every instance in the base $iD_2[KA] \subseteq iT[KA]$.

But in the general case these properties may only be verified by triggering two mechanisms, the *key completeness mechanism* and the *entity completeness mechanism*, when modifications are made to the database, since queries take priority over modifications (h3). We say that these two mechanisms *guarantee* as non-overflowing the preceding decompositions D_1 and D_2.

The entity completeness mechanism will in the preceding case ensure that each new value k of $iD_1[K]$ is found in $iT[K]$; if it is not, it creates a new entity t such that t.K = k and it thus completes T. The entity completeness mechanism will ensure that each new entity (xa) of $iD_2[KA]$ is found in $iT[KA]$; if not, it creates a new entity t of T such that t.KA = ka. The *limit* to the application of this mechanism is that it only refers to intrinsic fds.
We say that these two mechanisms guarantee as non-overflowing the preceding decompositions D_1 and D_2 respectively for K and KA.

Property
The entity completeness mechanism guarantees every decomposition D_1 concerned by f, *valid* for f, and every decomposition D_2 incompatible with T for f, *compatible* with T and *non-overflowing* for T.
For every instance in the base we have: $iD_2[KA] \subseteq iT[KA]$.

Proof

If D_1 is invalid for f, it does not contain T. Application of the entity completeness mechanism forces the fact that for every instance in the base $iD_1[KA] \subseteq iT[KA]$. As $iT[KA]$ verifies f because of the keys mechanism (h2), $iD1[KA]$ also verifies f.

Thus D_1 is forced to verify f.

If D_2 is not compatible with T for f, it does not contain T.

Application of the entity completeness mechanism forces the fact that for every instance in the database $iD_2[KA] \subseteq iT[KA]$.

So $iD_2[KA] \cup iT[KA]$ is equal to $iT[KA]$ and verifies f. D_2 is forced to be compatible with T for f_1.

Structure of a decomposition

The preceding properties (2,3,4) and theorem (1) show that for an intrinsic fd $K \rightarrow A$ of a relation T, it is sufficient to guarantee artificially that the minimal decompositions for f do not overflow for KA, verify f and are compatible with T for f, in order that all the other functional decompositions containing KA may have the same properties.

DEFINITION

The minimal decompositions containing KA not reduced to a single relation are said to be *minimal cyclic decompositions for f (or for KA)*.

The preceding property (1) shows that for a key K to a relation T, it is sufficient to guarantee that the minimal decompositions in relation to K do not overflow for K, in order that all the other decompositions containing K may have the same property.

DEFINITION

The minimal decompositions containing K not reduced to a single relations are said to be *minimal cyclic decompositions for K*.

(LUONG86) has shown that if the relation graph obtained using the algorithm in chapter 4 from the initial decomposition does not contain any functional cycle, then the minimum decompositions are not cyclic.

We will set out the list of minimal cyclic decompositions for each relation T of the compact decomposition (section 4.0) and for each key K to T. For each we have:

the source relation, the relations that make it up,

the relation for which it is cyclic (that is, relation T),

the keys of the relation T (including K) which are involved,

the fds which are involved in the fact that this decomposition is cyclic (there is at least f: $K \rightarrow A$).

Example

We consider a relation U which decomposes using the following relations forming a compact decomposition of U. The set of fds derived from the keys of each of these relations here forms a *base* of fds which is *circuit-less*. Each relation has a key whose attributes are italicised:

RS(*SIJG*)   RP(*A*)
RV(*GADH*)   T(*BCA*)
R$_1$(*I*B)   R$_2$(*J*C)
R$_3$(*H*BC)   R$_4$(*ADE*)
R$_5$(B)   R$_6$(C).

The relation graph obtained from this decomposition using the RG algorithm is as shown in figure 7.2.

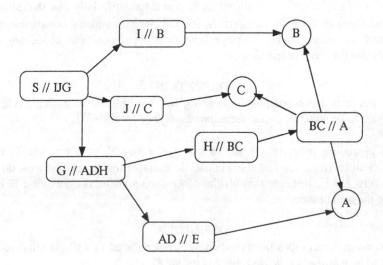

Figure 7.2 Cyclical decompositions and mechanisms

a) The minimal decomposition D$_1$ formed only from RS(SIJG) *overflows* for I, J and G but it is not cyclic. It is possible to create an entity (sijg) in iRS without there being an entity of key i in iR$_1$, one of key j in iR$_2$, one of key g in iRV.

The key completeness mechanism will make it mandatory to create these entities or prevent the creation of entity (sijg).

b) The minimal decomposition D_2 {(SIJG), (IB), (JC)} *overflows* for BC which is key to the relation T.

In fact it is possible to create entities (sijg) and (ib) and (jc); by join we obtain entity (sijgbc) and by projection on BC: (bc).

Without the use of the key completeness mechanism, it could be that there was no entity in iRT having bc as key.

This minimal decomposition is *cyclic* for T: its source is the relation RS, BC is the involved key.

c) The minimum decomposition D_3 {(SIJG), (IB), (JC), (GADH)}

– overflows of course for BCA: in fact a possible instance of the possible database, without using the entity completeness mechanism, is as follows: (sijg),)ib), (jc), (gadh), (bc-) (- means an obscure value);

– does not verify f: BC $\rightarrow$ A: in fact, without using the entity completeness mechanism, a possible instance in the database is:

    (sijg) and (s'ijg') in iRS,
    (gadh) and (g'a'd'h') in iRV,
    (ib) in iR_1 and (jc) in iR_2.

The join of these entities gives two entities in iD_3:
    (sijgbcadh), and
    (s'ijg'bca'd'h');
iD_3 does not verify BC $\rightarrow$ A.

– is not compatible with T: without using the entity completeness mechanism, a possible state of the database is as follows:

        (sijg), (ib), (jc), (gadh), (bca');

iD_3[BCA] $\cup$ iT[BCA] contains the entities (bca) and (bca') which do not verify BC $\rightarrow$ A.

This minimal decomposition D_3 is *cyclic* for T:
its source is the relation RS, the key BC and the fd BC $\rightarrow$ A are involved.

In this example there are other minimal cyclic decompositions like for example D_4 {RS, RV, R_3} for R_4 of source RS, concerning the key I of R_1 and the fd I $\rightarrow$ B.

7.5   Conclusions

The solution that we propose to solve the problem of risky fds, is to add to the functions of a DBMS two mechanisms: key completeness and entity completeness. These two mechanisms allow a database to be used in a "natural" way and partly ensure that the initial decomposition is *guaranteed safe*. This result is not complete because it only applies to intrinsic fds.

In Chapter 10 we will extend the application of these two mechanisms to fds that are not intrinsic, by integrating them with other very useful mechanisms for generating database applications.

Installing such mechanisms, which are needed even for simple and direct decompositions (such as the INVENTORY example), allows one to work with decompositions obtained from covers C of fds that are not necessarily non-redundant. In fact, the redundant fds of such covers are risky fds of the decomposition (property of section 6.3.3) and their verifications are ensured by the mechanisms that guarantee the decompositions to be safe.

The aim of the next chapter is to take advantage of this freedom to highlight a special fd cover which is not necessarily a non-redundant base, and which allows a first decomposition to be obtained automatically in which all the keys to each relation have an equivalent role. This decomposition will be the departure point for the subsequent design work.

8 Basic decomposition

8.1 Introduction

The aim of this chapter is to study a form of relation decomposition which on the one hand respects the equivalence of keys to relations and on the other hand facilitates the embedding of key and entity completeness mechanisms.

We have described the basic properties of fds in Chapter 2.4. Having shown the mathematical properties of fds, we propose our solution: the basic decomposition of a relation (it is unique for each relation).

In the subsequent chapters we integrate the determination of the basic decomposition with the database design process and from that describe the specifications for the mechanisms that need to be embedded in DBMSs.

NOTATION

Take f: $X \rightarrow A$ to be an fd.
$g(f)$ and $d(f)$ respectively designate the left (X) and right (A) parts of the fd.

Throughout the whole of this chapter, U designates a relation on which is defined a set of fd F; R designates the projection of the relation U on the set of attributes R^+ (which is included in that of U: U^+).

Property 1 and definitions (see section 2.4.3):
For each set of fds F, there corresponds a closure F^{**} that contains all the fds that can be generated for F by application of the derivation properties of the fds and a complete base F^*, the set of the elementary fds of F.

G is a *cover* of F if $G^{**} = F^{**}$; this cover is a base if it is included in F^*.
G is a *non-redundant cover* if every set G' obtained by removal of an fd of G is not a cover of F.

8.2 Keys to a relation

We will extend the definition of the elementary fd to the case of dependencies that have several attributes in the right part.

DEFINITION

$X \to Y$ is an *elementary* fd if and only if:
$\forall Y_i \in Y \quad X \to Y_i \in F^*$.
$X \to Y$ is a *quasi-elementary* fd if and only if:
$\exists Y_i \in Y \quad X \to Y_i \in F^*$ and $X \to Y \in F^{**}$.
$X \to Y$ is a *structurally elementary* fd if and only if:
$\forall X' \subseteq X \quad X' \to Y \notin F^{**}$ and $X \to Y \in F^{**}$.

Note
The set of these properties may be ordered: elementary, quasi elementary, structurally elementary; then every fd that allows one of these properties allows the rest.

Example 3 U(ABCMN):
if $F^* = \{AB \to M; AC \to N\}$
        then $ABC \to MN$ is structurally elementary;
if $F^* = \{ABC \to M; A \to N\}$ then $ABC \to MN$ is quasi elementary;
if $F^* = \{ABC \to M; ABC \to N\}$ then $ABC \to MN$ is elementary.

Property 2
Take K to be a key to relation R;
take K' to be a subset of R^+.
Then K' is another key to R if and only if:
$K \to K' \in F^{**}$, and $K' \to K$ is a structurally elementary fd.

Proof
If K and K' are keys to R, then $K \to K'$ and $K' \to K \in F^{**}$.
Take $K'' \subseteq K'$ such that $K'' \to K \in F^{**}$ then $\forall X \subseteq R^+ \ K'' \to X$;
K" is a key to R;
as K' is also a key to R, K', K" are identical and $K' \to K$ is structurally elementary.

Reciprocally:
If $K \to K' \in F^{**}$ and $K' \to K$ is structurally elementary, then $\forall X \in R^+ \ K' \to X \in F^{**}$ and $\forall K'' \subseteq K \ \exists B \in K$ such that $K'' \to B \notin F^{**}$ since $K' \to K$ is

structurally elementary. Consequently, K' is a key to R.

Property 3

Take K to be a key to R $(K \subseteq R^+)$.

If there is $K' \subseteq U^+$ such that $K \to K'$ and $K' \to K$ belong to F^{**}, then the relation $T = U[R^+ \cup K']$ allows K and K" as keys where $K" \subseteq K'$.

Proof

If there is $K_1 \subseteq K$ such that K_1 is a key to T,

then $K_1 \to K \in F^{**}$ is a key to R;

since K is also a key to R, $K = K_1$ and therefore K is a key to T.

As $K' \to K \in F^{**}, \exists K" \subseteq K'$ such that $K" \to K$ is structurally elementary. According to the preceding property, K" is also a key to T.

DEFINITION

If K is a key to R contained in R^+

and if $U[R^+ \cup K']$ allows K and K' as keys,

then K' is a *potential key* to R.

Property 4

Take two relations R and S, respectively projections of U on R^+ and S^+ and such that $KR \to KS$ and $KS \to KR$ belong to F^{**} where KR and KS respectively designate a key to R and a key to S.

Then $KR \to KS$ and $KS \to KR$ are structurally elementary and KR and KS are two keys to the relation T that is a projection of U on the union of R^+ and S^+.

Proof

If $KR' \subseteq KR$ such that $KR' \to KS \in F^{**}$ then $KR' \to KR \in F^{**}$ since $KS \to KR \in F^{**}$.

Since KR is a key to R, $KR = KR'$ and $KR \to KS$ is structurally elementary.

$KR \subseteq R^+$ as key to R and $KR \to KS \to S^+$; if $KR' \subseteq KR$ is a key of T,

$KR' \to KR$ and KR' is a key of R: thus $KR' = KR$ and KR is a key of T.

KS is as well.

Property 5

Take K_1 and K_2 as two keys of R. Take $K \subseteq U^+$. If $K \to K_1$ belongs to F^{**} and is structurally elementary, then $K \to K_2$ belongs to F^{**} and is also structurally elementary.

Proof

$K \rightarrow K_2 \in F^{**}$ since $K \rightarrow K_1 \in F^{**}$ and $K_1 \rightarrow K_2 \in F^{**}$.

Take $K' \subseteq K$ such that $K' \rightarrow K_2 \in F^{**}$, then $K' \rightarrow K_1 \in F^{**}$ and because $K \rightarrow K_1$ is structurally elementary, $K' = K$.

Thus $K \rightarrow K_2$ is structurally elementary.

DEFINITION

R *contains all its keys* if and only if, K being a key to R belonging to R^+, $\forall$ K' $\in U^+$ such that $K \rightarrow K' \in F^{**}$ and if $K' \rightarrow K$ is structurally elementary of F^{**}, then $K' \subseteq R^+$.

Example 4

Take U(ABC) to be a relation provided with the set of fds:

$F = \{A \rightarrow C; A \rightarrow B; B \rightarrow A\}$.

$R = U[AC]$ is a relation that does not contain all its keys; the key of R is A but B can be added to R^+;

and then $R1 = U[ABC]$ allows as key on the one hand A and on the other B.

8.3 Minimum fd equivalence classes

Throughout this chapter the fds considered have only one attribute in the right part. The fd properties of additivity and projection mean that this hypothesis in no sense detracts from the generality of the results.

8.3.1 Fd consensus and generation

The results of this section are derived from (GAROCHE-LEONARD78).

DEFINITION

The *consensus* of two fds f: $X \rightarrow A$ and g: $Y \rightarrow B$ is, when it exists, a new fd h: $Z \rightarrow C$ obtained by pseudo-transitivity of f and of g and described as:

h = f +> g.

Also, for the consensus to exist, it is necessary for $A \in Y$;

then: $Z = X \cup (Y - A)$ and $C = B$.

This concept of consensus is that of (KUNTZMANN72) who defined it in the more general context of the monomials of a boolean function.

Example 5
MN → A +> AP → B = MNP → B.

Pseudo-associativity theorem
Take three fds: f, g, h.
If (f +> g) +> h exists, then f +> (g +> h) also exists and, furthermore,
((f +> g) +> h) < (f +> (g +> h)).
The proof is provided in the appendix 8.11.1.

Example 6
f: M → A; g: AN → B; h: ABO → C;
i = (f +> g) +> h: MNAO → C; k = f +> (g +> h): MNO → C;
Thus i < k.

Lemmas relating to the consensus
Take f, g, f', g' to be fds such that f < f' and g < g'.
If f +> g exists, then f' +> g exists and (f' +> g) > (f +> g).
If f +> g' exists, then (f +> g') > (f +> g).
The proofs of these lemmas are obvious.

DEFINITION

A *generation* of f in the set F of fd, and from the fd f_0 of F, is the following recurrent sequence of consensus operations:

$$m_0 = f_0,$$
$$m_1 = f_1 +> m_0,$$
$$m_2 = f_2 +> m_1,$$

.
.
.

$$m_i = f_i +> m_{i-1},$$

.
.
.

$$m_n = f_n +> m_{n-1},$$
$$f < m_n,$$

where $\forall$ i $\in$ (1,n) $f_i \in$ F and $d(m_i) = d(f_0)$ and where n designates a finite number (possibly 0). It is then said that f_0 *generates* f in F or that f may be generated from f_0 or that f is generated by (f_0, f_1...f_n) in F.

GENERATION THEOREM

For every fd of F** there is a corresponding generation in F.

Proof

It is sufficient to prove the theorem for the elementary fds of F* since the others are deduced from these by augmentation which is a special generation.

By the definition of the complete base F*, every dependency f of F* is constructed from dependencies of F by a succession of consensus operations: proving that this succession of consensus operations can be realised using a generation is based on the recursive application of the pseudo associativity. The proof is to be found in section 8.11.1.

Property 6 (proof in section 8.11.3)

If f is generated by $(f_0, f_1...f_n)$ in F then $\forall\ i \in (l,n)$

$\forall\ A_i \in g(f_i): g(f) \rightarrow A_i \in F^{**}$.

Note

The concept of generation is as general as, but more precise than, that of derivation introduced in (BEERI-BERNSTEIN79) because it shows the most appropriate order for carrying out the consensus operations. The preceding lemma is the equivalent of lemma 2 in their paper in the context of generation.

8.3.2   Order relation on the set of fd equivalence classes of F**

DEFINITION

The fd f of F** is *generated* by the fd f_0 of F** if there is a generation of f in F** from f_0. It is also said that f_0 *generates* f in F**.

Theorem (proof in section 8.11.4)

The relation "f_0 generates f in F**" defines a *preorder* on the set of fd F**.

Note

If there is a generation of f from f_0 in F and if there is a generation of f' from f in F, then there is a generation of f' from f_0 in F.

This relation is *not antisymmetric* as the following example shows:

Take $F = \{AB \rightarrow C, A \rightarrow B, A \rightarrow C\}$.

$A \rightarrow C$ generates $AB \rightarrow C$ (by augmentation);

but $AB \rightarrow C$ also generates $A \rightarrow C$ because

$(A \rightarrow C) = (A \rightarrow B) +> (AB \rightarrow C)$.

DEFINITION

The relation "f_1 *generates* f_2 *in* F^{**} and f_2 *generates* f_1 *in* F^{**}" is an equivalence relation defined on F^{**}. We describe as f^* the equivalence class of the dependency f of F^{**}.

THEOREM

The relation $f^* < h^*$ (where f and h belong to F^{**}) defined on the set of equivalence classes in the following way:
$f^* < h^* \exists f_1 \in f^*, \exists h_1 \in h^*$ such that f_1 generates h_1 in F^{**}
is an *order relation*.

Note

If $f^* < h^*$ then $\forall f_1 \in f^*, \forall h_1 \in h^*$ f_1 generates h_1 in F^{**}.

These results are conventional results derived from a preorder relation.
The notation $f^* << h^*$ is if $f^* < h^*$ and if there is no other class g^* ($g^* \neq f^*$ and $g^* \neq h^*$) such that $f^* < g^* < h^*$.

8.3.3   Minimum equivalence classes

8.3.3.1   Structural aspects

DEFINITION

An equivalence class f^* is *minimal* if there is no other equivalence class h^* such that $h^* < f^*$.

Property 7 and definition

A minimum equivalence class contains at least one elementary fd. The elementary fds of a minimal class are said to be *minimal* and FMIN will designate the set of elementary fds of the different minimal classes.

Proof

Take $X \to A$ to be a non-elementary fd of a minimal class; then there is a elementary $Y \to A$ such that $Y \subseteq X$. Since $X \to A$ can be generated by $Y \to A$ by augmentation and since the equivalence class of $X \to A$ is minimal, $Y \to A$ belongs to this class.

Property 8

If f: $X \to A$ and h: $Y \to A$ are two elementary fds of the same minimal equivalence class, then the two fds (whose right parts are sets of attributes) $X \to Y$ and $Y \to X$ belong to F^{**} and are in addition structurally elementary.

Proof
Since f and h belong to the same equivalence class, f generates h and h generates f. According to the preceding lemma $X \to Y$ and $Y \to X$ are fds of F^{**}. If X' such that $X' \subseteq X$ and $X' \to Y$, then by transitivity $X' \to A$ and, since $X \to A$ is elementary, $X' = X$. Thus $X \to Y$ and $Y \to X$ are structurally elementary.

Note
X and Y are then *keys* to the relation formed on the attributes of the dependencies of f* and provided with the fds of f*.
X and Y are said to be *keys to* f*.

8.3.3.2   Algorithmic formation of minimal classes

Property 9
Take B to be an attribute.
Take f* and h* to be fd equivalence classes.
influence (f*) = {B, $\exists$ K key to f* and $K \to B \in F^*$};
infl nonr (f*) = {B $\in$ influence (f*); $\forall$ h* < f* B $\notin$ influence (h*)}.
Then FMIN = {$X \to B \in F^*$, $\exists$ h* and X is key to h* and B $\in$ infl nonr (h*)}.

Proof
$\forall$ f: $X \to B \in$ FMIN f* is a minimal class and X is a key to f*. Since f* is minimal, B $\in$ infl nonr (f*).

Reciprocally:
$\forall$ f: $X \to B \in$ h* such that X is key to h*, B $\in$ infl nonr (h*) and $X \to B \in F^*$.
Take $Y \to B \in F^*$ such that $Y \to B$ can generate $X \to B$; take e* to be the class of $Y \to B$; then e* < h* and B $\in$ influence (e*).
Since B $\in$ infl nonr (h*), e* = h* and h* is a minimal class.

8.3.3.3   Minimal equivalence classes and bases of F

Property 10
Every base of F contains at least one elementary fd of every minimal equivalence class.

Proof
Take G to be a base of F.
$\forall$ f $\in$ F*, there is a generation of f from f_0, dependency of G according to the

generation theorem. In particular, if f belongs to a minimal class, then since f_0 generates f, f_0 belongs to the same minimal class; thus G contains at least one elementary fd of each minimal class.

Property 11
Every fd f of F* can be generated by an fd of FMIN.

Proof
If $f \in$ FMIN, the proof is terminated.
Otherwise, $\exists\, h \in$ F** such that h* < f* and h* is minimal: then there is $h_1 \in$ h* such that $h_1 \in$ F* and h_1 generates f.

Note
FMIN is not always a base as the following example shows.

Example 7
F = {S → A; S → B; A → B; B → A}. F is a complete base.
The equivalence class of S → A cannot contain B → A because if B → A generates S → A, the inverse is false: B → does not belong to F**.
The equivalence class of S → A is not minimal; nor is that of S → B. The only minimal equivalence classes are those containing on the one hand A → B and on the other B → A. Thus FMIN = {A → B, B → A}.
FMIN is not a base of F.

8.4 Block of attributes and groups of fds

The aim of this section is to explain the concept of groups of fds and two partial order relations defined on the set of groups.

DEFINITION
Two sets of attributes X and Y are equivalent if X → Y and Y → X are fds of F**.

Property 12
This relation defines an equivalence relation. The proof is obvious.

DEFINITION
The name *block* of X is given to the equivalence class formed around X by the preceding equivalence relation. Its notation is b(X).

DEFINITION

$b(X) > b(X')$ if and only if $X \rightarrow X'$ belongs to F^{**}.

Property 13

This relation is a partial order relation defined on the set of blocks determined from F^{**}. The proof is obvious.

The notation $b(X) >> b(X')$ means that there is no other block $b(Y)$ verifying $b(X) > b(Y) > b(X')$; block $b(X)$ is immediately superior to block $b(X')$.

DEFINITION

$b^+(X)$ designates the set of attributes that belong to at least one set of attributes Y equivalent to X and therefore an element of $b(X)$. A *key* of a block $b(X)$ is a key of relation $Rb = U[b^+(X)]$.

Property 14

Relation Rb contains all its keys.

Proof

Take Y to be a potential key to Rb; then $Y \rightarrow X$ belongs to F^{**}. Furthermore, since Rb is constructed from the block of X, X is a key to Rb or X contains a key to Rb. In all cases, $X \rightarrow Y$ belongs to F^{**}; thus Y belongs to $b(X)$ and Rb contains all its keys.

DEFINITION

Block $b(X2)$ is *dependent* on block $b(X1)$ if and only if the set of key attributes of $b(X1)$ is contained in that of $b(X2)$.

Property 15

If block $b(X2)$ is dependent on block $b(X1)$, then every key K1 of $b(X1)$ and every key K2 of $b(X2)$ verifies: $K2 \rightarrow K1$ belongs to F^{**}.
The proof is obvious.

Property 16

The dependency relation defines a partial order relation on the set of blocks.

Proof

It is reflexive by construction.

It is antisymmetric: $b(X1)$ being dependent on $b(X2)$, if the reciprocal is true, then $K1 \rightarrow K2$ and $K2 \rightarrow K1$ belong to F^{**}.

K1 and K2 belong to the same block and thus $b(X1) = b(X2)$.

It is transitive: if $b(X3)$ is dependent on $b(X2)$ and $b(X2)$ is dependent on $b(X1)$, then every key to $b(X1)$ is contained in the set of key attributes to $b(X2)$ and thus in that of $b(X3)$.

Notation

G designates a subset of F**.

DEFINITION

A *group* r of G is a subset of fd of G whose left parts belong to the same block denoted as b(r) and called the block of group r. r^+ designates the set of attributes on which the fds of r are formed.

Property and definition

The potential keys to relation $Rr = U[r^+]$ are the keys to b(X). They are called the *keys* to group r.

Proof

Group r contains at least one fd $X \rightarrow A$ and the block of r is by definition the block of X. Every key Y of b(X) verifies that $Y \rightarrow X$ and $X \rightarrow Y$ belong to F** and thus Y contains a potential key to Rr: Y'.

Since Y' is a potential key to Rr, $Y' \rightarrow X$ is an fd of F**; $Y = Y'$ because otherwise Y would not be a key to b(X).

Y is a potential key to Rr.

Every key Z of Rr verifies that $Z \rightarrow X$ and $X \rightarrow Z$ belong to F**.

Z therefore belongs to b(X) According to the two preceding fds, it contains a key Z' to b(X): Z' must be equal to Z for Z to be a key to Rr.

Z is therefore a key of b(X).

Property 17

The left parts of the fds of F* belonging to a group are keys of this group.

Proof

If $X \rightarrow A$ belongs to F* and to a group r, then by definition of the group, X contains a key to r: let X' be this key. Then $X' \rightarrow X \rightarrow A$. Since $X \rightarrow A$ belongs to F*, X' is equal to X and X is a key to r.

DEFINITION

$r > r'$ if and only if $b(r) > b(r')$.

Property 18

This relation is a partial order relation defined on the set of groups of G. The groups that do not have inferiors are called *minimal*.

The proof is obvious.

The notation $r >> r'$ describes the fact that there is no other group r" that verifies $r > r" > r'$.

DEFINITION

Group r is *dependent* on group r' if and only if b(r) is dependent on b(r').

Property 19
This relation is a partial order relation defined on the set of groups of G.
The proof is obvious.

DEFINITION

Group r is *directly dependent* on group r' if and only if r is dependent on r' and if no other group r" verifies that r is dependent on r" and r" on r'.

DEFINITION

MIN(r) (respectively MIN(b(r))) designates the set of groups r' of G (respectively blocks b(r')) verifying that r >> r' or r is directly dependent on r'.

Note
An equivalence class of fd of G (section 8.3.2) contains fds whose right parts are equal and whose left parts belong to the same block. They therefore belong to the same group of G.

Example 8
$G = \{S \to A; S \to B; A \to B; B \to A\}$.
G allows four equivalence classes each of which allows one of the fds of G. G has two groups:
$r = \{S \to A; S \to B\}$; $r' = \{A \to B; B \to A\}$ and $r > r'$.

8.5 Invariance of non-redundant bases

DEFINITION

A group r_0 of F* is *mandatory* if and only if each of its fds f_0 verifies that every generation of f_0 in F* contains an fd of r_0.
The block of a mandatory group is a *mandatory block*; every key to a mandatory block is a *root* of attributes.

Note
A minimal group r of F* only contains fds of FMIN: an fd can only be generated by an fd of r because r is minimal. Thus a minimal group is mandatory.

Property 20
The set of fds of mandatory groups B_0 forms a base of F*.

Proof

Take B_0 to be the set of fds of mandatory groups.

Given the order relation defined previously for groups, it is possible to attribute a rank to each group (topological sort (KNUTH73)):

the minimal groups have as rank 1;

the non-minimal group r has as rank i(i > 1) if all the groups r' such that r > r' have a rank lower than i and if there is among them one that has the rank i-1.

We formulate the following recurrence hypothesis: the fds of the groups of rank n can be generated in B_0.

This property is true for rank 1 because the minimal groups are mandatory.

We assume this property to be true for those ranks lower than n (n > 1).

Take r to be a non-mandatory group of rank n. Then for every dependency f of r there is a generation of f in F*: GN = $\{f_1, f_2,...f_p, f'\}$ where none of the fds fi and f' belongs to r.

Since in addition according to property 6 there is $g(f) \rightarrow g(f_i)$ (i=1..p), each fd of GN belongs to a rank group than is strictly lower than that of r.

Assuming the recurrence property to be true up to rank n-1, each dependency of GN can be generated in B_0; the same goes for f.

The property is verified for rank n. B_0 is a base of F*.

Property 21 (proof in section 8.11.5)

Every base contains at least one fd of every mandatory group.

Property 22 (proof in section 8.11.5)

Every fd of a non-redundant base belongs to a mandatory group.

THEOREM

The roots of F*, that is the keys to the mandatory groups of F*, are keys to the groups of every non-redundant base of F*. This property constitutes an invariant of the non-redundant bases of F*.

The proof derives from the two preceding properties.

8.6 Homogenous coverings and the basic covering

DEFINITION

G is a *homogenous covering* of F if and only if:

a) G is a covering of F: G** = F**.

b) G contains no trivial fd.

c) If $X \to A$ belongs to G, and if Y is another key to block $b(X)$ in F^{**}, then $Y \to A$ belongs to G unless it is trivial;

also, for every attribute B of Y, $X \to B$ belongs to G unless it is trivial.

d) For every block b' of $MIN(b(X))$ in G and for every key attribute B of b', $X \to B$ belongs to G unless it is trivial.

Example 9

a) Take $F = \{S \to A, S \to B, A \to B, B \to A\}$.

$CV = \{S \to A, A \to B, B \to A\}$. CV is a covering of F, it is even a non-redundant base.

CV is not a homogenous covering because A and B are two equivalent keys and $S \to B$ is missing from CV;

$CV' = \{S \to A, S \to B, A \to B, B \to A\}$ is a homogenous covering.

b) Take $F = \{AB \to G, DF \to G, AB \to D, G \to E, AB \to E, DE \to AB, DG \to AB\}$.

The complete base is:

$F^* = \{AB \to DEG, DF \to ABEG, G \to E, DE \to ABG, DG \to AB\}$.

This is a covering of F:

$CV = \{AB \to GD, DE \to ABG, G \to E, DF \to G\}$; it is not homogenous because AB, DE and DG are equivalent keys, and DF and ABF are too.

There are in fact three blocks:

   b_1 which has DF and ABF as keys,

   b_2 which has AB, DE and DG as keys,

   b_3 which has G as key.

b_2 is dependent on b_3. In addition $b_1 > b_2 > b_3$.

$MIN(b_1)$ contains only b_2.

The following is a homogenous covering constructed from CV:

$CV' = \{DF \to ABEG, ABF \to DEG, AB \to GDE, DE \to ABG, DG \to ABE, G \to E\}$.

Notation

B_0 designates the set of elementary fds belonging to the mandatory groups of F^*.

DEFINITION

The *basic covering* CF of F^{**} is formed from a set of fds f:

$X \to A$ of F^{**} each verifying that:

a) it is not trivial;

b) X is a root, a key to mandatory group r_0;

c) it belongs to FMIN,

or A is a key attribute of the block of X,

or A is one of the key attributes of a mandatory group belonging to $MIN(r_0)$.

Property 23

The basic covering CF of F** is a homogenous covering of F* and it is unique.

Proof

We will prove that CF allows B_0 to be generated.

Take X to be a root and f: $X \rightarrow A$ to be an elementary fd.

Take r_0 to be the mandatory group of f.

If f belongs to FMIN, then f belongs to CF.

Otherwise, there is an fd g: $Y \rightarrow A$ of FMIN which allows f to be generated. g belongs to CF.

Take r_n to be the mandatory group of g. If r_n does not belong to $MIN(r_0)$, there is a mandatory group r_1 of $MIN(r_0)$ such that r_1 is dependent on r_n or that r_1 is greater than r_n.

There is thus a sequence of mandatory groups r_0, r_1...r_n such that r_{i+1} belongs to $MIN(r_i)$ (perhaps n = 0 or 1). Taking K_0...K_i K_n to be a key to each group, the fds $K_i \rightarrow K_{i+1}$ belong to CF by construction. $K_0 = X$ and $K_n = Y$ in particular.

Thus $X \rightarrow K_1$, $K_1 \rightarrow K_2$,...$K_{n-1} \rightarrow Y$ and $Y \rightarrow A$ provide a generation of $X \rightarrow A$ in CF except if A is an attribute of a key Ki.

Then the same reasoning applies in considering $X \rightarrow K_1$,...$K_{i-1} \rightarrow A$.

CF is thus a covering of F since it allows a base of F to be generated. CF is homogenous and unique by construction.

Algorithm for forming the basic covering of F

- calculate F* the complete base;
- calculate FMIN (property 9);
- calculate a non-redundant base F+ algorithms of BERNSTEIN76, PICHAT-DELOBEL79, LUCAS81;
- for each root X and its mandatory group r, generate the equivalent keys (LUONG86) and calculate MIN(r);
- for each root X, derive the fds of CF (property c of the definition) which are added to the fds of FMIN.

Example 10
We extend example 9b and we will calculate the basic covering.
a) *Calculation of FMIN*

We form the equivalence classes of the fds of F*:
$1 = \{G \rightarrow E\}; 2 = \{AB \rightarrow D\}; 3 = \{AB \rightarrow G, DE \rightarrow G\};$
$4 = \{DG \rightarrow A, DE \rightarrow A\};$
$5 = \{DG \rightarrow B, DE \rightarrow B\}; 6 = \{AB \rightarrow E\};$
$7 = \{DF \rightarrow A\}; 8 = \{DF \rightarrow B\}; 9 = \{DF \rightarrow E\};$
$10 = (DF \rightarrow G\}.$

They are ordered in the following way:
$1 < 6 < 9; 3 < 10; 4 < 7; 5 < 8.$
The minimal equivalence classes are therefore 1,2,3,4,5.
FMIN $= \{G \rightarrow E, AB \rightarrow D, AB \rightarrow G, DE \rightarrow G, DG \rightarrow A, DE \rightarrow A,$
$\qquad DG \rightarrow B, DE \rightarrow B\}.$

b) *Calculation of a non-redundant base*

BNONR $= \{AB \rightarrow G, DF \rightarrow G, AB \rightarrow D, G \rightarrow E, DE \rightarrow A, DE \rightarrow B\}.$
The groups of BNONR are:
$r_1 = \{G \rightarrow E \}$ key: G;
$r_2 = \{AB \rightarrow G, AB \rightarrow D, DE \rightarrow A, DE \rightarrow B\}$ keys: AB, DE, DG;
$r_3 = \{DF \rightarrow G\}$ keys: DF, ABF.
We have the following order: $r_1 << r_2 << r_3$.

c) *Calculation of the basic covering*

For root G: $G \rightarrow E$ which belongs to FMIN.
For roots AB, DE, DG:
  – $AB \rightarrow G, AB \rightarrow D, DE \rightarrow A, DE \rightarrow B$ which belong to FMIN;
  – $AB \rightarrow DE, DE \rightarrow AB, DG \rightarrow AB, AB \rightarrow DG, DE \rightarrow G, DG \rightarrow E$
    because of the different keys;
  – $AB \rightarrow G, DE \rightarrow G$ because $r_2 >> r_1$;
For roots DF, ABF:
  – $DF \rightarrow AB$ and $ABF \rightarrow D$ because of the different keys;
  – $DF \rightarrow ABEG$ and $ABF \rightarrow DEG$ because of $r_3 >> r_2$.

To summarise, the basic covering is:
CF $= \{G \rightarrow E, AB \rightarrow DEG, DE \rightarrow ABG, DG \rightarrow ABE, DF \rightarrow ABEG,$
$\qquad ABF \rightarrow DEG\}.$

8.7 Homogenous decompositions and the basic decomposition of a relation

DEFINITION

A decomposition D of a relation U is a *homogenous decomposition* of U if it is obtained from a homogenous covering of the fds defined on U by application of the theorem (decfd2) (see section 6.1.3) and if there is a special relation of D containing all the keys of U.

Property 24

A homogenous decomposition verifies the following properties:

a) Every relation R_i of D contains all its keys.

b) The relation: $R_i > R_j$, defined on the set of relations of D and signifying that there is the fd $K_i \rightarrow K_j$ in U, is a partial order relation.

c) The relation: R_i *is dependent on* R_j, defined on the set of relations of D and signifying that the set of key attributes to R_i contains the set of key attributes of R_j, is a partial order relation.

These are properties that can be easily demonstrated.

Example 11

The homogenous decomposition obtained from the homogenous covering CV' of example 9b is as follows:

U = U[ABDFEG] * U[ABDEG] * U[GE].

The keys to U are ABF and DF and are the keys to the first relation.

DEFINITION

The *basic decomposition of* U is the homogenous decomposition of U obtained from the basic covering of the fds of U by application of theorem (decfd2).

Example 12

The basic decomposition obtained from the CF of example 10 is the same as that obtained in example 11.

ALGORITHM

To obtain the basic decomposition of a relation U, it is sufficient to:

– construct the basic covering and form the corresponding relations R_i;

– determine the keys to U;

– if the keys to U are not roots, form the relation UK obtained by projection of U on the keys to U.

8.8   Completely homogenous decomposition

Our aim is to obtain a decomposition D that does not favour any key of a
relation of D when the latter allows several. This result is almost attained if D
is a homogenous decomposition. But there is still one detail missing which we
will illustrate by means of the following example.

Example 13
Take the relation U(ABCDSUVX).
F = {S → ABCDU; AB → CUV; UB → ACV; CD → UVA; UD → ACV;
    AC → XUV; UV → XAC}.
F is the basic covering.
The basic decomposition is formed from the relations:

U_1	= U[SABCDU]	key: S;
U_2	= U[ABCUV]	keys: AB; BU;
U_3	= U[CDUVA]	keys: CD; DU;
U_4	= U[ACUVX]	keys: AC; UV.

The relation U_1 contains a key to U_4: AC without containing the other UV.

To resolve this difficulty, a simple algorithm is applied recursively to each
relation R_i of a homogenous decomposition:
if R_i contains in its attributes a key to another relation R_j, all the key attributes
of R_j are added to it.
This algorithm finishes because necessarily $R_i > R_j$.

DEFINITION
The *completely homogenous decompositions* D guarantee the equivalence of
keys of the relations that form them because if K_j, key to a relation R_j of D, is
found in R_i^+ then all the other keys of R_j are found in R_i^+. The aim of
preserving the equivalence of keys (see section 7.1.3) is thus achieved.

8.9   Relation graph of a completely homogenous
decomposition

Take RG to be the relation graph obtained from a *completely homogenous*
decomposition D_h made *compact* (chapter 4) by application of the algorithm
RG.

INF(R_i) is the set of relations R_j of D_h such that $R_i > R_j$ or R_i is dependent on R_j, and the key attributes of R_j are attributes of R_i.

MINFD(R_i), the set assigned to a relation R_i of D_h by the construction process of a relation graph (section 4.1.1.E3), is the set of relations R_j of INF(R_i) such that there is no relation R_k of INF(R_i) dependent on R_j.
All the relations Rj of D_h to which R_i is directly superior or on which it is directly dependent belong to MINFD(R_i).
The following properties are proved in section 8.11.6.

Property (RG1)
RG has no circuit.

Property (RG2)
If relation R_1 is dependent on relation R_2 then there is a path linking the node of R_1 to that of R_2.

Property (RG3)
If relation R_2 belongs to INF(R_1) then there is a path in RG linking the node of R_1 to that of R_2.

Property (RG4)
If A is an attribute of a hinge of two relations R_1 and R_2, there is a node whose relation R_i allows A as key attribute and verifies that $R_1 > R_i$ and $R_2 > R_i$.

Property RG5
RG is connected.

Property RG6
If X is a linear risky key (or if f: X → A is a linear risky fd) in a homogenous decomposition D_h of U, then these risks are represented in the directed relation graph RG by paths linking the node of a relation containing X (or f^+) to the relation having X as key.
If X is a cyclic risky key to R_i (or if f: X → A is an intrinsic cyclic risky fd of R_i) in a homogenous decomposition, then these risks are represented in the directed relation graph RG by functional cycles containing R_i and allowing as key-attributes of the well attributes of X (or A in the case of a cyclic risky fd).

8.10   Conclusions

Our aim is to build an initial data structure which on the one hand retains the
equivalence of keys and on the other facilitates the use of mechanisms for the
completeness of keys and entities.

This study shows us that for a relation U provided with a set of fds F, there is a
unique covering, the basic covering that allows one subsequently to obtain a
unique homogenous decomposition of U preserving optimally the equivalence
of keys: this is the basic decomposition D_b of U.

In order for this equivalence to be realised completely, this decomposition
must be made *completely homogenous*.

In addition, we have shown that cyclic risky fds and cyclic keys correspond
precisely to cycles in the directed relation graph RG_b obtained from D_b, and
that linear risky fds and linear risky keys correspond in RG_b to paths.

In part 4 we will show how the latter properties allow the functions of the two
completeness mechanisms to be extended.

Note
We can now prove that the data structure built from a RG_b will preserve access
(section 4.3), since RG_b is connected (property RG4), the join of all relations
of D_b is embedded in RG_b (section 3.5).

8.11   Appendix FD

8.11.1   Pseudo-associativity theorem

Take three fds f,g,h.
If $(f +> g) +> h$ exists, then $f +> (g +> h)$ also exists and moreover
$(f +> g) +> h < f +> (g +> h)$.

Proof
Take f: $X \rightarrow A$; g: $Y \rightarrow B$; h: $Z \rightarrow C$.
A,B,C are attributes, X,Y,Z are sets of attributes.

As $i = (f +> g) +> h$ exists, $A \in Y$ and $B \in Z$:
        i: $X \cup (Y-A) \cup (Z-B) \rightarrow C$.

$j = g +> h$ exists since $B \in Z$; j: $Y \cup (Z-B) \rightarrow C$;
$k = f +> j$ exists since $A \in Y$; k: $X \cup ((Y \cup (Z-B))-A) \rightarrow C$.

If $A \notin Z$ then k: $X \cup (Y-A) \cup (Z-B) \rightarrow C$ and $k = j$.

Conversely, if $A \in Z$, then $g(k) \cup A = g(i)$ and $k > i$.

8.11.2 Generation theorem

For every fd of F** there is a corresponding generation in F.

Proof
a) By the very definition of the closure F**, every fd f of F** is constructed by a succession of consensus operations from dependencies of F and from trivial dependencies: $h_1...h_n$.
This sequence of consensus operations may be written down using an *evaluation tree*:
– an fd is assigned to each terminal node other than the root;
– the consensus operation is assigned to each other node of the tree.

Example of evaluation tree to construct $ABEHI \rightarrow L$

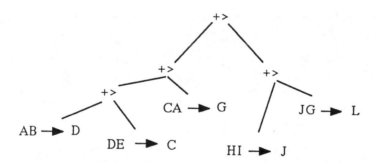

Figure 8.1 Evaluation tree

The *predecessor* node N of node N_1 in the tree is the node that is located on the path of N_1 to the root of the tree and which is adjacent to N_1. N_1 is then a *successor* to N. Every non-terminal node has two and only two successors N_1, the left successor, and N_2, the right successor.

b) *Evaluation* of the tree is a recursive process which requires:
– choice of any pair of terminal nodes N_1 and N_2 having the same predecessor N;

– destruction of N_1 and N_2 and assignment to N of the consensus f_{12} of the fds h_1, h_2 assigned respectively to N_1 and N_2: $h_{12} = h_1 +> h_2$;
– repeat a) and b) for as long as the root is not reached: once it is reached, the final result is assigned to the root.

An evaluation tree is *well formed* if in fact its evaluation leads to an fd assigned to its root.

Note
Every evaluation tree extracted from a well formed evaluation tree is itself well formed.

In the case of a generation, the evaluation tree verifies by construction that all the left successors of the non-terminal nodes are terminal nodes since the left part of every consensus operation in a generation is an fd of F. Such an evaluation tree is called a *generation tree*.

Example of generation tree of ABEHIHG → L

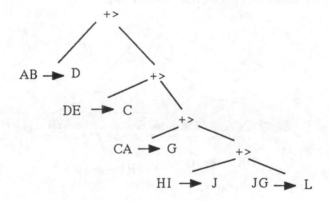

Figure 8.2 Generation tree

c) The *switching* of an evaluation tree A into another evaluation tree A' is defined only if the left successor LN of the root R of A is not terminal, and obeys the following rules:
root R' of A' is LN;
the left successor LN' of R' in A' is the left successor LS of LN in A;
the right successor RN' of R' in A' is the root R of A;
the left successor of RN' in A' is the right successor of LN in A;
the other nodes of A' are the same as those of A with the same predecessors and successors.

The nodes of A' are assigned to the same references (consensus operators or fd of F) as the corresponding nodes of A.

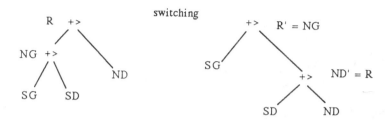

Figure 8.3 Switching

Property A1

The switching of an evaluation tree A of an fd of F** gives a well formed evaluation tree A', whose result is greater than or equal to that of A.

The proof is an obvious application of the property of pseudo-associativity of the consensus operation.

d) Transformation of an evaluation tree A of an fd f of F* into a generation tree.

– Make as many switches as there are nodes separating in A the root from the leftmost terminal node; this gives an evaluation tree A_1 whose left successor of the root is terminal and which leads to the same result as A since f belongs to F*.

– The right successor of the root can be considered to be the root of an evaluation tree A_1' a sub-tree of A_1; A_1' is an evaluation tree of an fd of F**. Its switching gives a new evaluation tree A_1'' whose result g' is equal to or greater than that g of A_1'; if it is greater, it is necessary to add a new consensus operation between a trivial fd (the right part is included in the left part) and the dependency g' to obtain g. We thus obtain an evaluation tree A_2 whose result is identical to A_1 and whose root R and its right successor allow as left successor a terminal node.

– Considering a new sub-tree of A_2 and making the same traverse, we transform gradually the initial evaluation tree A into a generation tree A' which allows the same result as A.

However, A' contains trivial fds.

e) The next part of the proof consists in showing that all the trivial fds of A'
that have been introduced can be eliminated.
The evaluation derived from A' is written

$$m_0 = f_0,$$
$$m_1 = f_1 +> m_0,$$

.

.

.

$$m_i = f_i +> m_{i-1},$$

.

.

.

$$m_p = f_p +> m_{p-1},$$
$$f < m_p.$$

From this evaluation we can derive another built on the following rules:

i) $e_0 = f_0$

ii) $\forall\ i \in (1,p)$: if f_i is not trivial and if the consensus of f_i and of e_{i-1} exists
       then $e_i = f_i +> e_{i-1}$;
       otherwise $e_i = e_{i-1}$;

iii) $f' = e_p$.

We will show that $\forall\ i \in (0,p)\ m_i < e_i$;
This property is true for $i = 0$.
We assume it to be true for $q(q < p-1)$ and we will show that it is true for
$q+1$: $m_q < e_q$.

– If f_{q+1} is trivial, then $g(m_{q+1}) = g(m_q) \cup g(f_{q+1})$ and thus
$m_{q+1} < e_q = e_{q+1}$;
– If the consensus does not exist between f_{q+1} and e_q, then $d(f_{q+1}) \notin g(e_q)$:
therefore $g(m_{q+1}) = (g(m_q) - d(f_{q+1})) \cup g(f_{q+1})$ and $g(m_{q+1}) \subseteq g(e_q)$
and thus $m_{q+1} < e_q = e_{q+1}$;
– If f_{q+1} is not trivial and if the consensus exists between f_{q+1} and e_q, then
$(g(m_q)-d(f_{q+1})) \cup g(f_{q+1})$ contains
$(g(e_q)-d(f_{q+1})) \cup g(f_{q+1})$ since $g(m_q)$ contains $g(e_q)$:
thus $m_{q+1} < e_{q+1}$.
– $f < f'$.
We have thus obtained an evaluation of f constructed only from an fd of F and
whose evaluation tree is a generation tree.

f) We will show that it is possible to construct a generation tree such that all the fds f_i of a generation tree $(i \neq 0)$ verify $d(f_i) \neq d(f_0)$.

Take $k \in (1,p)$ such that $d(f_k) = d(f_0)$ and $\forall i > k \; d(f_i) \neq d(f_0)$ and $e_k = f_k \mathbin{+>} e_{k-1}$.

If the evaluation tree is well formed, then $d(f_0) \in g(e_{i-1})$.

Since $d(e_{i-1}) = d(e_0) = d(f_0)$, e_{i-1} is in fact a trivial fd and $f_k > e_k$.

We can derive a new evaluation:
i) $h_0 = f_k$;
ii) $\forall i \in (k+1,p)$: if the consensus of f_i and of h_{i-1-k} exists
       then $h_{i-k} = f_i \mathbin{+>} h_{i-1-k}$;
       otherwise $h_{i-k} = h_{i-1-k}$;
iii) $f' = h_{p-e}$.

We will show that $\forall i \in (k,p) \; h_{i-k} > e_i$.

This property is true for $i = k$ since $h_0 = f_k > e_k$.

We assume it to be true for $q(q < p-1)$ and we will show that it is true for $q+1$: thus $h_{q-k} > e_q$:

– If the consensus of f_{q+1} and of h_{q-k} does not exist then $h_{q+1-k} = h_{q-k}$;
    if $e_q = e_{q+1}$ then $h_{q+1-k} > e_{q+1}$;
    otherwise $g(e_{q+1}) = (g(e_q) \cup g(f_{q+1})) - d(f_{q+1})$;
    since $d(f_{q+1}) \notin g(h_{q-k})$ and $g(h_{q-k}) \subseteq g(e_q)$,
    then $g(h_{q-k}) \subseteq g(e_{q+1})$ and $e_{q+1} < h_{q+1-k}$;
– If the consensus of f_{q+1} and h_{q-k} exists,
    then $g(h_{q+1-k}) = (g(f_{q+1}) \cup g(h_{q-k})) - d(f_{q+1})$
    and $g(h_{q+1-k}) \subseteq (g(f_{q+1}) \cup g(e_q)) - d(f_{q+1})$;
    thus $h_{q+1-k} > e_{q+1}$
– Thus $f'' > f' > f$.

8.11.3   Property 6

If f is generated by $(f_0, f_1 ... f_n)$ in F then
$\forall i \in (1,n) \; \forall A_i \in g(f_i): g(f) \rightarrow A_i \in F^{**}$.

Proof
$m_i = f_i \mathbin{+>} m_{i-1}$. Thus $g(m_i) = g(f_i) \cup (g(m_{i-1}) - d(f_i))$.

Thus $g(m_i) \rightarrow A_i \in F^{**} \ \forall \ A_i \in g(f_i)$.

$g(m_i) \rightarrow d(f_i) \in F^{**}$. $g(m_i) \rightarrow B_{i-1} \in F^{**} \ \forall \ B_{i-1} \in g(m_{i-1})$.

Thus, by successive applications of the pseudo-transitivity

$\forall \ i \in (1,n)$, $\forall \ j \in (1,i-1)$, $\forall \ B_j \in g(m_j)$, $g(m_i) \rightarrow B_j$.

Since $f < m_n$, $\forall \ A_n \in g(m_n) \ g(f) \rightarrow A_n \in F^{**}$ and

$\forall \ i \in (1,n) \ \forall \ B_i \in g(m_i) \ g(f) \rightarrow B_i \in F^{**}$;

thus $\forall \ A_i \in g(f_i) \ g(f) \rightarrow A_i \in F^{**}$

8.11.4   Theorem of the preorder defined on F**

The relation "f_0 generates f in F^{**}" defines a *preorder* on the set of fds F^{**}.

Proof

The relation is reflexive by the very construction of a generation. It is transitive: if f_0 generates f and if f generates f' in F^{**} then there are two generations S and S':

S: $m_0 = f_0$; $\forall \ i \in (1,n) \ m_i = f_i +> m_{i-1}$; $f < m_n$,

and S': $m_0 = f$; $\forall \ j \in (1,p) \ m'_j = f'_j +> m'_{j-1}$; $f' < m'_p$,

with $\forall \ i \in (1,n) \ f_i \in F^{**}$ and $\forall \ j \in (1,p) \ f'_j \in F^{**}$.

From S', we can construct a new generation S" verifying: $m''_0 = m_n$,

$\forall \ j \in (1,p)$, if $d(f'_j) \in g(m''_{j-1})$, $m''_j = f'_j +> m''_{j-1}$,

otherwise $m''_j = m''_{j-1}$.

We show by recurrence that $\forall \ j \in (0,p) \ m''_j > m'_j$;

this property is true for $j = 0$ since $m''_0 = m_n > f = m'_0$.

We assume it to be true for $\forall \ j \in (0,q)$ where $q < p$.

Then if $d(f'_{q+1}) \in g(m''_q)$, the consensus exists:

$g(m''_{q+1}) = (g(m''_q) - d(f'_{q+1})) \cup g(f'_{q+1})$;

since $g(m''_q) \subseteq g(m'_q)$, $g(m''_{q+1}) \subseteq g(m'_{q+1})$ and $m''_{q+1} > m'_{q+1}$

Otherwise $d(f'_{q+1}) \notin g(m''_q)$: then $g(m''_q) \subseteq g(m'_q) - d(f'_{q+1})$

and $g(m'_{q+1}) = (g(m'_q) - d(f'_{q+1})) \cup g(f'_{q+1})$ contains $g(m''_q)$;

since $g(m''_q) = g(m''_{q+1})$, $m'_{q+1} < m''_{q+1}$.

Thus S" is a new generation of $f'(f' < m'_p < m''_p)$ from m_n. The joining of the

two generations S and S" thus provides a generation of f' from f_0.
The relation is therefore transitive.

8.11.5 Mandatory groups

Property 21
Every base contains at least one dependency of every mandatory group.

Proof
The mandatory group r_0. contains the dependency f which does not belong to the base B. Since B is a base, there is f' in B which generates f in B: thus $g(f) > g(f')$ and the rank of the group of f' is less than or equal to that of r_0 If it is equal, then f and f' belong to the same group r_0: B contains a dependency of r_0. If it is not equal, then since the generation in B which constructs f from f' is also a generation in F*, it necessarily contains a dependency of r_0 by definition of a mandatory group.

Property 22
Every fd of an non-redundant base belongs to a mandatory group.

Proof
Each dependency f of a non-mandatory group r can be generated in F* by means of a generation G such that $G = (f_1, f_2...f_n, f')$ and $f_1, f_2...f_n$, f' do not belong to r. Thus the ranks of the groups containing the dependencies of G are strictly less than that of r.

Take BNONR to be a non-redundant database and BNONR(n) the dependencies of BNONR belonging to groups whose ranks are less than n (n is the rank of r).

Since BNONR is a base, each dependency of G can be generated in BNONR by means of dependencies belonging necessarily to BNON(n); in fact if the generation of f_1 in BNONR contains the dependency fnonr, then $g(f_1) \rightarrow$ g(fnonr) (property 6) and thus the group of f_1 has a rank greater than or equal to the rank of the group of fnonr.

Thus f belongs to the closure formed from BNONR(n). f cannot therefore belong to BNONR.

8.11.6   Relation graph of a completely homogenous decomposition

8.11.6.1   Property (RG1)

RG is without a circuit.

Proof
If the nodes of the relations $(R_1 R_2 ... R_n)$ form a circuit, then $R_1 > R_2 ... R_{n-1} > R_n$ and $R_n > R_1$. This is impossible, because the relation defined on the relations is an order relation.

8.11.6.2   Property (RG2)

If relation R_1 is dependent on relation R_n then there is a path linking the node of R_1 to that of R_n.

Proof
R_n belongs to $INF(R_1)$ because KR_n^+ is included in KR_1^+. If R_n belongs to $MINFD(R_1)$, the property is proved.
Otherwise, there is R_2 of $MINFD(R_1)$ by construction of the relation graph such that KR_n^+ is included in KR_2^+: R_2 is dependent on R_n. The nodes of R_1 and R_2 are linked by an arc from the node of R_1.

The same reasoning may be applied to relations R_2 and R_n, while noting that the dependency relation is a partial order relation: also, there is a sequence of relations $R_2 ... R_n$ such that:
– R_1 is dependent on R_j if $i < j$ (i and j included between 2 and n).
– R_{j+1} belongs to $MINFD(R_i)$ for every $i \in (2, n-1)$. There is therefore a path linking the node of R_1 with that of R_n.

8.11.6.3   Property (RG3)

If relation R_1 belongs to $INF(R_n)$ then there is a path in RG linking the node of R_1 to that of R_2.

Proof

If R_1 belongs to $INF(R_n)$, there is a relation R_2 that belongs to $MINFD(R_n)$ and which is dependent on R_1 according to the third stage of the algorithm: it is possible for R_1 and R_2 to be identical. There is an arc linking the node of R_n to that of R_2, and there is a path linking the node of R_2 to that of R_1 according to the preceding property.

8.11.6.4 Property (RG4)

If A is an attribute of a hinge of two relations R_1 and R_2, then there is a node whose relation R_i allows A as key attribute and verifies that $R_1 > R_i$ and $R_2 > R_i$.

Proof

If relations R_1 and R_2 allow a hinge Hi_{12}, then D_h which is compact contains a relation R_{12} whose keys are identical to those of Hi_{12}. If A is not a key attribute of R_{12}, D_h contains a relation R_{121} whose keys are identical to those of $Hi_{121} = Hi_{12} - KR^+_{12}$ Thus, step by step, there is a relation R_i whose A is a key attribute. By construction $R_1 > R_i$ and $R_2 > R_i$.

Conversely, the fourth stage in the construction of the relation graph (section 4.4.4) might eliminate R_i. But, it should be noted that by construction R_i belongs to $INF(R_1)$ and to $INF(R_2)$. There is also a relation R_3 of $MINFD(R_1)$ which is dependent on R_i (possibly equal to R_i). R_3 therefore allows A as key attribute.

Similarly, there is a relation R_4 of $MINFD(R_2)$ which is dependent on R_i. If R_3 and R_4 are identical, their node is linked to two distinct nodes, that of R_1 and that of R_2 and it cannot be removed during the course of the fourth stage; otherwise, there is a relation R_5 (possibly equal to R_i), dependent on R_i and on which R_3 and R_4 are dependent.
R_5 cannot be removed during the fourth stage.

At the end of the algorithm, there is at least one relation allowing A as key attribute.

8.11.6.5   Property (RG5)

RG is connected.

Proof

D_h being a homogenous decomposition of a relation U, there is, by definition, a relation R source of D which allows as keys, the keys to U, and which is greater than all the other relations R_i of D.

In the directed graph of relations obtained at the end of the third stage of the algorithm for transforming a compact decomposition into a relation graph (section 4.1.1), R is assigned to a node.

According to the preceding property (RG3), this node is linked to all the other nodes by a path since $R > R_i$.

The directed relation graph is connected.

The next stages of the algorithm do not alter this characteristic even if relation R is no longer assigned to a node but to an edge in the final relation graph.

8.11.6.6   Property (RG6)

If X is a linear risky key (or if f: $X \rightarrow A$ is a linear risky fd) in a homogenous decomposition D_h of U, then these risks are represented in the directed relation graph RG by paths linking the node of a relation containing X (or f^+) to the relation allowing X as key.

If X is a cyclic risky key of R_i (or if f: $X \rightarrow A$ is an intrinsic cyclic risky fd of R_i) in a homogenous decomposition, then these risks are represented in the directed relation graph RG by functional cycles containing R_i and allowing as key attribute of the well, attributes of X (or A in the case of cyclic risky fds).

Proof

1. X is a key to the relation R_i of D_h. There is a partial functional decomposition D' of D_h which overflows for X; D' is minimal and take R to be the source of D'. R is greater than R_i because $K \rightarrow X$ is an fd of U. There is therefore a path linking the node of R to that of R_i (property RG3). In D', there is a relation R_k such that R_k^+ and X allowing at least one common attribute B. Since R_k is a relation of D', $R > R_k$.

According to property (RG4), there is a node in RG whose relation R_{ik} allows

B as key attribute and verifies: $R_k > R_{ik}$ and $R_i > R_{ik}$.

1a) If $R_{ik} = R_k$, then $R > R_i > R_k$.

Since R_i does not belong to D', there are two paths that link R to R_k and there is therefore a functional cycle of source R, of well R_k, containing R_i of which a key attribute of the well is B, a key attribute of R_i.

1b) If $R_{ik} = R_i$, then $R_k > R_i$.

The keys to the common attributes of R_k and of R_i are those of R_i. Since the decomposition is completely homogenous, R_k^+ contains KR_i^+ and therefore X.

Then $R = R_k$ and X is a linear risky key: there is a path linking the nodes of R_k and of R_i.

1c) Otherwise there are three distinct relations R_i, R_k, R_{ik}.

A path from R to R_k does not pass through R_i because R_i is not a relation of D'. There is then a cycle of source R and of well R_{ik}, containing R_i and allowing as key attributes of the well, at least one attribute of X.

2. f: $X \to A$ is an intrinsic fd of a relation R_i of D_h. There is a partial functional decomposition D' of D_h which overflows for f; D' is minimal. It contains a relation R_k which allows A as attribute. The reasoning is as previously.

9 Appendix: Smoothing functional cycles

We have shown in an earlier chapter (chapter 7) the role of fds at cyclic risk in the maintenance of a coherent database. Fds at cyclic risk are associated with functional cycles (section 3.4.3) that can be detected in the relation graph of a basic structure RG_b. Even if each functional cycle of a RG_b does not necessarily contain a fd at cyclic risk, a large number of them do contain one and require for the maintenance of a coherent database the triggering of *mechanisms* for the completing of entities and keys. Because these mechanisms are relatively costly in the cycle control, we now propose to minimise their use.

With this aim in view, we will *"smooth"* some functional cycles, that is, we will transform them. We then obtain a new relation graph RG_{sm}.

This approach comes from (LUONG86).

After explaining the principle of such an operation, we will set ourselves the task of describing the conditions that must be fulfilled to ensure that such an operation is *valid*. This validity is closely linked with the fidelity (section 3.2) of RG_{sm} in relation to the initial decomposition.

Thus the conditions for validity will ensure that the intended smoothing of a functional cycle preserve:

(f1) the contents of the database
(f2) access to the entities
(f3) the effectiveness of the validation of the fds.

We begin with an example.

Example 1

Figure 9.1 shows the relation graph RG_b obtained by our algorithm.

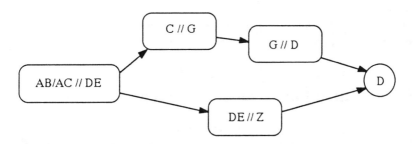

Figure 9.1 Functional cycle to be smoothed

The relations of the initial decomposition were R_s (ABCDE), R_1 (CG), R_2(GD) and R_{so}(DEZ).

Smoothing this functional cycle leads to the relation graph RG_{sm} shown in figure 9.2.

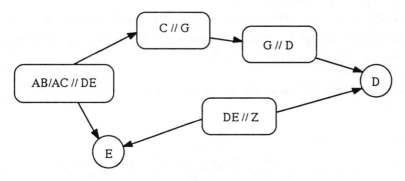

Figure 9.2 Functional cycle after smoothing

RG_{sm} no longer contains a functional cycle.

The fd $G \rightarrow D$ which is at cyclic risk in RG_b : $((R_s*R')$ [GD]), is no longer so in RG_{sm}.

The relations deduced from RG_{sm} are $R_s^!$ (ABCE), R_1 (CG), R_2(GD) and R_{so} (DEZ).

Because we can easily rediscover R_s by forming $R_s^!$ R_1 and R_2, the contents of the database are preserved. The set of intrinsic fds in RG_{sm} allow $AB \rightarrow D$ and $AC \rightarrow D$ to be obtained.

Access to the entity of R_{so} relative to an entity of R_s' is via R_1 and R_2. We will consider this smoothing to be valid and keep RG_{sm} as the structure of the database.

At the same time, there remains a cyclic key DE and the following must be assured: $(iR_s'*iR_1*iR_2)$ [DE] $\subseteq iR_{so}$ [DE].

9.1   Smoothing a functional cycle

DEFINITION

Take a relation graph RG containing a set of functional cycles (FC) with the same source R_s.

Smoothing FC consists of transforming R_s into a new relation R_s' such that:

(sm1) $R_s'^+ + \subseteq R_s^+$ and $\forall\ A \in R_s^+ - R_s'^+$ there is a relation T_i of $MINFD(R_s)$ (section 4.1. E3) such that A is a key attribute of T_i;

(sm2) $KR_s^+ = KR_s'^+$;

Each relation T_i of $MINFD(R_s)$ such that KT_i^+ is not included in $R_s'^+$ is called the *smoothing origin*; from now on, we will describe it by R_{soi}.

Take RG_{sm} to be the relation graph obtained after this transformation; because it no longer contains an arc joining the nodes of R_s' and R_{soi}, it contains less functional cycles than RG.

Example 2 Figure 9.3 shows a relation graph RG_b .

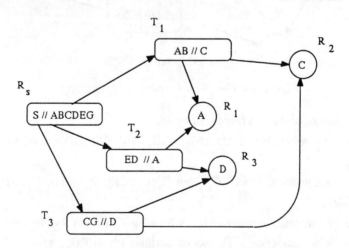

Figure 9.3 Functional cycle (FC)

R_s is formed on attributes SABCDEG.

There are three FCs, with the same source R_s and respective wells R_1, R_2, and R_3.

Figure 9.4 shows one possible way of smoothing these cycles (RG_{sm1}).

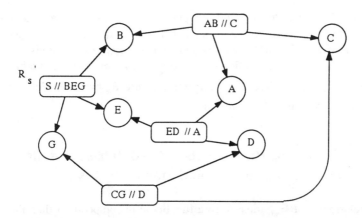

Figure 9.4 Smoothing CF (method 1)

R'_s is formed on attributes SBEG.

Figure 9.5 shows another possible way of smoothing these cycles (RG_{sm2}).

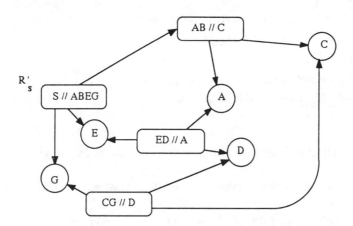

Figure 9.5 Smoothing CF (method 2)

RG_{sm2} contains no functional cycle.

The following section will show that RG_{sm1} and RG_{sm2} are not valid and we will not keep them.

9.2   Validation of a smoothing

In the introduction to this chapter, we placed the validation of a smoothing in the context of respect for the conditions of fidelity to the initial decomposition. We will now describe these conditions in the framework of this study.

Take RG to be the initial relation graph, RG_{sm} the relation graph obtained after smoothing, R_s the relation of RG transformed into R_s' by smoothing, and R_{soi} the relations originating from the smoothing.

9.2.1   Preserving the contents of the database and the effectiveness of the validation of the fds

Some relations of RG_{sm} must form a functional decomposition that allows R_s to be found. Therefore, the set F_{sm} of intrinsic fds of the relations of RG_{sm} must have the same closure as the set F of those of RG.

(sm3) $(F_{sm})** = F**$.

Example
In example 2, RG_{sm1} does not verify this condition:
$S \rightarrow ADC$ does not belong to $(F_{sm})**$;
$F_{sm} = (S \rightarrow BEG; AB \rightarrow C; ED \rightarrow A; CG \rightarrow D)$.
Thus RG_{sm1} is not valid.
In contrast RG_{sm2} verifies this condition.

9.2.2   Do not increase the number of fds at cyclic risk

(sm4) The set of the fds at cyclic risk of RG_{sm} must be included or equal to that defined in RG.
If this condition is not fulfilled, the smoothing serves no purpose.
It may even lead to worse situations, as shown in the following example.

Example
In example 2, GR_{sm2} does not verify this condition.

In RG_b, there is no fd at cyclic risk (despite the cycles): for example $ED \rightarrow A$ is intrinsic to T_2 and is defined in R_s: it is only at linear risk.

At the same time, this same fd $ED \rightarrow A$ is at cyclic risk in RG_{sm2} : it is intrinsic to T_2 and is defined in $R_s' * T_1 * T_3$ which is a minimal decomposition for this fd.

9.2.3 Preserve access

Take $R_s'*$ to be the relation that can be obtained by composition of all the relations of RG_{sm} whose nodes can be reached by an outflow of the node of R_s'.

All the keys to a relation R_{so}, the origin of a smoothing, that belongs to the set attributes of $R_s'*$ are said to be *privileged* with respect to the other keys of R_{so}.

(sm5) RG_{sm} preserves the access if for each relation originating from the smoothing R_{so}, the designer accepts that the association of an entity rs' of R_s' and of an entity r_{so} of R_{so} necessarily proceeds by the knowledge of the value associated to a privileged key of R_{so} and can no longer be made by the knowledge of the value associated to another key of R_{so}.

Example
Take the following RG_b shown in figure 9.6.

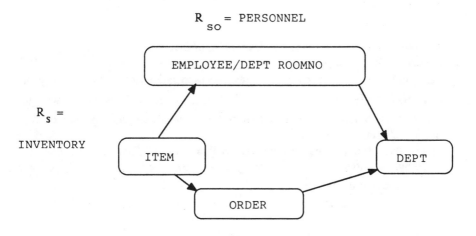

Figure 9.6 Inventory

Relation INVENTORY
An item of material is bought when an order is placed, it is used by an employee and is located in a departmental room (NOROOM DEPT).

Relation ORDER
An order is passed through a single department.

Relation PERSONNEL
An employee works in a single room in his department. Only one employee works in a room.

Figure 9.7 shows the RG_{sm} obtained.

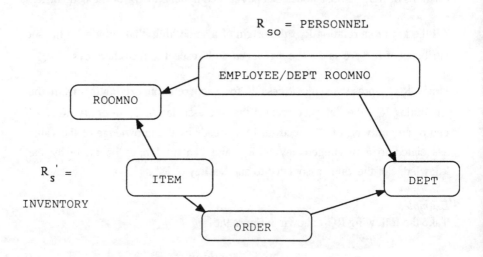

Figure 9.7 Smoothing of Inventory

RG_{sm} is valid only if for the designer, the associations between an entity of INVENTORY (R_s) and one of PERSONNEL (R_{so}) are made by the knowledge of the room where the item of material is located and not by that of the employee who uses the item.

At the same time, if the designer thinks that some of these associations are made by the knowledge of the employee who uses the item, then RG_{sm} is not valid and RG_b must be conserved.

PART 4

PERSPECTIVES

10 Perspectives

Throughout the previous chapters we have attempted to deal with a new subject matter, that is, structured data that can be stored in a database. Such subject matter is common to the field of information and to the field of management. It brings the computing expert and the manager together when a database is being installed and enables them to understand one another. It is tantamount to providing them with a language for their needs (relation, relational graph, etc). Our aim is to contribute to the training of database designers and, for us, such people must become experts in this new subject matter.

In section 10.1 we review the different parts of the design process of a database structure by repositioning the framework of the designer's actions.

Using these results, we introduce in section 10.2 some extensions to the relational data model that derive from several sources. We have left such a discussion until now, as we did not want to overcomplicate the exposition. These extensions offer managers and computing specialists a richer language for comprehension and designers more scope for specification. But these specifications must be easily embedded in software tools. The DBMSs must evolve and provide broader data models than the simple relational data model. In conjunction with other researchers, we (JUNET-FALQUET-LEONARD 86), have developed an example of a new DBMS that we call ECRINS. To conclude, in section 10.3 we describe some new mechanisms that future DBMSs should contain in order (in our view) greatly to facilitate the realisation of database applications. We discovered these mechanisms through our study of the design domain and the fact that we include them at the very end indicates the importance that we attach to them.

10.1 Design process for databases

Our approach to the design of a database structure divides into three parts, like many others, namely:

– determining a first data model
– determining a logical data structure
– determining an internal data structure.

10.1.1   Determining a first data model

This stage forms part of the analysis of the field of application. The relational data model allows the results of analyses to be stored precisely. We have shown how integrity rules can be stored precisely. We have shown how integrity rules can be an effective aid in this part. For analysis, it is not simply important for them to emphasise these rules to guarantee the coherence of the data in the future database, they can also strengthen their model by finding such rules in particular situations: inclusion dependencies are an especially valuable aid to the understanding of cycles in a model.

We have also shown how necessary it is to determine the spaces and contexts for more computer data models: future bold users might ask questions that lie outside such spaces and contexts: this would be at their risk, but the responsibility of the designers will be absolved if such bold and careless users were to ask questions without due reflection that exceeded the bounds of space and context.

In the end, the model file will include:
– the domains
– the attributes, each with its domains
– the relations, each with its attributes
– its keys (including one mandatory)
– the permitted unknown values
– the integrity rules, each with its context, its range
– the spaces and contexts

For each space U we shall work with one of its *completely homogenous decompositions*, so that at this stage in the process no key is advantaged (a design approach different from others, for example (BERNSTEIN76)). With this aim, we have two alternatives which correspond to two approaches that we have already met:
– fd approach (also known as the synthetic approach). This entails considering the set of fds defined on U and a decomposition of U is built only from the fd. In this case, we advocate the use of one basic decomposition of U.

– decomposition approach. One retains the decomposition of U formed with the help of relations previously obtained at the modelling stage. In this case, we advocate the adding to each relation of all its potential keys and then making it completely homogenous and compact.

With one or other of these approaches we obtain a completely homogenous decomposition D_h of U, which gives no advantage to any key.

10.1.2 Determining a logical data structure

The RG algorithm automatically transforms the homogenous decomposition D_h into a relational digraph RG_h. The designer's skill will enable him to eliminate some hinges and even rename some attributes and smooth some cycles: for each cycle the designer must, if he wishes to smooth it, accept that the key to one relation must be privileged in respect to the others. It is of course an algorithm that indicates which cycles can be smoothed and, for each of them, the relation and the key that should have the privilege.

Once all this work has been done, an algorithm introduces the possible binary edges (4.1.1. E6).

10.1.3 Determining an internal data structure

This part depends on the DBMS system used. The main aspects of this were presented in chapter 5.

The designer can:
> double the nodes
> delete access paths
> insert relations

These transformations are controlled by an algorithm that, for example, guarantees that there is always a simple algorithm for obtaining entities of the space relation.

In order to be able to do his job properly, the designer must possess the results of an analysis of future processing, especially information on the frequency of entity deletion and entity access.

10.1.4 Comment

The transformation of the initial homogeneous decomposition into an internal data structure demands skill from the designer. His work is assisted by algorithms that guarantee that the final internal structure remains faithful to the initial homogenous decomposition.

Our approach confronts the designer of a database with the choices whose relative values can be clearly understood. Questions as well known as normal relational forms are partially reduced to a single optimisation point of view and can be handled in a purely algorithmic way.

We shall compare our results with those of other approaches using some examples.

10.1.4.1 Example

Take the relation R (SABCEGHX) provided with following set of fds:
$F = \{S \rightarrow ABCEGH, E \rightarrow C, H \rightarrow A, AB \rightarrow CG, CG \rightarrow ABX\}$.
The purely boolean approach would offer the following choice of non-redundant databases to the designer:

$FNONR_{11} = \{S \rightarrow EHB, E \rightarrow C, H \rightarrow A, AB \rightarrow CGX, CG \rightarrow AB\}$,

$FNONR_{12} = \{S \rightarrow EHB, E \rightarrow C, H \rightarrow A, AB \rightarrow CG, CG \rightarrow ABX\}$;

$FNONR_{21} = \{S \rightarrow EHG, E \rightarrow C, H \rightarrow A, AB \rightarrow CGX, CG \rightarrow AB\}$;

$FNONR_{22} = \{S \rightarrow EHG, E \rightarrow C, H \rightarrow A, AB \rightarrow CG, CG \rightarrow ABX\}$.

AB and CD being keys to R[ABCGX], we can consider that the designer must choose between on the one hand $FNONR_{11}$ (or $FNONR_{12}$) and on the other hand $FNONR_{21}$ (or $FNONR_{22}$), which leads to two possible decompositions of R:

D_1:R = R[SEHB]*R[EC]*R[HA]*R[ABCGX];

D_2:R = R[SEHG]*R[EC]*R[HA]*R[ABCGX].

The RG associated with D_1 is as follows:

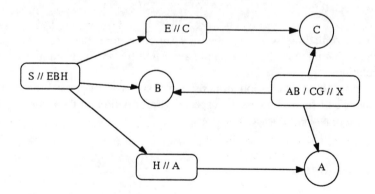

Figure 10.1 RG constructed from a non-redundant base

In D_1 there is a cyclic risk for the fd $E \rightarrow C$.

Entity creations of relations of D_2 cannot therefore be executed independently from one another if one wants to guarantee global coherence; in fact the existence of (sb) in R[SB], (sh) in R[SH], (ha) in [RHA], (abcgx) in R[ABCGX], (se) in R[SE], (ec') in R[EC], requires c = c'.

D_2 leads to the same problem.

Our approach is not to smooth the functional cycle and obtain the relational graph shown in figure 10.2.

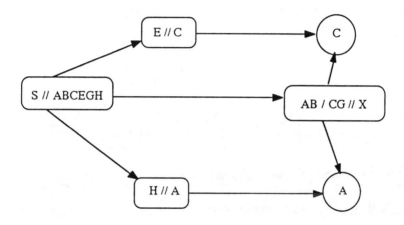

Figure 10.2 Our solution

This RG corresponds to the following basic decomposition:
R = R[SABCEGH]*R[EC]*R[HA]*R[ABCGX]*R[C]*R[A].
The fds $E \rightarrow C$ and $H \rightarrow A$ are only at risk linearly and smoothing puts one or the other at cyclic risk (property am4 of chapter 9).

10.1.4.2 Example (PICHAT-DELOBEL79)

Take the relation R(ABCDEFG) provided with a set of fds from which the following is from the non-redundant bases:
$\{G \rightarrow F, AF \rightarrow E, A \rightarrow BC, C \rightarrow A, D \rightarrow A, H \rightarrow I, I \rightarrow J\}$.
DHG is the key to R.

Here is the direct decomposition that can be deduced from it.
R = R[DHG]*R[GF]*R[AFE]*R[ABC]*R[DA]*R[HI]*R[IJ].

It gives preference to the role of A in relation to that of C when they are two equivalent keys to R[ABC].

With our approach, we obtain the following basic decomposition:
R = R[DHGACF]*R[GF]*R[ACFE]*R[DAC]*R[ACB]*R[HIJ]*R[IJ]*R[F].

Relation R[ACFE] is the source of a valid smoothing (chapter 9) and we get the relational graph of figure 10.3.

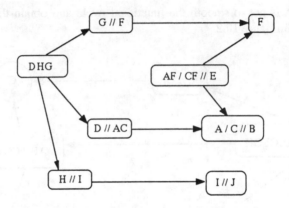

Figure 10.3 RG obtained for the Pichat-Delobel example

10.1.4.3 Example (BEERI-BERNSTEIN79)

Take the relation R[ABCDE] provided with the fds set:
F = {A → BC, BC → A, AD → E, E → C}.
We suggest the basic decomposition D of R
R = R[ABC]*R[ABCDE]*R[EC]*R[C] whose RG is as shown in figure 10.4.

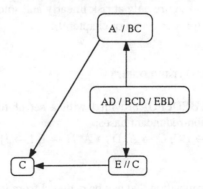

Figure 10.4 RG obtained for the Beeri-Bernstein example

The authors propose two decompositions:
D_1 = {R_1= R[ABC], R_2 = R[ADE], R_3 = R[EC]};
D_2 = {S_1 = R[ABC], S_2 = R[BCDE], S_3= R[EC]}.

The only difference between D_1 and D_2 on the one hand, and D on the other, is that R_2 and S_2 do not contain all their keys.

The authors note that the structure deduced from D_1 is of the Boyce Codd Kent (BCKNF) normal form while that deduced from D_2 is not. If it is true that updates of a relation in BCKNF can be executed independently, on the other hand, updates of isolated relations, all in BCKNF and forming a decomposition, must sometimes be controlled in a global way to facilitate interrogation.

So, for D_1, if (abc) $\in$ iR_1 (ade) $\in$ iR_2 (ec') $\in$ iR_3, global control requires c = c'.

The differences between D_1 and D_2 no longer appear clear, and we suggest the decomposition D which has the advantage of giving an equivalent role to the keys AD and BCD.

10.1.4.4 Example (BERNSTEIN76)

Take relation R(ABCX1X2) provided with the set of fds:
F = {X1X2 $\rightarrow$ A, C $\rightarrow$ X1X2, AX1 $\rightarrow$ B, BX2 $\rightarrow$ C}.

(BERNSTEIN76) provides as final decomposition:
D' = {R'_1 = R[X1X2CA], R'_2 = R[AX1B], R'_3 = R[BX2C]}
giving as keys to R'_1: X1X2 and C,

R'_2: AX1

R'_3: BX2

In fact BX2 is also a key to R'_1 because X1X2 $\rightarrow$ AX1 $\rightarrow$ B on the one hand and BX2 $\rightarrow$ C $\rightarrow$ X1X2 on the other.

We have no information about the merits of the decomposition of the relation R_1 = R[X1X2CAB] in the two relations R'_1 R'_3. Furthermore, this decomposition D' requires that each update be verified with the help of the instances of the 3 relations, if one wants to avoid contradictions.

Our proposition causes a functional cycle which, when handled by the mechanisms that we suggest (section 10.3), avoids contradictions.

This is the decomposition that we suggest:
D = {R$_1$ = R[X1X2CAB], R$_2$ = R[AX1B], R$_3$ = R[B]};
Keys to R$_1$: X1X2, C, BX2.

This decomposition does not favour any key and provides all the keys to the relations.

10.2   Extended relational data model

Since Codd's (CODD70) introduction of the relational data model, a number of other data models have appeared. They all try to have a richer syntax in order to move easily to accommodate quite complex models. They thus facilitate the determination of a first data model. We will now describe four concepts.

10.2.1   Sub-sequence of a relation's attributes

A relation is formed on a set of attributes arranged in sequence. A *sub-sequence of attributes* in this relation is controlled by an attribute of the relation called a *generic attribute* of the sub-sequence whose domain must be of type word.
It is subjected to a one variable proposition that takes its values in the domain of the generic attribute.
An entity of a relation accepts values for the attributes of this sub-sequence only if the proposition is verified by the value taken by the entity for the generic attribute.

Example
Let the relation PERSON formed on the attributes NAME, CIVIL-STATUS and the sub-sequence of attributes DATE-OF-MARRIAGE, PLACE-OF-MARRIAGE.
DATE-OF-MARRIAGE and PLACE-OF-MARRIAGE constitute an attribute sub-sequence of the relation PERSON.
An entity of PERSON only takes values for these attributes if the value taken for the generic attribute CIVIL-STATUS is not "unmarried".
Note that the sub-sequences can be nested one within the other.

10.2.2   Sub-relation
A *sub-relation* SR is a relation defined with reference to a *reference relation* R and controlled by an attribute of R, called *generic attribute* of SR (SMITH77).

The generic attribute must have a domain of type word and not belong to any sub-sequence of R.

The sub-relation SR is limited to a single value of the generic attribute domain. An entity of R is an entity of SR only if it takes this value for the generic attribute. Conversely, an entity of SR can always be considered to be an entity of R. Two sub-relations of R cannot be assigned to the same value of the same generic attribute.

It is recursively possible to define a new sub-relation SSR that accepts SR as reference relation; it may then be said that SSR is also a *sub-relation* of R. This expression is justified by the fact that an entity of SSR is an entity of SR and therefore of R.

A sub-relation SR of R may have its own attributes.

Example

Take the relation PERSON that accepts as attributes:

NAMEPERS providing the name and forename of the person and serving as key to the PERSON relation; EMPLOYMENT indicating whether a person is "working", "unemployed", "non-working" or "retired".

UNEMPLOYED, WORKING are the sub-relations that accept PERSON as reference relation; they accept EMPLOYMENT as generic attribute.

An entity of PERSON is an entity of UNEMPLOYED if it takes the value "unemployed" for EMPLOYMENT; it is an entity of WORKING if it takes the value "working" for EMPLOYMENT.

UNEMPLOYED accepts its own attribute NBYRUN that indicates the number of years that the person has been unemployed.

10.2.3 Association relation or associate relation

An association relation (CHEN 76) is a relation defined with reference to two *reference relations* R_1 and R_2. The entities of an association relation allow one entity of one of the two reference relations to be linked with an entity of the other. Each reference relation fulfils a role in the association and each role has allocated to it a parameter *maxcard* that shows the maximum number of entities (RA) that may be constructed from an entity of the reference relation that fulfils this role. There can be several distinct association relations that have the same reference relations.

Example

Take the relations PERSON and TOWN which are not association relations and take the two association relations BIRTH and ABODE that both accept PERSON and TOWN as reference relations. PERSON fulfils the role of "person born in" in BIRTH, and a person has allocated a maximum of 1 entity in BIRTH (since a person has only one birth place). PERSON fulfils the role of "person living in" in ABODE. TOWN fulfils the role of "birthplace of" in BIRTH, and a town may have an unknown maximum number of entities of BIRTH: the maximum number of persons born in a town has no meaning as an integrity rule. It plays the role of "place of abode of" in ABODE, again with an unknown maxcard.

In the case where the two reference relations R_1, and R_2 are either the same relation, or sub-relations of the same relation R, where R may be one of the two relations R_1 or R_2, the association relation is then called a *loop*.

If the loop applies to the same relation, it may be symmetric if the two roles are identical, or *asymmetric* in the opposite case; if not, it is necessarily asymmetric.

Example

Take the same relation PERSON and take the loops FRIEND and RELATIONSHIP which accept PERSON as reference relation. FRIEND is a symmetric loop if "person X is a friend of person Y" is equivalent to "person Y is a friend of person X". In this case, the two roles of FRIEND are identical with an unknown maximal cardinality. RELATIONSHIP is asymmetric and accepts two distinct roles: PARENTS OF and CHILD OF. The maximal cardinality assigned to the role CHILD OF is 2. So, for an entity of PERSON, it is possible to create through the role of CHILD OF a maximum of 2 entities of RELATIONSHIP.

The reference relation R_1, of RA fulfils a *determinant* role in RA if its key is included in the key of RA. If the keys are equal, there corresponds to an entity of relation R_1 at most one entity of RA through this role (maximal cardinality equal to 1).

In the preceding example, PERSON fulfils a determinant role in BIRTH but not in ABODE.

10.2.4   Complementary relation

A complementary relation CR is a relation that has a reference relation R; the key to CR is formed from the key K to R to which has been added one or more attributes that belong to CR. An entity of CR may only exist if the entity of R that has the same values for K exists.

Example

The relation QUALIFICATION is a complementary relation of the relation PERSON: it accepts as key the attribute NAMEPERS, forming the key to PERSON, and NOQUALIF (qualification number) which accepts a rank type domain. The other attributes of QUALIFICATION provide the label (LABEL) of the qualification, the number of years experience of this person in this qualification (NBYEARS), the main place of work where this person did the work requiring this qualification (PLACEOFWORK), the main diploma that the person obtained in this qualification (DIPLOMA) and the date on which it was obtained (DATEOFDIPLOMA).

It is therefore possible to allocate the different qualifications of a person to that person, that is, an entity of the relation PERSON, through the entities of the complementary relation QUALIFICATION with the data that belongs to each qualification.

To create a QUALIFICATION entity of a person X, there must be a PERSON entity in the database for this person X. If a PERSON entity is deleted, so are the QUALIFICATION entities attached to it.

The parameter *maxcard* of a complementary relation CR designates the maximum number of entities that are assigned to an entity of reference relation R.

In our example, the maxcard of QUALIFICATION is 5 if there are a maximum of 5 qualifications to a person in the database considered.

10.2.5   Base relation

A *base relation* is a relation that is not a sub-relation, a complementary relation, or an association relation.

10.2.6   Graphical representation

The graphical representation of a set of relations forming a data structure can be constructed from a graph whose edges represent association relations, while the nodes represent the other relations (BOUILLE 78).

A node is assigned to one and only one relation R that is not association. The name of R is written inside the closed curve representing this node. It may itself contain other modes that are assigned to relations $R_1...R_n$. The latter must then be sub-relations of R. The nodes of sub-relations relating to the same generic attribute of R are linked to the name of R by the same tree that has the exclusive or symbol as root.

An edge may be assigned to a single association relation AR. It has the name of this relation for information. It joins nodes N_1 and N_2 of the reference relations R_1 and R_2 of AR.

It may be directed or not: an arrow in the direction of N_1, towards N_2 means that at most one entity of R_2 through AR may relate/correspond to an entity of R_1. A non-directed edge of N_1 to N_2 therefore means that several entities of R_2 may correspond to an entity of R_1.

If an edge is not assigned to an association relation, it then joins the node of a complementary relation to that of its reference relation. It is then shown by a thick line.

Example

Take the relations of the preceding examples: PERSON, TOWN, ABODE, BIRTH, QUALIFICATION, UNEMPLOYED, WORKING, FRIEND, RELATIONSHIP. We add the association relation WORKPLACE, which has as reference relations WORKING and TOWN. We assume that the maxcard of the role of WORKING in WORKPLACE is 1; at most only the entity of TOWN through WORKPLACE can correspond to an entity of WORKING.

Figure 10.5 shows the graphical representation of this set of relations.

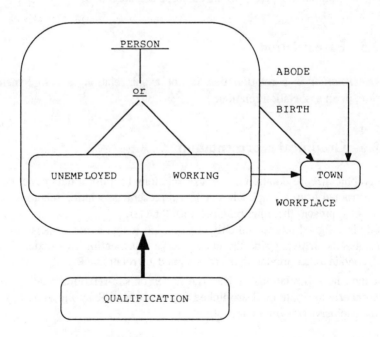

Figure 10.5 Model with the extended relational model

10.2.7 Conclusion

The concepts of association relation and complementary relation may be very easily translated into terms of the simple relational data model. They commonly appear simpler to use in the establishment of a model and this is the reason for their use.

On the other hand the concepts of attribute sub-sequence and of sub-relations can only be translated into terms of the simple relational data model by means of complicated terms with the writing of exhaustive integrity rules. However, if one is using relational DBMSs, whose data model is the simple relational data model, then this road must be followed. We believe that the solution for the future is to establish a DBMS whose data model integrates these concepts (VELEZ-LOPEZ 87, TIGRE project, for example).

In fact, as databases come to be used in the most diverse domains, it has to be recognised that a general data model for databases is no longer sufficiently relevant. In our view there will increasingly be specific data models and it is to be hoped that there will be DBMSs that accept these specific data models: we give one example in the domain of the CAO (RIEU 84), another in the domain of econometrics (SNELLA 84, PIREE project), another in the analysis of data (LEONARD 86, FARANDOLE project). In these three examples, the researchers developed both the specific data model and the DBMS that accepted it.

10.3 Control mechanisms

To guarantee the decompositions to be safe we have developed two mechanisms: the completeness of keys and the completeness of entities. We will specify them in the case of completely homogenous decompositions and we will see that they are included in a broader range of mechanisms that appear to us to be basic.

In the first sub-sections we will introduce all of these mechanisms. We will then show that they allow a *completely homogenous and compact decomposition* to be guaranteed safe and that they verify intrinsic or non-intrinsic fds.

Notation
RG_h describes the relation digraph derived from a completely homogenous and compact decomposition D_h of a relation R by the algorithm RG; '-' denotes an obscure value.

DEFINITIONS

An *extended relation* R* of a relation R is obtained by join of the relations that form an outflow of source R in RG_h. An *extended entity* r* corresponds to an entity r of R, and is the entity of R* such that $r^*.R^+ = r$.

A *path of entities* $(r_1. r_2...r_n)$ is a set of compatible entities whose relations $R_1 R_2...R_n$ form a path in RG_h.

The instances of the relations of D_h that we will discuss form *an instance of the database*.

10.3.1 Keys mechanism

For each relation R_i of D_h and for each key K_i to R_i, the keys mechanism guarantees that there can only exist in an instance iR_i two entities taking the same value for K_i.

10.3.2 Linear mechanism

Take a relation R_i whose set of attributes contains a key K_j of another relation R_j.
If an entity r_i of iR_i takes a clear value k_j for K_j, *the linear mechanism guarantees* that there is an entity r_j of iR_j taking the value k_j for K_j.

Furthermore, if R_i^+ contains another key K_{j1} of R_j, *this mechanism guarantees* that for each attribute A_{j1} of K_{j1} :
if $r_j.A_{j1}$ is clear then $r_j.A_{j1} = r_i.A_{j1}$ else $r_i A_{j1}$ is obscure.

This mechanism solves problems relating to keys with linear risk and fds with linear risk: in fact, in both cases, given that the minimum decompositions to be considered come down to a single relation, the preceding mechanism guarantees that:

$iR_i [K_j] \subseteq iR_j [K_j]$ and even $iR_i[K_jK_{j1}] \subseteq iR_j [K_jK_{j1}]$ with the exception of obscure values (cf mechanism of partial keys).

10.3.3 Complementary association mechanism (off track)

The simplest instance of its use is illustrated by the example of the relation U(ABCXYZ) which decomposes according to R_1 (ABX) R_2 (BCY) and R_3(CZ).

Figure 10.6 shows the relation graph RG_{h1}.

Figure 10.6 Off track mechanism

In using this database, it may be that we know entity (ac) of U[AC] before knowing entities (ab) of U[AB] and (bc) of U[BC]. But, with the decomposition provided, it is not possible to store entity (ac) in the database.

The aim of the complementary association mechanism is to make this possible. We introduce the concept of the *directed complementary arc* from the node of (AX) to that of (CZ) and the complementary association between the relations (AX) and (CZ) and the complementary association between the relations (AX) and (CZ). It means that if no entity (by) of R_2 corresponds to an entity (ax) of R_1, it is possible to assign to it an entity (cz) of R_3 by a complementary association. This mechanism will guard against storing redundancy in the database: so, as soon as we know the entity (by) corresponding to entity (ax), the complementary association between (ax) and (cz) is destroyed; but as the facts (ac) and (ab) exist and there is the fd B $\rightarrow$ C, the mechanism will deduce the creation of the association between (by) and (cz). Of course, if entity (by) is already assigned to another entity (c'z'), the mechanism will refuse the association of entity (ax) with that one (by) if c and c' are different.

An *entity path is complementary* if it contains at least one association between entities that is complementary. The usefulness of complementary associations is not restricted to the storage of data in the database; it applies equally to the deletion of data from the database.

So, in the first example, let us assume that the database contains entities (abx), (bcy) and (cz). Whether we remove (bcy) or remove the association (ab) or (bc) by updating entities (a-x) or (b-y), the normal method of storing data in a database causes the association (ac) to be removed. This behaviour may cause data to be lost. The use of complementary associations provides a useful remedy for this. If a complementary association exists between relations (AX) and (*CZ*), the deletions described previously would only be executed if the user had indicated to the system that it should also delete or retain (ac).

To simplify the description of this mechanism, we will assume that there is systematically a complementary association between two relations R_i and R_j, with R_i being greater than R_j without being immediately superior to it. Of course, it would be possible to refine this scenario: the database designer could design the necessary complementary associations. To a finer degree, it would be possible to distinguish complementary associations serving for the creation of associations, those serving for the removal of entities or associations or those serving for both!

Before arriving at this stage of detail, those responsible for DBMSs must be convinced of the relative ease of implementing such a mechanism; in our view, it could considerably assist the development of applications in a database and the definition of a database structure.

Take the case where $R_i > R_j$ and R_i is not directly superior to R_j.
The complementary association mechanism guarantees that if one association exists between two entities r_i and r_j, then there is no path between r_i and r_j in the database; in addition, there is no complementary association between r_i and r_m for any entity r_m of iR_m with $R_i > R_m > R_j$.

10.3.4   Partial keys mechanism: obscure entity

Here is the simplest situation that illustrates how this mechanism functions. Take the relation U(SABXY) which decomposes into $R_1(SAB)$, $R_2(ABX)$, R_3 (*A*Y). Figure 10.7 shows the corresponding relation graph.

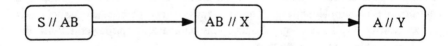

Figure 10.7 Partial keys mechanism

In the use of this database, it may be that the entity (sa-) is known. Implicitly, this entity makes an association between an entity r_1 of iR_1 of key s and an entity r_3 of iR_3 of key a. Because R_1 is not directly superior to R_3 it is sufficient to create a complementary association between r_1 and r_3. In this particular case (R_2 is dependent on R_3), the mechanism of partial keys will implant it simply by creating an entity (a--) in iR_2. Such an entity is called obscure because it does not take a clear value for any key.

An obscure entity may be associated with another entity or not (see cycle mechanism). On creation it takes the obscure value for each non-key attribute. Two obscure entities are non-comparable except in one case:
take two relations R_i and R_j, with one key of one K_i containing a key of the other K_j. One can also write $K_i = K_jX$. There is an obscure entity r_j and two entities r_{j1}, r_{j2} of iR_i, that are also obscure, such that the values of $r_{j1}.X$ and $r_{j2}.X$ are clear and identical. If r_{j1} and r_{j2} are both associated with the same entity r_j, they are then identical.
Figure 10.8 shows a simple example that illustrates this situation.

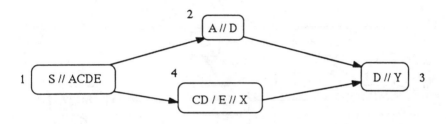

Figure 10.8 Situation where obscure entities can be equal

The relations are R_1 (SACDE), R_2 (AD), R_3 (DY) and R_4 (CDEX). The database contains r_1=(sac--) and r_1'=(s'ac--) in iR_1, r_2=(a-) in iR_2, r_3 in iR_3 and r_4=(c---) and r_4'=(c---) that are obscure in iR_4. The entity paths are $\{r_1, r_2, r_3\}$ $\{r_1', r_2, r_3\}$ $\{r_1', r_4, r_3\}$.
Here, r_4 and r_4' are identical because they are associated with the same entity r_3 and take the same value for C. Thus their values for the key CD can only be identical.

Note that the partial keys mechanism is an extension of the linear mechanism.

Take two relations R_i and R_j and a key K_j to R_j contained in R_i^+.

The *partial keys mechanism guarantees* that, for each entity r_i of iR_i such that $r_i.K_j$ is obscure, there is an entity r_j in iR_j that may be obscure such that $r_i.K_j = r_j.K_j$ and that there is an entity path (perhaps complementary) linking r_i to r_j.

It furthermore guarantees that if $r_j.K_j$ becomes clear, then $r_i.K_j$ also becomes clear, and reciprocally.

10.3.5   Cyclic keys mechanism

The following example illustrates this mechanism.
Take the following basic decomposition of a relation:
$$U = R_1(SACDEX) * R_2(AB) * R_3(CDY) * R_4(CEZB) * R_5(BCV) * R_6(C) *$$
$$R_7(B)$$
and the corresponding relation graph as shown in figure 10.9.

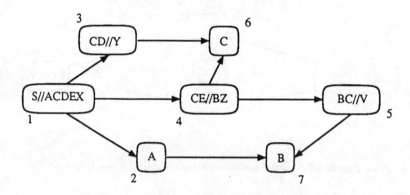

Figure 10.9 Cyclic keys mechanism

The entities stored in the base are (cdy) and (ab).
We create the entity r_1=(sacd-x). What does the cyclic keys mechanism do?
This mechanism will create r_4=(c---) in iR_4 and associate r_1 and r_4. The mechanism will note that BC is a cyclic risk key because of the partial functional decomposition $R_1*R_2*R_3$; it sees the creation of a new value (bc) of BC. As iR_5 is for the moment empty, it creates the entity r_5=(bc-) in iR_5. It will then trigger the complementary association mechanism between r_1 and r_5: it will create the association between r_4 and r_5.

The *cyclic keys mechanism guarantees that* if there is an entity s whose extended entity s* takes a clear or obscure value for a key KR to a relation R, then
- there is an entity r that may be obscure in iR such that for each attribute A of KR such that s*.A is clear, r.A = s*.A;
- there is a path between s and r that is perhaps complementary.

This mechanism concerns cyclic risk keys. For each partial functional decomposition D' of D_h that does not contain R, and of which KR is a subset of attributes, this mechanism guarantees that iD'[KR] $\subseteq$ iR[KR]. It intervenes as soon as an entity of an instance of a relation of D' is created or as soon as an attempt is made to remove an entity of iR.

Note that this cyclic keys mechanism may be considered an extension of the linear mechanism. It is an extension of those put forward by (SMITH 77; ZANIOLO 79; KUCK-SAGIV 83).

10.3.6 Cycle mechanism

The simplest situation that corresponds to this mechanism is illustrated by the relation U(SABCDWXYZ) which decomposes following $R_1(SAC)$, $R_2(ABX)$, $R_3(BDY)$, $R_4(CDZ)$, $R_5(DW)$.
Figure 10.10 shows the relation graph.

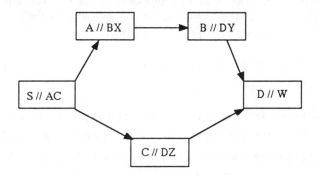

Figure 10.10 Cycle mechanism

This is a database state that includes the entities (sac) (a-x) (cdz) (dw) and (d'w'). We then create the entity (bd'y) and the association (ab). This state of the base is incoherent because there are two entity paths:
(sac) (abx) (bd'y) (d'w) and (sac) (cdz) (dw).

The first path associates s with d', the second s with d while there is the fd
$S \rightarrow D$ derived from the others by transitivity.
The cycle mechanism will verify that the two entity paths converge towards
the same entity of the well of the cycle.

To do this it will always try to anticipate rather than be in the cruder position
of finding an "error". So, from the first status of the database, it confirms that
there is a path that leaves from one entity of the source of the cycle $r_1=(sac)$
and comes to associate with r_1 an entity of the relation well (sac) (cdz) (dw).
The other path is: (sac) (a-x).
The mechanism will trigger the complementary association mechanism to
create a complementary association between (a-x) and (dw): in fact, from data
stored in the database it is possible to deduce the entity (ad) of U[AD].
This complementary association is established with the help of an obscure
entity of R_3.

The *cycle mechanism* is applied in the case of a functional cycle of source S
and of well P; for each entity s of iS, it *guarantees* the existence of an entity
path for each of the branches of the cycle that joins s to the same entity p of iP.
Each entity path is formed from an entity that may be obscure for each relation
of the branch.
This mechanism comes into play as soon as an association between two entity
relations belonging to the same cycle is created or removed. (LUONG 86)
contains a description of part of this mechanism.
This mechanism is finer than that proposed by (SAGIV 81) and (BROSDA-
VOSSEN85) as (LUONG 86) has shown. It is very close to the chase process
(MAIER-MENDELZON-SAGIV 79) applied only to fds.

In the preceding example, we now assume that the database contains a single
entity $r_2 = (a-x)$ in iR_2.

The creation of the entity $r_1(sa-)$ in iR_1 triggers the cycle mechanism; the latter
causes the association between r_1 and r_2 and in particular creates the obscure
entities r_3 r_4 r_5 in such a way that $(r_1 r_2 r_3 r_5)$ and $(r_1 r_4 r_5)$ form two entity
paths.

Then, the creation of the entity $r_1'=(s'a-)$ in iR_1 also triggers the cycle
mechanism, which confirms the entity path $(r_1' r_2 r_3 r_5)$, and causes the creation
of an obscure entity r_4' to form the path $(r_1' r_4' r_5)$.

10.3.7   Usefulness of these mechanisms

THEOREM

The keys mechanism, the complementary associations mechanism, the cyclic keys mechanism, the cycle mechanism and the partial keys mechanism guarantee the validity of the intrinsic fds and the fds that are able to be generated from the intrinsic fds. Two partial functional decompositions D_1 and D_2 concerned by one of these fds are compatible. These mechanisms guarantee the initial homogenous decomposition to be safe.

We prove this theorem in the appendix (section 10.5) .

A prototype (ALCOREZA 88) of all these mechanisms has been constructed for a single functional cycle.

10.3.8   Examples

(a) Here are the relations that form the decomposition:
    {S(SABCEGH); R_1(EGHX); R_3(AB); R_4(BCE),R_5(E),R_6(B)}.

The keys to R_1 are EG and H; the fds are deduced from the keys.

Figure 10.11 shows the relation graph.

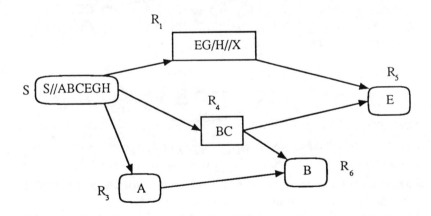

Figure 10.11 Use of the mechanisms (1)

The fd f:AC → E is deduced from A → B and BC → E; it is defined in the relation S. Of course, as AC is not a key to S, the key mechanism applied to iS is not empowered to verify it.

Take the partial functional decomposition D' formed from S[SABC], R_3 and R_4. Two entities s and s' verifying s.AC = s'.AC as clear, exist in iS if there is an entity r_3 verifying r_3.A = s.A in iR_3.

In addition, the partial keys mechanism creates if required an entity r_4 of iR_4: r_4.C = s.C, and another r_4': r_4'.C = s'.C.

The cycle mechanism, applied to the functional cycle of source S and well B, guarantees that r_4.B = r_3.B = r_4'.B. From this r_4 and r_4' are derived as identical. s and s' are thus linked to the same entity of iR_4; their extended entities at D' take the same value for E. f is valid in iD'.

It is also valid in S because of the cycle mechanism applied to the functional cycle (SR_1R_4); it guarantees that the entities r_1 assigned to s and r_1' assigned to s' verify:

$$r_1.E = s.E = r_4.E = s'.E = r_1'.E.$$

(b) Figure 10.12 shows the relation graph of another example.

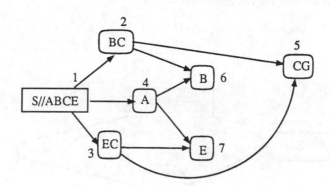

Figure 10.12 Use of mechanisms (2)

The fd f: AC → G is not intrinsic to any relation; it emerges just as well from A → B and BC → G as from A → E and EC → G.

There are two partial functional decompositions affected by f: on the one hand {S[SABC], R_2} and on the other {S[SACE], R_3}.

If there is in the database an entity s of iS such that s.AC is clear, then if required the partial keys mechanism constructs an entity r_2 in iR_2 such that s.C = r_2.C, and an entity r_3 in iR_3 such that r_3.C = s.C.

The cycle mechanism applied to the functional cycle of source S and of well R_5 and that of partial keys assign to these two entities an entity r_5 of iR_5 such that $r_5.C = r_3.C = r_2.C = s.C$.

Thus s is assigned to a single entity of R_5 and to a single value of G, whether via the path through R_2 or via the path through R_3.

If there is now another entity s' of iS that verifies s'.AC = s.AC as clear, it is easy to show by the same reasoning as before that s and s' are assigned to the same entities r_2 and r_3 because of the partial keys and cycle mechanisms applied respectively to the functional cycle of source S and of well R_6, and to that of source S and of well R_7.

Thus s and s' are assigned to the same entity r_5.

Not only do the two functional decompositions validate f, but they are mutually compatible for f.

(c) Figure 10.13 shows the relation graph of a final example.

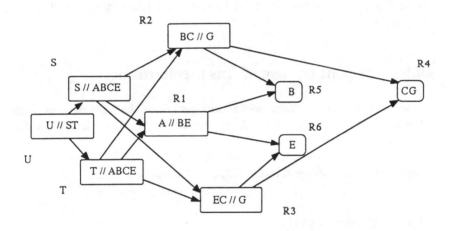

Figure 10.13 Use of mechanisms (3)

AC → G emerges from A → B and BC → G and also from A → E and EC → G. If there is an entity s = (sac--), there is the entity r_1 = (a--) and in addition if necessary the partial keys mechanism creates r_2 = (-c-) and r_3 = (-c-).

The cycle mechanism applied to the cycle $(SR_2R_4R_3)$ prescribes that $r_2.G = r_3.G$. It also prescribes that $r_2.B = r_1.B$ because of the cycle $(SR_2R_5R_1)$ and also $r_3.E = r_1.E$ because of the cycle $(SR_3R_6R_1)$.

If now we create an entity $t = (tac\text{--})$, it is linked to r_1 and thus to r_5 and r_6. The partial keys mechanism joins it to a new entity $r_3' = (\text{-c-})$. The cycle mechanism applied to $(TR_1R_6R_3)$ prescribes that $r_3'.E = r_1.E$ and thus that $r_3'.E = r_3.E$. r_3 and r_3' are identical.

So s and t are assigned to the same entity of R_4 and AC $\rightarrow$ G is validated.

10.4   Conclusion

As we explained in the introduction, we provide no design methodology for a database structure. Although we divide the design process into three parts, we provide no design method. We do not say that a designer must begin with the first part, then the second part then end with the third part. These three parts only serve to distinguish between the design problems.

For us this book is neither a methodology, nor a database design method but only a reflection on the databases.

10.5   Appendix: use of this mechanism

We will show that all these mechanisms guarantee the validation of each intrinsic fd and the safety of the decomposition for the intrinsic dfs and for each key.

In addition they also validate the fds that are not intrinsic.

Take the relation T of key X and the fd $X \rightarrow A$ intrinsic to T.

10.5.1   Property (M1)

The fd $X \rightarrow A$ is validated in iT thanks to the keys mechanism.

10.5.2   Property (M2): guaranteed safety with reference to X

The linear mechanism guarantees that for each relation R that is directly superior to T, if iR contains an entity r such that r.X is clear, then there is an entity t in iT such that r.X=t.X. The cyclic keys mechanism extends this result to each relation R which is not directly superior to T, but of which each extended relation that does not contain T contains one or more keys of T as attributes.

These two mechanisms thus guarantee each partial functional decomposition with reference to X to be safe.

In particular, the linear mechanism guarantees the existing integrity rule of dependence between relations.

10.5.3 Property (M3): linear safety

Lemma

Take R > T and two entities r and t in the base linked by an entity path, complementary or not. A is an attribute common to R and T. r.A and t.A are clear values. With the application of the preceding mechanisms r.A and t.A are identical.

Proof

There is a hinge RT between R and T that accepts A as a key attribute because the initial decomposition is compact.

(a) If the keys to RT are not those of T, then RT is distinct from T. According to the partial keys mechanism, there are two entities of iRT, rt and rt' such that rt.A = r.A and rt'.A = t.A and two entity paths on one hand between t and rt' that extend the path between r and t, and on the other hand between r and rt.

If there is a cycle of source R and of well RT, with one branch of the cycle passing via T, the other not, and if the two preceding entity paths correspond to these two distinct branches, then the application of the cycle mechanism goes to guarantee that rt = rt' and thus r.A = t.A = rt.A.

Otherwise, there is a single entity path linking r to rt. Application of the complementary associations mechanism guarantees that this path passes through t; as there is only one entity of iRT that can be joined to t, rt and rt' are identical: rt.A = t.A = r.A.

(b) If the keys to RT are those of T, then RT is merged with T and A is a key attribute of T. According to the partial keys mechanism, r may only be joined with an entity t of iT such that r.A = t.A.

If a relation R accepts XA as attributes, then for each entity r of iR such that r.X is clear, there is an entity t of iT such that r.X = t.X according to the cyclic keys mechanism: it even guarantees the existence of an entity path from r to t.

If now r.A is clear, the preceding lemma may be applied, to deduce r.A = t.A. Thus iR[XA] $\subseteq$ iT[XA].

By this means any partial functional decomposition affected by XA is guaranteed to be linearly safe.

10.5.4 Property (M4): cyclic safety

Lemma

Take R > T and two entities r and t in the base joined to one another by a complementary or non-complementary entity path.
Take R* to be an extended relation of R not containing T.
A is an attribute common to R* and T. With application of the preceding mechanisms, r*.A and t.A are identical when one of them at least is clear.

Proof
This lemma becomes the previous lemma when R* = R. Take V to be a relation that has served to build R* and of which A is an attribute. V is distinct from R. R is superior to V by construction.
In addition, iV is such that it contains an entity v joined to r by an entity path and r*.A = v.A.
TV is the hinge between T and V which accepts A as a key attribute because the decomposition is compact.

(a) If the keys to TV are not those of T, then TV is distinct from T. According to the partial keys mechanism there are two entities of iTV, tv and tv', such that tv.A = v.A and tv'.A = t.A, and two entity paths linking r to an entity of iTV: (r,v,tv) and (r,t,tv'). If these paths are distinct, there is a functional cycle of source R and of well TV, and the cycle mechanism guarantees that tv and tv' designate the same entity; otherwise, it is guaranteed by the complementary association mechanism. So tv.A = v.A = t.A = r*.A.

(b) If the keys to TV are the same as those of T, then TV and T are merged and A is a key attribute of T. According to the partial keys mechanism, v must be linked to an entity t' of iT that verifies v.A = t'.A. As r is joined to v by an entity path, it is also joined to t'; according to the cycle mechanism or the complementary association mechanism it is guaranteed as before that t = t'; thus t.A = r*.A.

If a relation R accepts an extended relation R* that does not contain T but whose set of attributes contains XA, then for each entity r of iR such that r*.X is clear, there is an entity t of iT such that r*.X = t.X according to the cyclic keys mechanism; this mechanism also guarantees the existence of an entity path from r to t.

If now r*.A is clear, the preceding lemma can be applied to produce r*.A = t.A. Thus iR* [XA] ⊆ iT[XA].

This guarantees the decomposition to be safe and iR* to validate X → A.

10.5.5 Theorem (M5)

The four mechanisms – keys mechanism, complementary association mechanism, cyclic keys mechanism and cycle mechanism – guarantee the safety of the partial functional decompositions in relation to the keys to the relations that form the decomposition and in relation to the intrinsic fds. They guarantee the validity of the intrinsic fds in the database.

We will now extend this result to the fds that are not intrinsic.

10.5.6 Case of fds that are not intrinsic

Take an elementary fd f:X → A that may be generated from intrinsic fds.

10.5.6.1 Property (M6)

We will show that if the preceding mechanisms are active, f is validated for each instance of a functional decomposition D that accepts XA as attributes. Take S to be the source of such a decomposition.

Proof

(a) There is a special functional decomposition DG of source S which accepts XA as attributes.

In fact, f:X → A may be generated from the fds $(f_1 f_2 ... f_n)$ that are intrinsic and which make a well formed generation tree (section 8.11). Take $R_1, R_2 ... R_n$ to be the corresponding relations. We have shown that X → $g(f_i)$ for i = (1...n) (where $g(f_i)$ designates the left hand side of f_i). Given that KS is a key to S, as S is the source of D, KS → X exists and therefore KS → $g(f_i)$. We have shown that $g(f_i)$ contains a key to R_i. So S is superior to R_i and there is a path in the relation graph linking S to each of the R_i relations (RG$_3$ property, see 8.11.6.3). All of these paths form a special functional decomposition DG of source S which accepts XA as attributes.

(b) We will show that iDG validates f:X → A thanks to the mechanisms. We assume that there are two entities of iS extended to DG, s* and s'*, such that s*.X and s'*.X are clear and identical. In the theorem for the generation of fds, we learnt that X is the set of source attributes of the tree, and A the well attribute. There is therefore at least one fd f_1 whose left-hand part is made up only from source attributes X_1 included in X. A key to R_1 is X_1 and the complementary association mechanism guarantees the existence of an entity path joining s and s' to the same entity r_1 of iR_1 such that $s^*.X_1 = r_1.X_1$. The same goes for all the fds $f_2...f_p$ (p ≤ n) such that g(f) is included in X. The complementary association mechanism guarantees the existence of an entity path joining s and s' to the same entity r_j (j ≤ p) of iR_j such that $s^*.X_j = r_j.X_j$. And so $s^*.A_j = s'^*.A_j$, where A_j designates the right-hand part of f_j.

The right-hand parts A_j of the fds f_j (1 ≤ j ≤ p) cannot be source attributes of the generation tree; they belong to the left-hand parts of other fds; there is at least one fd f_k such that g (f_k) contains only attributes X_k of X and of A_j, through tree construction. Take R_k to be the corresponding relation. There is a path linking S to R_k in the relation graph. According to the cyclic keys and partial keys mechanisms, there is an entity path linking s to an entity r_k of iR_k and another linking s' to an entity r'_k of iR_k. As $s^*.X_k = s'^*.X_k$, $r_k.X_k = r'_k.X_k$. If $s^*.A_j$ is clear, $r_k.A_j$ is as well, and $r_k.A_j = r'_k. A_j = s^*.A_j$.

Because s and s' are linked to the same entity r_j, $r_k.A_j$ and $r'_k.A_j$, whether obscure or not, are identical (cycle or complementary association mechanism). Thus, s and s' are joined to the same entity r_k (=r'_k) of iR_k.

By degrees, it can be shown that s and s' are linked to the same entity for each iR_i (1 ≤ i ≤ p) that forms DG. Thus $s^*.A = s'^*.A$, whether the value is clear or obscure.

So iDG validates f:X → A.

(c) We will show that iD validates X → A and that iD is compatible with iDG for f_1.

Take S* to be the extended relation of S to DG. Take S_1^* the extended relation of S to D.

XA forms a subset of S^{*+} and of S_1^{*+}. For each attribute A_i of XA, there is a relation R of DG and a relation R_1 of D (perhaps equal to R) such that A_i is an attribute of R and of R_1 There is therefore a hinge CH between R and R_1 that accepts A_i as a key attribute because the decomposition is compact: this hinge can be R or R_1. Thus in the relation graph, there exists either a path linking S R and R_1 or there exists a cycle of source S and of well CH.

If we consider an entity s of iS, its extended entity s* to DG and its extended entity s_1^* to D, then thanks either to the cycle mechanism in the case of the cycle, or to the complementary association mechanism in the case of a path joining S, R and R_1, $s^*.A_i = s_1^*.A_i$ and thus $s^*.X = s_1^*.X$.
Similarly, $s^*.A = s_1^*.A$.
If we consider another entity s' of iS, its extended entity s'* to DG, and its extended entity $s_1'^*$ to D such that $s_1^*.X = s_1'^*X$ as clear, then we can deduce from the preceding paragraph that $s^*.X = s'^*.X$ as clear. Again, from the preceding paragraph, because iDG validates $X \rightarrow A$, $s^*.A = s'^*.A$. Finally, also, $s_1^*.A = s_1'^*.A$.

iD also validates $f:X \rightarrow A$ and furthermore it is compatible with iDG for f. We even know that iD[XA] and iDG[XA] contain the same entities containing clear values for X.

10.5.6.2 Property (m7)

If two functional decompositions D and D' are affected by f: $X \rightarrow A$, they are compatible for f when the mechanisms are active.

Proof:
This result has already been shown if D and D' have the same source. Now, we have to consider decompositions of different sources, S for D, S' for D'.
We consider the preceding decomposition DG of source S and we adopt the same notation. Because $KS' \rightarrow X$ is verified, and $X \rightarrow KR_i$ ($1 \leq i \leq n$), we also have $KS' \rightarrow KR_i$, thus $S' > R_i$ ($1 \leq i \leq n$).
There is therefore, a decomposition DG' of source S' constructed from the relations R_i.

Take s to be an entity of iS, s* the entity s extended to DG; take s' to be an entity of iS', s'* the entity s' extended to DG'; we assume that $s^*.X = s'^*.X$ as clear. By the same reasoning as before (see 10.5.6.1.b), we will obtain by degrees that $s^*.A = s'^*.A$.
Thus iDG and iDG' are compatible for f.
Because from the foregoing, on the one hand iDG[XA] and iD[XA] and on the other hand iDG'[XA] and iD'[XA] contain the same entities that take clear values for X, iD and iD' are compatible for f.

10.5.6.3 Theorem (m8)

Thus, they key mechanisms, the complementary association mechanism, the cyclic keys mechanism, the cycle mechanism, the partial keys mechanism guarantee the validity of the fds that may be generated from the set of intrinsic fds. They guarantee the functional decompositions in relation to these fds to be safe.

The proof of this theorem derives from the preceding theorem for the cases of intrinsic fds and the preceding properties for the other fds.

Bibliography

ABITEBOUL85 Abiteboul S., Cocktail de dépendances, thesis, Paris 11, 1985

ABITEBOUL-VIANU85 Abiteboul S., Vianu V., Transaction and constraints, PODS Conference, 1985

ABRIAL74 Abrial J.R., Data semantics, IFIP Conference in Data Management Systems, North Holland, 1974

ADIBA-DELOBEL-LEONARD76 Adiba M., Delobel C., Léonard M., A unified approach for modelling data in logical data base design, IFIP Workshop TC2, Freudenstadt, Jan 1976

AHO-BEERI-ULLMAN79 Aho A.V., Beeri C., Ullman J.D., The theory of joins in relational databases, ACM TODS, 4, 3, Sep 1979

ALCOREZA88 Alcoreza J., Mécanismes de cohérences dans les cycles functionnels, Mémoire de licence d'Informatique de Gestion, University of Geneva, Feb 1988

ARMSTRONG74 Armstrong W.W., Dependency structures in relational databases, IFIP Conference, 1974

BEERI-BERNSTEIN79 Beeri C., Bernstein P., Computational problems related to the design of normal form relational schemas, ACM TODS, 4, 1, Mar 1979

BEERI-FAGIN-HOWARD77 Beeri C., Fagin R., Howard J.H., A complete axiomatization for functional and multivalued dependencies in database relations, ACM SIGMOD, 1977

BEERI-RISSANEN80 Beeri C., Rissanen J., Faithful representations of relational database schemes, IBM RJ 2722 (34837), 1980

BENCI-ROLLAND79 Benci G., Rolland C., *Bases de données: conception canonique pour une réalisation extensible*, Editions SCM, Paris, 1979

BERGE70 Berge C., *Graphes et hypergraphes*, Dunod, Paris, 1970

BERNSTEIN76 Bernstein P.A., Synthesizing third normal form relations from functional dependencies, ACM TODS, 1, 4, Dec 1976

BLAUSTEIN81 Blaustein B.T., Enforcing database assertions: techniques and applications, PhD thesis, Harvard, 1981

BODART-PIGNEURS83 Bodart F., Pigneur Y., *Conception assistée des applications informatiques: 1. étude d'opportunité et analyse conceptuelle,* Masson, Paris, 1983

BOUILLE78 Bouille F., A survey of the hypergraphed based data structure application to cartography and mapping, International User's Conference of Computer Mapping Software and Data Bases, Cambridge, Mass., 1978

BRIAND-COCHET77 Briand H., Cochet C., *Analyse fonctionnelle en informatique de gestion,* Dunod, Paris, 1977

BROSDA-VOSSEN85 Brosda V., Vossen G., Updating a relational database through a universal relational interface, Report 101, Technical University of Aachen, Schriften zur Informatik und Angewandte Mathematik, Aug 1984

BRY-MANTHEY86 Bry F., Manthey R., Checking consistency of database constraints: a logical basis, VLDB Conference, 1986

BULA78 Bula E., Méthode d'approche pour la conception d'une banque de données, thesis, University of Neuchâtel, 1978

CASANOVA82 Casanova M.A., A theory of data dependencies over relational expressions, PODS Conference, 1982

CASANOVA-FAGIN-PAPADIMITRIOU82 Casanova M.A., Fagin R., Papadimitriou C.H., Inclusion dependencies and their interaction with functional dependencies, PODS Conference, 1982

CAVARERO-HERIN-AIME82 Cavaréro J.L., Hérin-Aime D., *La conception des systèmes d'information. Un modèle, un dossier standard, des méthodes,* Masson, Paris, 1982

CHEN76 Chen P.P.S., The entity relationship model: towards a unified view of data, ACM TODS, 1, 1, Mar 1976

CODD70 Codd E.F., A relational model for large shared data banks, CACM, 13, 6, June 1970

CODD79 Codd E.F., Extending the relational database model to capture more meaning, ACM TODS, 4, 4, Dec 1979

COSMADAKIS-KANELLAKIS84 Cosmadakis S.S., Kanellakis P.C., Functional and inclusion dependencies: a graph theoretic approach, PODS Conference, 1984

DATE75 Date C.J., *Introduction to database systems*, Addison- Wesley, Reading, Mass., 1975

DELOBEL73 Delobel C., Contributions théoriques à la conception et l'évaluation d'un système d'informations appliqué à la gestion, thesis, University of Grenoble, Oct 1973

DELOBEL78 Delobel C., Normalisation and hierarchical dependencies in the relational data model, ACM TODS, 3, 3, Sep 1978

DELOBEL-ADIBA82 Delobel C., Adiba M., *Bases de données et systèmes relationnels*, Dunod, Paris, 1982

DELOBEL-CASEY72 Delobel C., Casey R.G., Decomposition of a database and the theory of boolean switching functions, IBM Journal of Research and Development, Sep 1972

DELOBEL-LÉONARD74 Delobel C., Léonard M., The decomposition process in a relational model, IRIA Workshop on Data Structures, Namur, May 1974

DEMOLOMBE-YAZDANIAN-NICOLAS85 Demolombe R., Yazdanian K., Nicolas J.M., Modèle complet, modèle irredondant pour un schéma de base de données relationnelle, Journées Base de Données, Grenoble, 1985

FAOUS-FORSYTH75 Fadous R., Forsyth J., Finding candidate keys for relational data bases, ACM SIGMOD, 1975

FAGIN77 Fagin R., Multivalued dependencies and a new normal form of relational databases, ACM TODS, 2, 3, Sep 1977

FAGIN82 Fagin R., Horn clauses and database dependencies, JACM, 29, 4, Oct 1982

FINKELSTEIN-SCHKOLNICK-TIBERIO88 Finkelstein S., Schkolnick M., Tiberio P., Physical database design for relational databases, ACM TODS, 13, 1, Mar 1988

FLORY82 Flory A., *Base de données: conception et réalisation*,
Economica, Paris, 1982

GALACSI86 GALACSI: Briand H., Crampes I.B., Ducateau C., Hebrail Y.,
Hérin-Aime D., Kouloumdjan J., Sabatier R., *Les systèmes d'information:
analyse et conception*, Dunod, Paris, 1986

GALLAIRE81 Gallaire H., Impacts of logic on databases,
VLDB Conference, 1981

GALLAIRE-MINKER-NICOLAS84 Gallaire H., Minker J., Nicolas J.M.,
Logic and databases: a deductive approach, ACM Computing Surveys, 16, 2,
June 1984

GARDARIN84 Gardarin G., *Bases de données: les systèmes et leurs langages*,
Eyrolles, Paris, 1984

GAROCHE-LÉONARD78 Garoche-Reynaud F., Léonard M., Basepirr:
algorithmes d'obtention de monômes premiers, des couvertures et bases
irredondantes des fonctions booléennes particulières, Journées des modèles
relationnels, Institut de Programmation de Paris, Mar 1978

GAROCHE-LÉONARD84 Garoche-Reynaud F., Léonard M., On a class of
boolean functions with matroid properties, Communications in Discrete
Mathematics 49, North Holland, 1984

GUYOT86 Guyot J., Un modèle de traitement pour les bases de données,
thesis, University of Geneva, Ed. Le Concept Moderne, Geneva, 1986

HAINAUT86 Hainaut J.L., *Conception assistée des applications
informatiques: 2. conception de la base des données*, Masson, Paris, 1986

HUONG87 Huong P., Dépendances d'inclusion et bases de données, internal
report, University of Geneva, June 1987

JUNET86 Junet M., Design and implementation of an extended entity-
relationship database management system (ECRINS/86), Entity-Relationship
Model Conference, Dijon, 1986

JUNET-FALQUET-LÉONARD86 Junet M., Falquet G., Léonard M.,
ECRINS/86: an extended entity-relationship database management system and
its semantic query language, VLDB Conference, 1986

KNUTH73 Knuth D., *The art of computer programming*, **3**, Addison-Wesley, Reading, Mass., 1973

KUCK-SAGIV83 Kuck S.M., Sagiv Y., Designing globally consistent network schemas, ACM SIGMOD Conference, San Jose, Calif., May 1983

KUNDU75 Kundu S., An improved algorithm for finding a key of a relation, PODS Conference, 1975

KUNTZMANN72 Kuntzmann J., *Théorie des réseaux-graphes*, Dunod, Paris, 1972

LAFAYE82 Lafaye M.C., Outils d'aides à la conception des bases de données relationnelles ou réseau (multigraphe de projection), thesis, University of Rennes, Dec 1982

LÉONARD83 Léonard M., Observation des dependances fonctionnelles non réduites à leurs propriétés booléennes, INFORSID seminar, Campo Dell'Oro, 1983

LÉONARD88 Léonard M., Conception d'une structure de données dans les environnenments de bases de données, thesis, University of Grenoble, May 1988

LÉONARD-GALLAND-JUNET-TSCHOPP85 Léonard M., Galland A., Junet M., Tschopp R., ECRINS: un modèle relationnel étendu et un système de gestion de petites bases de données, Latin Informatics Convention, Barcelona, Apr 1985

LÉONARD86 Léonard M., Snella J.J., Abdeljaoued A., FARANDOLE: a RDBMS for statistical data analysis, 7th Symposium on Computational Statistics, COMPSTAT, Rome, 1986

LUCAS81 Lucas S., Metodologias de concepçao de bases de dados, thesis, Lab. Nacional de Engenharia Civil, Lisbon, Nov 1981

LUCCHESI-ORSBORN76 Lucchesi C.L., Orsborn S.L., Candidate keys for relations, technical report, University of Waterloo, Ontario, Canada, 1976

LUONG86 Luong Dong Thi B.T., Une approche de conception d'une base de données cohérentes et complètes, thesis, University of Geneva, Ed. Le Concept Moderne, Geneva, 1986

MAIER83 Maier D., *The theory of relational databases*, Computer Science Press, USA, 1983

MAIER-MENDELZON-SAGIV79 Maier D., Mendelzon A., Sagiv Y., Testing implications of data dependencies, ACM TODS, **4**, 4, Dec 1979

MAIER-ULLMAN83 Maier D., Ullman J.D., Maximal objects and the semantics of universal relational databases, ACM TODS, **8**, 1, Jan 1983

MAIER-ULLMAN-VARDI84 Maier D., Ullman J.D., Vardi M.Y., On the foundations of the universal relation model, ACM TODS, **9**, 2, June 1984

MELKANOFF-ZANIOLO80 Melkanoff M.-A., Zaniolo C., Decomposition of relations and synthesis of entity relationship diagrams, in Entity-relationship approach to system analysis and design, North-Holland, 1980

MENDELZON79 Mendelzon A.O., On axiomatizing multivalued dependencies in relational databases, JACM, **26**, 1, Jan 1979

MIRANDA-BUSTA84 Miranda S.M., Busta J.M., *L'art des bases de données: 1. Introduction aux bases de données*, Eyrolles, Paris, 1984

MITCHELL83 Mitchell J.C., Inference rules for functional and inclusion dependencies, PODS Conference, 1983

NICOLAS78 Nicolas J.M., Mutual dependencies and some results on undecomposable relations, VLDB Conference, 1978

PARADAENS-JANSSENS81 Paradaens J., Janssens D., Decomposition of relations: a comprehensive approach, in *Advances in database theory*, **1**, Plenum Press, New York, 1981

PÉPIN85 Pépin, *Introduction aux systèmes de gestion de bases de données*, Eyrolles, Paris, 1985

PICHAT-DELOBEL79 Pichat E., Delobel C., Designing third normal form for relational data base schema, research report, IMAG, 149, University of Grenoble, 1979

PORTAL75 Portal D., Conception d'un système automatisé de gestion de la scolarite de l'enseignement superieur, thesis, University of Grenoble, Mar 1975

REITER84 Reiter R., Towards a logical reconstruction of relational database theory, in *On conceptual modelling*, Springer-Verlag, 1984

REYNAUD75 Reynaud F., Théorie des ecoulements dans les graphes orientés sans circuit, Discrete Mathematics 12, North-Holland, 1975

RIEU84 Rieu D., Modèle et fonctionnalités d'un SGBD pour les applications CAO, thesis, University of Grenoble, July 1984

RISSANEN77 Rissanen J., Independent components of relations, ACM TODS, **2**, 4, Dec 1977

ROLLAND78 Rolland C., Concepts for information system conceptual schema and its utilization in the REMORA project, VLDB Conference, 1978

SAGIV83 Sagiv Y., A characterization of globally consistent databases and their correct access paths, ACM TODS, 8, 2, June 1983

SAGIV-DELOBEL-PARKER-FAGIN81 Sagiv Y., Delobel C., Parker D.S., Fagin R., An equivalence between relational database dependencies and a subclass of propositional logic, JACM, **28**, 3, July 1981

SCIORE82 Sciore E., Complete axiomatization of full join dependencies, JACM, **29**, 2, Apr 1982

SCIORE83 Sciore E., Inclusion dependencies and the universal instance, PODS Conference, 1983

SMITH77 Smith J.M., Smith D.C.P., Database abstractions: aggregation and generalization, ACM TODS, **2**, 2, June 1977

SNELLA84 Snella J.J., Léonard M., Pirée: un système de gestion de bases de données economiques, INFORSID Conference, Bandol, 1984

TARDIEU-ROCHFIELD-COLLETTI83 Tardieu H., Rochfield A., Colletti R., *La méthode MERISE; principe et outils*, Les Editions d'Organisation, Paris, 1983

ULLMAN80 Ullman J.D., *Principles of database systems*, Computer Science Press, USA

VARDI82 Vardi M.Y., The implication and finite implication problems for types template dependencies, PODS Conference, 1982

VELEZ-LOPEZ87 Velez F., Lopez M., Projet TIGRE: bilan et enseignement, Troisième Journée des Bases de Données Avancées, Port-Camargue, May 1987

VETTER-MADDISON81 Vetter M., Maddison R., *Database design methodology*, Prentice-Hall, New York, 1981

WASSERMAN83 Wasserman T., The unified support environment: tool support for the user software engineering methodology, in CRIS 2.IFIP Conference, York UK, July 1983

ZANIOLO76 Zaniolo C., Analysis and design of relational schemata for data base systems, PhD, UCLA, USA, 1976

ZANIOLO79 Zaniolo C., Design of relational views over network schemas, ACM SIGMOD, June 1979

ZANIOLO-MELKANOFF81 Zaniolo C., Melkanoff M., On the design of relational database schemata, ACM TODS, 6, 1, Mar 1981

Index